Indian Railways' Journey with Coal 1855–2023

Ashim Kumar Maitra

Indian Railways' Journey with Coal 1855–2023

Changing Policies and Outcomes

PETER LANG

Chennai · Berlin · Bruxelles · Lausanne · New York · Oxford

Bibliographic Information published by the Deutsche Nationalbibliothek
The Deutsche Nationalbibliothek lists this publication in the Deutsche Nationalbibliografie; detailed bibliographic data is available in the internet at http://dnb.d-nb.de.

Library of Congress Control Number: 2025004108

Library of Congress Cataloging-in-Publication Data
Names: Maitra, Ashim Kumar, 1954- author
Title: Indian Railways' journey with coal (1855-2023) : changing policies and outcomes / Ashim Kumar Maitra.
Description: Oxford ; New York : Peter Lang, [2025] | Includes bibliographical references and index.
Identifiers: LCCN 2025004108 (print) | LCCN 2025004109 (ebook) | ISBN 9781803745671 paperback | ISBN 9781803745688 ebook | ISBN 9781803745695 epub
Subjects: LCSH: Indian Railways | Railroads--India--History | Coal trade--India--History | Railroads and state--India--History
Classification: LCC HE3300.I53 M35 2025 (print) | LCC HE3300.I53 (ebook) | DDC 385.0954--dc23/eng/20250403
LC record available at https://lccn.loc.gov/2025004108
LC ebook record available at https://lccn.loc.gov/2025004109

ISBN 978-1-80374-567-1 (Print)
ISBN 978-1-80374-568-8 (E-PDF)
ISBN 978-1-80374-569-5 (E-PUB)
DOI 10.3726/b22023

Published by Peter Lang Pvt Ltd, Chennai (India)

info@peterlang.com

This publication has been peer reviewed.

www.peterlang.com

In memory of
Baba and Ma
for their unconditional love and nurturing

Foreword

The three keywords in the book title – Coal, India, Railways – are the hot topics now in climate change discourse, the most complex problem humanity is trying to navigate for safe survival on earth now and in the future. Research output on the solution space with scientific evidence to show what is feasible, possible and doable is growing in leaps and bounds. The main message from global discourse is that it is possible to manage climate change within safe limits of planetary boundary for sustainable human living, but some disruptive choices are to be made by the current generation of decision makers now. Besides technology and innovations, two major identified 'enablers' of such change are policy plus institutions and redirection of financial resources to drive the desired change at scale and within a reasonable time. International negotiation in Conference of Parties (COP) of UNFCCC (United National Framework Convention for Climate Change) has agreed in recent past to eventually phase out unabated fossil fuel use as extraction and combustion of it are the major causes of GHG emissions. The globally agreed strategy is to start with phase down of coal use and finally close all unbated coal-based power plants and reduce use of fossil fuel in transportation of freights and passengers by promotion of railways where ever feasible.

In the context of current debate, the book is a 'treasure-chest' for those who want to understand why coal phase out/down is seen as a socio-political-economic struggle for India. Book is written with rich evidence support and let us not forget the contribution comes from Ashim Kumar Maitra who is a practitioner served both Indian Railways at the top managerial rank. He was also advisor to the chairman of Coal India Ltd. and was an Independent Director of West Bengal Power Development Corporation. So, he has seen the dynamics of the three sectors during his professional career. He was a trained economist and is an expert on transportation and logistics. The book is substantially new and one of its kind for the Indian context with global relevance because the book provides a chronological narrative of how policy priority, policy design and institutional structure for coal, railways and power sector in India co-evolved in phases with changing national priorities as decided by the federal government keeping in view both the political economy and economic growth. Past contributions in the thematic area have either covered only one sector coal industry, Indian railways or Indian power sector. Mr. Maitra consulted in preparation of this book all such references. However, his value-added contribution is in taking a systemic approach of cross sector collaboration, their coevolution and changing phases and current situation. It is a first attempt that dared to cover with authority such vast temporal scale for India to make the narrative comprehensive. The narrative starts from the colonial period 1855 and extends up to 2023. There is no such comprehensive rich source of evidence-based written narrative and insights on the subject in one place. The author has toiled and written down the facts in such a way that it will make life easy for all future researchers trying to understand transition challenges and policy design for a sustainable future of India and for rest of the world.

Mr. Maitra explains why coal and railways developed concurrently right from the beginning as coal was the only fuel for railways and distribution of coal was not possible without railways. After independence the government specifically planned for their development to foster industrial growth. Over the long period of time covered by this study despite regime changes from colonial period to independent India and political regime changes in the latter period coal-railways nexus grew to support India's industrialization and then to provide access to modern electricity to boost the economic growth. It is noteworthy that systemic approach did not overlook how with cheap liquid fuel invention boosted road transport and how politically that was embraced in India and how through incentive design and market-based instruments freight movement was shared by railways and road transport with former almost exclusively keeping the monopoly in coal transport to meet emerging electricity demand. Mr. Maitra ends the book with a futuristic view and raises a pertinent research question how coal-rail-power nexus might be dwindling in future and can this transition be done proactively by adopting policy-institution nexus to avoid unwanted socio-political-economic struggle.

He shows that without policy makers playing a catalytic role the railways-coal-power sector nexus in India could not have boosted the economic growth. This is true for both the colonial period and independent India, although beginning was with railways-coal nexus. This presentation reestablishes the human agency and reminds me of the age-old proverb where there is a (political) will there is a way.

Foundation of Maitra's argument rests, however, in the view that policy and institution can be very strong catalyst in shaping the economic developmental of a nation like India. He argues that policy and institutional reforms become more productive by paying explicit attention to changing market conditions, developmental paradigm and challenges for humanity. This also helps in positioning a country in a global context.

I have served the energy economics, resource and environmental economics, climate change economics and policy space for more than forty years. I believe that this book is extremely timely contribution and will surely help inject new insights and clear perspective for researchers and policy makers not only in India but has potential to inform the global discourse on shaping the smooth transitions for sustainable future for coal rich countries like India. The hope lies in his narrative around how political will can drive and bend and twist and redirect policy, institutions and finance which current climate change solution space developers are looking for.

Besides technology and innovations, two major identified 'enablers' of such change are policy plus institutions and redirection of financial resources to drive the desired change at scale and within a reasonable time. As it accepted globally that it is now time for roll back of unabated coal use appropriate priorities, institutions, incentives, compensations, upskilling of manpower, promotion of a portfolio of appropriate new technologies and related infrastructure assumes priority. Keeping an eye on growing geopolitics of materials and resource in near future there cannot be any global technology determinism or technology winner for various scientific reasons as well. India must make a prudent choice in the best interest of its people because demographically India will have the largest productive population globally in two decades time. So, while deciding on the resilient infrastructure, priorities and human capability building how '*creative but disruptive choice set*' includes various low/zero GHG emitting technologies and in that how coal-railway-power sector nexus gets reconfigured will determine prosperous India's development trajectory.

The book will be of considerable interest and use to the authors of global assessment reports and development community including academia, decision makers like national governments, bilateral and multilateral funding agencies, civil societies engaged in developmental actions in the region and will generate more interest for taking forward more extensive studies in many other countries to advance deeper regional debate, struggle and understanding of way forward.

Joyashree Roy
Distinguished Professor and Director SMARTS center, Asian Institute of Technology, Thailand.
Former Professor of Economics, Jadavpur University, Kolkata, India.

Table of Contents

List of Maps

List of Tables

Preface

This book traces the progress of railways and coal industry in India from the middle of the nineteenth century to present times. The long journey was shaped by changing political scenarios, economic conditions and the perspectives of the ruling governments. It also witnessed changing management styles, priorities and applications of technology. A study of the impact of all these diverse factors on shaping the development of the two industries is especially interesting as their contemporaneous development was important for India's industrial progress and they continue to play pivotal roles in sustaining the economy to the present day.

India today consumes nearly a billion tonnes of coal, and the Indian Railways moves more than two thirds of it. Energy consumption in India is increasing at a rapid pace and driven by the expanding population and quest for better living standards, this trend is likely to continue. However, the unbridled use of coal, a polluting fossil fuel, cannot continue at the present rate. As the world progresses to the use of renewable energy to ensure a cleaner environment, India has committed to generating 500 giga watts of electrical energy from renewable sources by 2030. Though providing adequate energy from renewable sources to replace coal would be a great challenge, the transition should occur as soon as possible. This is the appropriate time to narrate the story of the wonderful concurrent journey of the railways and coal in India.

Systematic records of coal mining in India are available from the 1820s, and for the last two centuries, the importance of coal in the energy firmament of the nation has steadily increased. The railway was introduced in India in 1853 and the first line of the East Indian Railway reached the Raniganj coalfields in Bengal in 1855. The narrative of the book begins from the period when the first railway line in India reached the coalfields.

The progress of railway transportation depended on the availability of coal as it was the basic fuel for the locomotives. Road and riverine transportation facilities were poor. Thus, railway transportation became the preferred mode for distribution of coal. The two industries became mutually dependent and developed contemporaneously. The industrial development of the nation was facilitated by the expansion of the railway network and increase in coal production and the performance of the two industries continue to be crucial to the economic growth of India.

During the period under study, political control over the country changed and along with it, the attitude of the government towards these two industries. Administrative structures, management methods and technology experienced radical changes over time. Progress was achieved by adapting to changing conditions and creating management structures to accept the change. Navigation of these huge changes was not easy, but was achieved with good leadership and commendable cooperation between the two industries.

The railways and coal are very large industries and any narrative about them covering a period between 1855 to 2023 has to necessarily make some choices about the areas of focus. I have chosen to make the study temporal, by periods rather than by subjects, the choice being determined by stages when certain changes in policies and economic thinking occurred. The second level of choice is the gradual development of coal production and railway transportation in the country, the philosophy of the government about the industries, the policies governing them, the management methods and the status of technology. All the parameters underwent changes over time and produced varied outcomes. The period under British rule is covered in the first two chapters and the other four are devoted to the major changes that took place after India attained independence in 1947. The segregation serves to highlight what role the railways and coal industry could have performed for the nation during the period of British rule.

My experience with coal started in 1980 when I joined the Eastern Railway as a young officer and was promptly posted to Asansol, in the heart of the Raniganj coalfield, then one of the leading coal handling railway divisions of the country. Thereafter, my professional life would be dominated by handling various aspects of coal logistics for the next four decades. Long years of working in coalfield areas in close association with officers of the coal industry provided the opportunity of observing both industries at close quarters and experience first-hand their cooperation, the impact of changing policies at the grass root levels and the immense contribution of coal and railways to the task of nation building. Experience of working at zonal railway headquarters and at the Ministry of Railways (Railway Board), provided a macro perspective about both industries. The criticality of dynamic and progressive policies to facilitate the complex exercise of production and distribution of a critical fuel to the numerous users in the country became evident, as also the need for continuous coordination between the producers, transporters and consumers. Experience of working with Coal India and WBPDCL deepened my understanding of producers' and users' perspectives.

Primary material for the work has been gathered from archival sources such as government documents and administrative reports. Secondary sources of data are books on railways and coal industry and commentary of scholars. My own observations through the four decades of lived experience in handling coal transportation and logistics appear at certain parts of the narrative.

The journey of coal and railways together in the service of the nation will continue for the foreseeable future, though the demand for coal will slowly decline. As this transition takes place, it is hoped that the readers of this book will enjoy the narrative about the stellar journey of the two industries from 1855 to 2023.

Ashim K. Maitra
Kolkata, India

Acknowledgements

Writing the book would not have been possible without patient support from several quarters and it is my pleasant duty to gratefully acknowledge this help.

Recording the historical journey of two large industries covering a period of more than one and a half century requires knowledge about various facets of working and I have accumulated this imperceptibly over the years through constant interactions with my esteemed colleagues and members of the staff. I owe a debt of gratitude to them for having helped me immeasurably in this journey.

Discussions with my wife Susmita and daughters Sulagna and Sreya helped me sharpen the focus of the narrative and reduce the level of technicality to render the book worthwhile for wider readership, including enthusiasts and professionals from other fields. Creative inputs from Sreya and Sulagna, both academicians of long standing, helped me finalize the manuscript.

Among my distinguished colleagues in the railways, I would like to record my gratitude to Mr. Gopal K. Mohanty, Mr. Ghanashyam Bansal, Mr. Rahul Aggarwal, Mr. Y. N. Babu, Mr. H. S. Bajwa and Dr. Avinash Mishra. They were always available for discussions, for clarifying ideas and for suggesting sources of data for supporting the arguments of the narrative.

I am grateful to Mr. M. K. Singh and Mr. P. S. Mitra, retired executives of Coal India for suggesting valuable reading materials on the coal industry. Mr. Sreekanth Roy, General Manager, Coal India offered precious insights regarding the gradual mechanisation of production processes in the coal industry and the new initiatives being launched by Coal India Ltd.

Most of the archival sources of information and data have been obtained by accessing the exhaustive repository available at the National Library, Kolkata, and the libraries of Ramakrishna Mission Institute of Culture, the British Council and the National Digital Library. Other relevant materials on policy issues have been obtained from official web sites of the relevant ministries and government organisations. Information about relevant books shared by well-wishers and some personal procurements have served as secondary sources of information.

Ms Indrani Dutta and Ms Padmavathy Subramanian of the Peter Lang Group guided me through the entire process of preparing the manuscript, reviewing it and making necessary editorial corrections. I am very grateful for their sustained support over the period.

Recording acknowledgements to individuals is always fraught with the danger of omission of some name or names. I have tried my best to recall all those who helped me through the period of writing. I beg apology in advance from those whose name(s) I may have omitted inadvertently.

List of Abbreviations

1. GSI: Geological Survey of India
2. EIC: East India Company
3. GIPR: Great Indian Peninsula Railways
4. EIR: East Indian Railways
5. BBCR: Bombay Baroda and Central Railway
6. BNR: Bengal Nagpur Railway
7. EBR: East Bengal Railway
8. NWFP: North West Frontier Province
9. MGMII: Mining Geological and Metallurgical Institute of India
10. CIC: Central Indian Coalfields
11. NCDC: National Coal Mines Development Corporation
12. CIL: Coal India Limited
13. IR: Indian Railways
14. ECL: Eastern Coalfields Limited
15. BCCL: Bharat Coking Coal Limited
16. CCL: Central Coalfields Limited
17. WCL: Western Coalfields Limited
18. NCL: Northern Coalfields Limited
19. SECL: South Eastern Coalfields Limited
20. MCL: Mahanadi Coalfields Limited
21. NEC: North Eastern Coalfields
22. CMPDIL: Central Mine Planning and Design Institute Limited
23. RDSO: Research Design and Standards Organisation
24. PTS: Preferential Traffic Schedule of Railways
25. DMR: Director Movement, Railways
26. EDRM: Executive Director, Rail Movement

27. CMAL: Coal Mines Authority Limited
28. SCCL: Singareni Coal Company Limited
29. DGMS: Directorate General of Mines Safety
30. NTPC: National Thermal Power Corporation
31. CC Rakes: Closed Circuit Rakes
32. CC: Carrying Capacity (of a wagon)
33. TISCO: Tata Iron and Steel Company
34. IISCO: Indian Iron and Steel Company
35. SAIL: Steel Authority of India Limited
36. BG: Broad Gauge
37. MG: Metre Gauge
38. NG: Narrow gauge
39. MGR: Merry Go Round
40. JBIC: Japanese Bank for International Cooperation
41. PIB: Press Information Bureau, Government of India
42. NEP: National Electricity Plan
43. NRP: National Rail Plan
44. BOG: Balance Other Goods
45. BU: Billion Units

Introduction

Modern industrialised economies source their energy requirements primarily from non-renewable fossil fuels. Coal is the most abundantly available fossil fuel on the earth, and has been in use since at least 400 CE.[1] The use of coal in industrial processes started in the eighteenth century and gathered momentum during the nineteenth and twentieth centuries. A series of scientific inventions, during the eighteenth and nineteenth centuries, such as the steam engine of James Watt, paved the way for a rapid increase in the use of coal in a variety of industrial processes. It would not be an exaggeration to state that coal is the fuel that propelled the Industrial Revolution in Europe and America.

Logistical support for supply of coal to industries was facilitated by the introduction of the coal fired steam locomotive, which paved the way for the introduction of the railways in England (1825) and in other countries. The benefits of this mode of transportation for men and materials soon became apparent. Steamships and railways together enabled the creation of a logistics chain that could cover intercontinental distances and provide reliable logistics support for the industries. Railways using coal as their primary fuel provided fast and reliable means of transportation of raw materials to industries and in the distribution of their finished products. Coal using industries, availing railway transportation, now broke the shackles of having to be located near the coal mines and could be situated at locations far away from the coal fields. Thus, the two industries, coal and railways, developed a wonderful synergy.

---

1 There are some accounts that mention that coal was used in China to smelt copper as early as 1000 BCE. Coal cinders have been found in England suggesting that the Romans used coal before 400 CE. (Source: Encyclopaedia Brittanica)

Records of efforts at coal mining in India are available from 1774. However, systematic mining of coal started in India only from 1820. The growth of coal production was seriously impaired by the lack of logistics support for the distribution of the coal. The advent of railways in India (under British rule) in 1853 provided the backbone for transportation of coal, which was also the primary fuel for the railway and hence indispensable for expansion of the railway network. The railways were, at that time, run by private companies. The Great India Peninsula Railway operated in the western part of the country. Their focus was on movement of cotton to the ports for export. The East Indian Railway (EIR) was headquartered at Calcutta and was keen to transport coal which was available in Bengal. The first railway line on EIR was between Howrah to Hooghly. It was extended up to Raniganj, at the heart of the coalfields in 1855. The coal industry and railways have progressed steadily from that time to provide energy and logistics support to the Indian economy. This narrative is about transportation of coal by railways. Hence the story begins in 1855.

Coal production and railway transportation have come a very long way since then. India today is one of the world's largest coal users and has one of the largest railway systems transporting more than 3.5 billion passengers and 1.5 billion tonnes of freight every year. Coal is the primary commodity in the Indian Railway's freight basket. Given the resource constraints, transporting coal to numerous coal consumers spread all over the country from multiple production points over an extremely busy railway network, carrying passenger and freight trains on the same track, is a gigantic optimisation exercise.

Coal deposits in India are largely concentrated in the eastern and east-central parts of the nation and hence railway transportation plays a crucial role in the distribution of coal to the various centres of demand all over the country. Transportation of coal to distant corners of the sub-continent entails a substantial cost, which is determined by the pricing policy of the railways. For large distances, the cost of transportation may be as much as the cost of the coal and sometimes even more. The economics of the location of industries and fuel consumption patterns is, thus, influenced greatly by the cost of transportation.

Through the evolution of coal production and transportation over more than one and a half centuries, both industries have witnessed changes in the policies governing the industries, in administrative systems, management methods, financial policies and upgradation of technology. Throughout the journey, they have maintained close cooperation and, together, played a crucial role in the industrial advancement of the nation. The story of the development of the coal and railway industries in India is, thus, a fascinating account of progress and growth.

The book is divided into six chapters which cover the following periods:

1) The Journey from 1855 to 1902
2) 1902–47: Progress Amidst Challenges
3) 1948–80: A New Beginning: Planned Development
4) 1981–2002: Impact of new policies
5) 2003–23: Paradigm Shifts
6) Looking Ahead

The periods chosen are those during which some major changes occurred in either or both the rail and coal industries. The narrative of each part is divided into smaller sections with sub titles mentioning the issue addressed.

The span of the narrative is from 1855, when the first railway line reached a coalfield, to 2023. It records the challenges faced during various phases owing to the prevailing government policies, and the political and socioeconomic environment. Presented in a chronological fashion, it identifies and comments on certain salient features discernable during the various phases of development. The features examined during the narration are, the administrative policies followed over time for the management of the railways, expansion of the railway network and the connections to the coalfields, the trends in coal production and transportation of coal by the railways, technology adopted by the coal industry and railways during various periods, changing contours of the tariff policy of railway with respect to freight, changes in the demand pattern for coal over time, the contribution of coal transportation by railway to industrial development. The book concludes with a chapter on the future of the coal industry and coal movement by railways as India moves towards a more climate sensitive economy.

Chapter 1 of the book describes the scenario from the middle of the nineteenth century till 1902. When the railway was introduced in India in 1853, the country was producing about a hundred thousand tons of coal. The distribution of coal was a major issue as both road and riverine transportation were slow and unreliable. The railway needed coal as its primary fuel and the introduction of the railways in any coal mining area provided a great fillip to both the production and distribution of coal. Coal mining began in Raniganj in Bengal and slowly spread to other areas, aided by the expansion of the rail network. Similarly, the discovery of coal deposits in an area prompted the railways to extend the network to that area. By the end of the nineteenth century, India had a fairly large railway network, which connected various parts of the country. Most of the coal producing areas at that time had been connected to the railway network.

Strategic control and exploitation of India's economic resources were the main objectives of the imperial government. It did not wish to invest directly in the construction of the railways in India and left this task to private entrepreneurs by providing them an attractive guaranteed return on investment. The administrative structure aimed at exercising considerable control over railway companies in areas of construction through setting of uniform standards. However, in areas of operations and tariff policy, there was considerable latitude. The consequence of this policy was that aberrations developed which hurt the interest of the consumers and also the government. Coordination amongst the railway companies was very poor. They did not adopt uniform tariffs or rules and standards of operation and the quality of service was not very satisfactory. The government introduced some modifications in its policies after a quarter of a century had elapsed. Necessary legislation was also put in place to provide uniformity in the behaviour of the companies. There was a growing realisation about the need for cohesive working of the railways and, to this end, some railway companies were brought under government control.

The development of the rail network followed the requirements for fulfilling strategic objectives of the British government, such as military movement, connecting the coalfields for supplying coal to the railways and other industries, and connecting the ports to the hinterland for supply of raw materials such as cotton for export to England.

The coal industry grew rapidly, particularly in Bengal and India became an exporter of coal. Though the railway network and coal production increased rapidly, the choice of technology and the tariff policies of disparate companies imposed hurdles on the free movement of coal, particularly over long distances. The trade policy of the British government did not support the development of industries in India and this naturally stifled the demand for further increase in demand for coal.

Chapter 2 covers the period from the beginning of the twentieth century to the attainment of independence in 1947.

Development of new coalfields resulted in rapid increase in coal production. The British government introduced a number of reforms in the railway early in the twentieth century, which were beneficial to the coal and other industries. Attempts were made to increase the level of centralised control on the railway companies. The First World War saw the imposition of strict controls on both the railways and coal industry. New administrative posts were introduced to enforce the rules. The supply of coal and its distribution was carefully controlled. After the war, controls were relaxed and demand for coal increased. This period saw a change in the attitude of the British government towards Indian industries.

Some protection was provided to selected industries, which increased demand for coal and rail transportation.

The coal industry had systemic problems with regard to its structure and level of technology. Intense competition among the companies had deleterious effects on the industry. Some commissions were appointed by the government to enquire into the problems but no major changes were attempted. From 1919, there were changes in the structure of legislatures and a major reform in the railway finances paved the way for improvement in railway services. Centralisation of control on railway companies increased and several major companies came under government control. Cohesion in working and uniformity of standards were sought to be implemented.

The Great Depression caused distress in the coal industry and its systemic structural problems came to the fore. Coal production reduced and availability of the requisite amount of coal became a major issue during the Second World War. The British government provided incentives for coal production which produced some results. This period once again saw the imposition of controls on coal production and rationing of coal distribution.

At the end of the War and the eve of independence, the railway and coal industries were well developed but had a number of infirmities that had to be addressed urgently by the free nation.

Chapter 3 carries the narrative forward from 1948 to 1980, outlining the various actions of the government to take control of the coal industry and railways and use them as instruments for rapid industrial development of a fledgling nation.

Soon after independence, the management system of the railways was completely overhauled. The existing railway companies were merged to form the Indian Railways, which was divided into administrative zones. A roadmap for industrial development was enunciated with sectors like railways and energy wholly under the government. Development was carefully planned in accordance with the objectives of the country as enunciated in the Five Year Plans. Coal was named as an essential commodity and legislation was put in place to control the production and distribution of coal. The government focused on setting right the infrastructural deficiencies in the railways through vertical integration by setting up factories for manufacturing locomotives and coaches. The focus was on the generation of transport capacity to match the demands of new industries.

Indian Railways introduced new freight wagons to carry larger volumes of traffic and operational management methods were modified to handle the burgeoning demand for transportation. The new freight wagons introduced by the railways necessitated radical changes in operational patterns that suited large industries but were not favourable for small units, which found themselves marginalised and slowly migrated to road. The shifting of consumers from rail to road resulted in the steady increase in the share of road transport in the national freight transport market. As the railway is a much more energy efficient mode of transport than road, the energy demand from the transport sector increased.

A well-meaning government policy[2] for ensuring balanced regional development increased real transportation costs, prompting the government to look for alternative instruments for balanced regional development. This policy was modified much later.

The Government of India loosened its control on coal in 1967. However, the allocation of coal was controlled by the railways through a very elaborate system of sanction of demand and allotment of wagons.

A new direction to policy was announced by the government after 1969 wherein the government decided to control the commanding heights of the economy. In line with its announced policy, the coal industry was nationalised in 1973, and all mines (except some coking coal[3] mines owned by the steel industry) were brought under the government under the aegis of Coal India Ltd (CIL). The change involved a gigantic management exercise of creating a new establishment, management structure, recruitment and training of personnel. The focus was on the introduction of modern technology to ramp up production. The Indian Railways (IR) had to develop coal evacuation infrastructure in tandem to keep the industries running. The allocation of funds for CIL and Railways was generous and capacity creation proceeded apace.

The allocation of coal for major industries was decided every quarter by a governmental committee. This provided a stable movement matrix for the coal industry and railways and was useful for the consumers.

Chapter 4 of the book covers the period from 1981 to 2002. This was the period when the loosening of governmental controls and liberalisation of economic policies was started. The economy grew at a faster pace, creating more demand for transport. The capacity of the railway network needed augmentation. The investment planning of the railways during the period did not accord adequate priority to this issue. There was a large shelf of investment proposals causing resources to be spread thinly.

The tariff and investment planning policies of the railways were completely under government control. Passenger tariff was kept low while freight tariff increased steadily, leading to migration of traffic away from railway. Due to substantial losses of revenue in the passenger segment, the profit margin of the

---

2 Freight equalisation policy. For a detailed analysis please see Chapter 3.

3 Coking coal is the type of coal that can be used in the manufacture of steel. Some steel companies like SAIL and TISCO have their captive coking coal mines.

railways was squeezed, while high dividends were paid to the central government on capital received for investment.

The financial support received from the government reduced in the 1990s leading to the borrowing of expensive capital for investment in infrastructure from the market via the Indian Railway Finance Corporation. Coal India also faced paucity of funds during this period, particularly after 1991.

To limit the incremental number of freight trains on an increasingly congested network, the railways opted for carrying more cargo per train. New and larger wagons were introduced, and longer trains were run. Very few industries require a very large volume of materials at one time. Hence, the policy of higher cargo per train increased the share of bulk commodities in the railway's freight basket. Coal to major industries was the most prominent among these commodities. The profile of wagons used by Indian Railways changed in favour of high sided open top wagons amenable for carrying loose materials, like coal.

This was also the period when the demand for coal from the power sector started increasing rapidly. The pattern of movement of coal by railway changed significantly owing to the emergence of new coal producing areas. The railway infrastructure in the older coalfields remained underutilised and the challenge was to create new infrastructure to keep pace with growing coal production from the new coal mines. The increase in coal production came from a few states and the movement by railways was confined to some specific corridors, which were already congested. The problem would exacerbate further in later years.

The new coalfields produced inferior quality coal, with high ash content. Transportation of large amounts of poor quality coal thus entailed carrying large quantities of ash. The concept of beneficiation[4] of coal was discussed in official documents but weakly implemented.

By the year 1999–2000, the financial position of the railways became such that the government appointed a committee with broad terms of reference to look into the workings of the railway.

There were several criticisms of railway working. The most often cited were the spreading of investment thinly over several projects, cost and time over runs of projects, high operations and maintenance costs and poor inter-departmental coordination. The congestion of the existing network and need for further investment were, however, not disputed, but not remedied by adding sufficiently to track network.

Chapter 5 covers the period from 2002 to 2023 and has been named Paradigm Shift as a number of fundamental changes in the management strategy of the

---

4 Beneficiation of coal is the process of reducing the percentage of impurities in the coal, thereby increasing the percentage of combustible material.

railways were introduced. In 2004, the railways enhanced the stipulated cargo-carrying capacity of existing wagons and changed the tariff policy thereby bringing about a radical increase in freight movement and revenue earning. However, the systemic issue of track capacity was not addressed. As traffic volumes increased, the old problem of route congestion resurfaced.

The demand for coal from the power sector continued to increase. The Ministry of Environment and Forests laid down guidelines for the use of beneficiated coal at power stations located at various distances from the coalfields. A number of coal washeries were set up by private operators. The level of washing, however, was much less than the requirement.

An ambitious new project named the Dedicated Freight Corridor (DFC) was unveiled, which envisaged two pure freight corridors from the north to the east and from the north to west. This was to be the long term solution for solving the line capacity[5] problem on Indian Railways. A new company named the Dedicated Freight Corridor Corporation of India (DFCCIL) was set up in 2006. The east to north corridor was completed in 2023. The north to west corridor is likely to be completed soon. Two more DFCs are proposed to be set up for the east to south and east to west routes. Are these the best investment choices?

As part of the liberalisation programme, a new coal distribution policy was announced by the government which changed the system of allocation of coal quantities for major consumers from coalfields through a government committee. The new system introduced bipartite agreements between buyers and sellers. The implicit assumption was that the transportation of coal from any source to any destination was feasible.

This was also the period which witnessed a huge surge in the demand for coal from the power sector due to participation of private power generators. The demand from the power sector increased so rapidly that the biggest coal producer in the country hesitated to sign all the agreements for coal supply brought before it. An order from the highest level of the government was issued directing the coal company to supply coal for a specific level of power generation.

In 2014 the new government appointed another committee to look into 'mobilisation of resources for major railway projects and restructuring of Railway Ministry and Railway Board'. This was yet another attempt to set right the deficiencies in the railways. An interim report was available in the public domain in March 2015. In February of the same year, the Hon'ble Minister for Railways

5 Line capacity of a line segment of railway track is the capability of that line segment to carry a specific traffic mix and volume of traffic (passenger and/or freight) while meeting the quality goals for each type of traffic.

had presented a White Paper on Indian Railways, laying bare the infrastructural and financial position of the organisation. In 2017, a fundamental shift in the mode of financing of the Indian Railways took place after the merger of the Railway Budget with the Union Budget, changing a system implemented as far back as 1924.

As part of the central government's emphasis on developing infrastructure, investment in railways increased. In 2019, the Union Cabinet took a major decision to unify the existing eight Group A services of the railways into one service known as the 'Indian Railway Management Service'. It was stated that this step would improve decision making in the railways by eliminating interdepartmental rivalries. It is too early to assess what effect a change of this magnitude would have on the organisation.

The government also announced that it planned to invest Rupees 50 trillion over the next twelve years to modernise and upgrade the railways. The constraint of funds that the railways faced in the past would perhaps no longer be an issue and this augers well for the future.

In view of the growing demand for coal and the steady increase in imports, the government decided to open up the coal sector for commercial mining. The Mineral Laws (Amendment) Act was passed in 2020. The coal sector was thrown open for private players and earlier conditions of captive use were withdrawn. Participation of foreign investors was allowed. This was a major departure from the earlier policy of the government to control extraction of this important mineral.

Chapter 6 of the book is entitled Looking Ahead. It reflects on the journey of the past and attempts to put into perspective the anticipated growth profile for coal movement by railways in the medium term as the economy moves towards more environment friendly energy alternatives. The alternatives available to the Indian Railways for sustaining freight traffic growth in the future are also examined.

At the COP 26 summit in 2021, the Hon'ble Prime Minister made five promises to reduce carbon emissions. From the perspective of coal demand, the most important declared objective was to generate 500 gigawatts (GW) of energy from non-fossil fuels by 2030. It is likely that the target of 500 gw will be achieved. The demand for energy in the country is growing rapidly and a decision regarding the future of coal-based power generation will have to balance the needs of environmental protection and energy security of the nation.

The demand for coal is influenced by complex factors such as geopolitical issues, availability of raw materials for generating green power and the progress of technology. The war in Ukraine has prompted some European nations to rethink the option of rapidly phasing out the use of coal. In recent years, the Government of India has taken several initiatives to bolster coal production in the country by encouraging private players to produce coal. Clearly, the anticipation is that in the medium term, the demand for coal will remain stable.

It is clear that the transportation of coal by railways in India will slowly undergo a fundamental change owing to the advent of new technology. In one era, smaller consignments were discouraged for moving bulk traffic and the smaller customers migrated to road. Now another fundamental change is occurring in the shape of power generation from renewable sources of energy, which would slowly replace coal as a fuel. For the railways in India, the wheel would have come a full circle. Smaller consignments may have to be wooed back to keep the revenue stream in good health.

The tapering of coal demand would take place gradually and the coal industry and the railways have time to prepare alternative plans to keep themselves afloat. The task is challenging and would require ingenuity and careful planning.

Looking at the longer term, a few suggestions are provided for managing the transition from coal to other traffic.

***

CHAPTER 1

The Journey from 1855 to 1902

The Industrial Revolution in Europe in the eighteenth and nineteenth centuries led to the transition from a society based on agriculture and handicrafts to one depending on industry, mechanised manufacturing and factories. New inventions such as the spinning jenny, the power loom, the cotton gin and the steam engine, opened new vistas of industrial production and transportation. Superior management techniques gradually enhanced the productivity of industries. The Industrial Revolution in Britain created an almost insatiable appetite for raw materials for British industry and the need for large markets for selling their finished products.

The British administrators and industrialists were aware of the vast wealth and the abundant natural resources of India. Development of maritime trade had provided the means of bridging the vast distances between countries and efficient movement of cargo. The control of the East India Company over the Indian subcontinent had increased slowly after 1757 and by the fifth decade of the nineteenth century, large parts of India had come under British administrative control. For administering the country effectively, the Imperial administration needed a mode of rapid mass transportation of troops and materials and the British industry required an efficient transport system for integrating the markets of India and England.

Railway had been introduced in England in 1825. Congruence of British strategic and commercial interests dictated that a railway system be developed in India as well. A means of rapid movement of men and materials would be an invaluable asset to the administration and the railway network would help in the export of raw materials for British industry and import of finished products. Coal was needed for running the railways and the coal industry needed the railways to distribute coal across the country. The development of the coal industry and the railways in India were thus logical extensions of the interests of the imperial government and the trade.

The British administration did not wish to invest government capital for railway construction. Instead, private entrepreneurs were encouraged to run railway companies. As an incentive to the investors, the government offered to guarantee a minimum return on the capital invested. This came to be known as the 'guarantee system'. Several companies invested in building railroads in India.

As a system of transportation, an efficient railway system needs (i) a philosophy of service that determines its overall policies, (ii) a legal mandate to operate, (iii) basic inputs such as fixed and mobile assets, (iv) a management structure, (v) rules of operation, (vi) a commercial policy determining the commercial goals, standards of service and (vii) a tariff policy with reference to costs of operation and service to the consumers.

Among the many facets of railway working, some, like legislation, standards of construction, rules for operation and tariff policy should ideally be centrally controlled. This, indeed, was the stated policy of the British government. However, with the presence of a large number of players, implementation of some of the policy issues, such as tariff policy, proved to be rather difficult. The railway companies operated under contracts with the government and enjoyed considerable freedom within the terms of the contracts. Their perspectives of management were not uniform and enforcing cooperation between them proved to be difficult. A number of aberrations developed which had to be corrected over the course of years. The quality of service to the consumer was adversely affected.

Coal deposits in India are located in the eastern and east-central parts of the country. The distribution of coal all over the large country by rail requires a system of close cooperation between railway companies, such that the consignments are delivered at the least possible cost. There were a number of hurdles in this path, which stemmed mainly from the structure of the system, and the lack of uniformity in the administrative policies. As the rail network expanded, the quantity of coal required by the railways increased. Systemic inefficiencies thwarted the seamless distribution of coal, resulting in its large-scale importation, even though domestic coal was available.

The free trade policy of the British government, which did not grant protection to nascent Indian industries, stifled the possibility of industrial growth. Leveraging of the advantage of ample coal supplies and a large railway system for development of industries could not be realised up to the end of the nineteenth century. The narrative of the development of the railways in India in the second half of the nineteenth century has to be viewed in the light of these political, organisational, economic and policy issues.

Our narrative starts by recounting the development of the coal industry prior to the advent of the railways. It then traverses, briefly, the history of setting up the railways in India and delves into the issues arising out of the interface between the railway companies and the coal industry.

Development of Coal Mining in India before Introduction of Railways

Records for mining of coal in India are available from 1774. It is not known whether coal was actually mined earlier. However, there is evidence of use of metals in India from the Harappan period (2500–1700 BCE). The Ashok Pillar created probably during the Gupta period (fourth to sixth century CE), and presently at the Qutab Minar in Delhi, is an example of use of complex alloy for producing a pillar that has not rusted even after being exposed to the elements for centuries. Such work on metals may not have been possible without generating considerable heat being provided by coal as fuel (Ghosh, 1977, p. 32) (*Gupta*, 2004, p. 12).

Coal Exploration in India

In the eighteenth and early nineteenth centuries, industries requiring coal operated mainly near Calcutta on the eastern coast and around Bombay and Ahmedabad in the western part of India. The coal used by these industries was imported from England at the large ports in both the cities. Calcutta had a locational advantage for using Indian coal, if available, as it was located near the coal deposits in Raniganj (180 kms). Bombay, however, had no coalfields in the vicinity, and had to depend on imported coal for a long time.

In 1774, Warren Hastings, who was then the British Governor General in India accorded permission to two serving officers, John Summer and S. G. Heatly to work coal mines in Bengal. The mines were near the Damodar River, in the Raniganj coalfield, and they commenced working mines as open or incline pits. The coal was, however, found to be of poor quality and this initiative ended in failure. At that time, coal required for foundry work, steam ships and other industries was imported from England. With the expansion of the activities of the East India Company, the need for use of coal increased steadily. In their paper entitled 'Beginnings of Coal Industry in Bengal' Indrajit Ray and Krishna Paul mention

> The matter came again to limelight in 1808 when the Court of Directors expressed its displeasure over the heavy expenditure on the import of British coal in India. They suggested that the ordnance works should be shifted to England if coal could not be mined in India. The Earl of Minto then sought the comments of the Military Board again about the prospect of coal mining in India. He subsequently ordered the Collector of Burdwan to procure and forward 50 to 100 maunds of local coal to the Commissary of Stores along with available information on the subject. (Ray & Paul, 2001, p. 839)

Acting on these orders, another attempt was made at analysing the coal sample sent from the Chinakuri area by one Mr. Marriott. This coal was sent by the Collector of Burdwan to the In-charge of Ordnance Works. After examination, this coal too was found inferior for use in iron works.

In 1813, Marquis of Hastings who was the Governor General of Bengal, decided to have the suitability of Indian coal for forging examined by a competent expert. A shipwright in Calcutta named Mathew Smith, who was using coal from Panchet area for forging, suggested the name of William Jones as a competent and knowledgeable expert.

William Jones was appointed in April 1814 and concluded that sufficient coal of superior quality was available at and around Raniganj. He submitted his report to the government in 1816. Initial progress of mining by private companies was slow. A company named Carr Tagore and Co.[6], set up in 1828, managed some mines. Later, Carr and Tagore started aggressive mining operations and opened new mines in 1840. The Carr Tagore and Co and another company named the Gilmore Homfrey & Co were amalgamated in 1843 to form the Bengal Coal Company which was the biggest coal company of that era. This company had its administrative office in a village named Egra near Raniganj. This was the first administrative office of an Indian coal company.

The decade 1844–54, saw the opening of a number of new mines by players who entered the mining industry.

Issues in Coal Mining

The development of the mining industry in Bengal faced some systemic problems. The Permanent Settlement introduced by Lord Cornwallis in 1793 had made the zamindars the owners of the land. Those who were earlier rent collectors and junior functionaries became owners of huge tracts of fertile and mineral bearing lands. The rapid spread of profitable coal mining spurred the demand for land and the coal mining companies engaged in fierce competition to acquire land. The government had not acquired the rights to the coal bearing land from their original owners and hence litigation over land issues was very common and time consuming. The companies which were able to acquire the land adjoining the transportation route tried their best to cut off their competitors from that route. This unsavoury practice was adversely commented upon and the government tried to rectify it, but with limited success. The issue of the ownership of land and the lease of small parcels of land for mining would continue to fester till the second half of the twentieth century.

---

6 Tagore of the Carr Tagore and Co, was Dwarkanath Tagore, grandfather of Nobel laurate poet Rabindranath Tagore.

The second problem identified by several reports and researchers is the availability of a regular and committed labour force for mining. The miners were recruited from the local agricultural labour. Their attendance at work was irregular, conditioned mainly by the needs of agriculture, which was their first priority. T. Oldham quoted in 'Beginnings of Coal Industry in Bengal' by Indrajit Ray and Krishna Paul observes, 'They worked when they liked, retired when they liked, were always ready with an excuse to stop work, and refused to work until some imaginary grievances were rectified. These strikes were not occasional but frequent.' (Ray & Paul, 2001, 840)

Some researchers contend that the slow development of the Raniganj coalfield of Bengal was also a result of the inadequate dissemination of knowledge regarding the coalfield and consequently the lack of inputs from outside. A committee for 'Investigation of Coal and Mineral Resources' was set up in 1837. John McClelland was the Secretary of the committee and he was the first to appoint a professional geologist. The report of the committee was submitted in 1838. Another detailed report submitted by the committee was published in 1846. This report recommended that the time had come for a proper geological survey of the coal deposits in India. Based on the conclusion of the report and the recommendation of the Government of Bengal, D. H. William of the Geological Survey of Great Britain was deputed to India in 1846 to begin the first systematic mapping of the deposits of the Raniganj Coalfield. His report was published in 1850. The Geological Survey of India (GSI) was set up in 1851. The first task of the GSI was to locate coal deposits for use by the railways, which was about to be launched in India.

The mapping of the Raniganj coalfield was done in 1858–59 mainly by H.W.T. Blanford and W. L. Wilson who was the Superintendent of the GSI. A report of the output of coal was submitted to the government in 1859.

Demand for Coal and Transportation Constraints in early nineteenth century

The Need for Railways

While the British government was trying to gauge the level of coal deposits in Bengal, the use of coal by industries in and around Calcutta had proliferated. The demand for coal increased but reliable transportation was a major constraint in ensuring regular supplies. There were two modes of transportation, rivers and roads. The navigable river adjoining the coalfields was Damodar. In 1818, the Calcutta authorities of the East India Company sent as many as 900 boats to carry coal from Panchet to Calcutta for forging. However, only 200 of the boats could reach the mines. Riverine transportation was constrained severely by seasonality and movement was always in limited quantity.

The other mode of transportation, road, was not worth considering seriously as carriages drawn by mules carrying small payloads of cargo would make very heavy weather of traversing the 150 miles to Calcutta. Further, there were very few roads that were usable throughout the year.

The demand for coal near and around Calcutta increased further from 1823 as a steam powered engine had been introduced at a paper mill in Srirampur. The mill required coal from Raniganj. Impetus to the demand for coal was also provided by the growth of inland steam-based river navigation, which started in India around 1828. With the opening of a few mines between 1820 and 1834, the output of coal increased from 400 tonnes during 1815–23 to 10,000–14,000 tonnes in 1832. Coal was transported during monsoon through the Damodar and Ajoy rivers when sufficient draught was available.

The Carr Tagore and Co had various businesses including flourishing indigo plantations in the land between the Ajoy and Damodar rivers. The company, owner of several coal mines, also focused on the logistics of coal transportation. Coal used to be taken to the banks of the rivers Nunia and Damodar and was stacked for loading into boats which would ferry the coal up to Amta (near Calcutta). Later, a company called the Calcutta Steam Tag Association was formed and Dwarkanath also procured two steamships for carrying coal. As Dwarkanath had interest in several companies in the Calcutta area which were using coal, the integration of the supply chain was quite strong. The Carr Tagore and Co. virtually had monopoly in the supply of coal to sugar mills, rayon mills and the Calcutta Mint (set up in 1757). In 1840 the government engaged steamers, which generated huge demand for coal. Industries such as cotton spinning, forging and paper mills located at Calcutta had started using steam powered engines and this created a continuous demand for coal.

With the progressive opening of new mines and the booming demand for coal, production increased rapidly.

Table 1.1: Trends in Coal Production 1815–46

Period	Coal Production in Tons
1815–23	400
1832	1,000–4,000
1839	36,000
1846	91,000*

*After the formation of the Bengal Coal Company Ltd
Source: Gupta, 2004, p. 25.

The overall transportation scenario, however, continued to remain dismal. Lord Dalhousie commented wryly: 'Great tracts are teeming with produce they cannot dispose of, others are scantily bearing what they could carry in abundance, only if it could be conveyed whither it is needed.' (Danvers, 1878, 41)

A committee was set up in 1845 to examine and recommend the best methods for transportation of coal. After great deliberations, the committee made four recommendations (Gupta, 2004, p. 30) which were:

- Construction of a canal from the Ajoy river.
- Connecting the river Damodar and the Hooghly River.
- Development of roads.
- Construction of railways in India

Setting up the Edifice: Policies for the Development of Railways in India

The railways had been introduced in England in 1825. The investors in Britain, having seen the benefits of a railway system were quite sure that similar advantages would accrue from India too. A strong vocal lobby emerged in England demanding the setting up of a railway system in India. Development of railways in India was strongly advocated by Lord Hardinge and Lord Dalhousie who were Governor Generals in India between 1844 and 1858. The decision to construct a railway system in India was taken due to the congruence of the strategic, administrative and business interests.

India was seen as a vast market for the supply of raw materials and consumption of finished products. With the logistical support of British steamships, India could provide crucial raw materials (particularly cotton) for British industries and would also be a huge market for the consumption of finished products such as cotton garments, steel goods and machinery. Many British investors were willing to set up railway companies in India if sufficient support was available from the government. In India too, some enterprising businessmen, who had seen the railways in England, realised the advantages of having a railway system. It is reported that Dwarkanath Tagore, who was already running a successful coal mining company, offered to pay one third of the cost of laying railway tracks up to the coalfields beyond Burdwan.

Investors in Britain started lobbying with the East India Company (EIC) and the Government. Several petitions were submitted. These proposals found support from Lord Hardinge, Governor General of India from 1844 to 1848. Lord Hardinge observed:

> From political, military and commercial considerations, … [he] thought that the Court of Directors of the East India Company should liberally give assistance to private capitalists, willing to make railways in India, without waiting for proof that the construction of railways will yield reasonable profit. The Governor-General stated that in his opinion, 'on military considerations alone, the grant of one million sterling, or an annual contribution of five lakhs of rupees, may be contributed to the great line when completed from Calcutta to Delhi, and a pecuniary saving be effected by a diminution of military establishments. (Khosla, 1988, p. 2)

Lord Dalhousie, who was the Governor General of India from 1848 to 1856, also played a very important role in moulding the opinion of policy makers in England regarding the construction of railways in India. He wrote two minutes in 1850 and 1853, the latter running into some 253 handwritten pages, in which he discussed various issues beginning with the political, economic and social benefits of installing a railway system, the standards of construction, the routes to be chosen at the outset, the levels of supervisory control of the government and the like.

A formal proposal for the construction of railways in India was first presented to the East India Company in London in 1844 by a private company headed by Macdonald Stephenson, who later became Agent of the East Indian Railway. Two private associations were formed in England in 1845. They were the Great India Peninsula Railway Company (GIPR) and the East Indian Railway Company (EIR). The management of the two associations found it impossible to raise funds for the construction of the railways in India without assistance from the government. Negotiations on the issue of a government guarantee continued for several years.

The development of a railway system in a vast country like India, which had a very rudimentary industrial base, was a gigantic exercise in the management of finance, engineering and human resources. Issues of legal authority to run a railway system and defining sound technical and commercial policies were also major challenges. It is worthwhile to trace, briefly, the evolution of various aspects of the policies governing the operation of railways in India, after which the narrative will turn to the development of the railways in connecting the coalfield areas and the growth of coal production.

Administrative Policies for the Development of Railways

The idea of building a railway system in India having been accepted, the Court of Directors of the East India Company conveyed to the Governor General of

India, through a dispatch dated 7th May 1845, the basic contours on which the development of a railway system through private enterprise could be considered. This was the first official communication by the British Government which recognised the need for development of railways in India. On 28 May 1845, the House of Commons ordered that this communication be printed. The communication pointed out, very presciently, that freight traffic was likely to be the main revenue earner for the railways.

After protracted discussions, the Court of Directors of the East India Company agreed to provide necessary assistance by developing a scheme to guarantee a rate of interest on the capital invested in the construction of the railways. This was accepted by the government.

Mr. Simms was selected as the Consulting Engineer and he reached India in September 1845. After arrival in India and examining the ground realities, Mr. Simms suggested that 'Government should grant leases to joint stock companies to construct and operate certain lines for a given number of years, give land free for the construction of railways and impose no tax or duty on railways' earnings' (Khosla, 1988, p. 3). He also suggested that a series of supervisory controls should be retained by the Government. The whole matter was remitted to a committee of Engineers, which submitted detailed recommendations underscoring the feasibility of and the need to develop a railway system in India. The recommendations of the committee were accepted. The Court of Directors resolved that the first line would be a trunk route connecting the seat of power in Calcutta to the Northwestern Provinces. Hence the first line would be from Calcutta to Delhi via Mirzapore. The strategic importance of the railways was underlined by this decision.

Terms of Guarantee

The terms and conditions of the guarantee could be finalised only after extensive negotiations between the Court of Directors of the East India Company, the Board of Control for India and the Government of India. It was agreed that land was to be given free. The guaranteed interest on capital invested would be 5 per cent and the Government would retain control over standards of construction. The government would also supervise the working of the railways. The contract period would be for 99 years. However, the government would retain the option of purchasing the lines after 25 or 50 years. The East Indian and the Great Indian Peninsula Railway Companies accepted the terms laid down and the legal agreements were ultimately signed on 17 August 1849. (Khosla, 1988, p. 8)

The first 'Report to the Secretary of State for India in Council on Railways in India' for year ending 1859, by Juland Danvers, Secretary, Railway Department, India Office states:

> Railways are, accordingly, being constructed in India under what is popularly termed the "guarantee" system, i.e., through the instrumentality of Companies, who receive from the Government the guarantee of a certain rate of interest upon the capital expended, with the approval of Government, upon their undertakings. The direct pecuniary interest which, under this arrangement, the Government have in the success of each railway, involved the necessity of some supervision and control, which is provided for in the contracts with the several Companies. The land required for the railway and works connected therewith is also given to the Companies, free of expense, by the Government. (Danvers, 1860, p. 1)

The contract was subject to several principal conditions, which are mentioned in the same report of Juland Danvers as follows:

- The guarantee was for a term of 99 years. It applied to all of the money paid to the Government Treasury and spent with the approval of the Government. Once the capital account was closed, any unspent amount paid into the Treasury would be returned to the company.
- The net receipts of the railways were to be paid into the government Treasury. If the net receipts were less than the guaranteed interest, the shortfall would be made up by the government. If the net receipts were more, half of the excess would be added to the dividend of the shareholders of the company and the other half would go towards repayment of the sums paid earlier by the government towards guaranteed interest.
- If the net receipts were less than the working expenses, the guaranteed interest payment would have to cover the shortfall.
- If the company were able to return the entire amount paid by the government as guaranteed interest, it would be entitled to retain the entire profits, so long as the operations remained profitable.
- Notwithstanding the 99 years lease, the Government retained the power of purchasing the Railway within six months after the expiry of 25 years or fifty years from the date of the contract. The price of purchase would be the mean value of the shares of the company in the London stock market during the past three years.
- If any railway company failed to execute the project or work the railway satisfactorily, the government retained the power to take over the company and return the money spent by the company within six months.
- After 99 years, the land would revert to the government. If the railway company had not, by then, used the option to surrender the company to the

government, the assets of the company such as track, locomotives, etc. could also be purchased by the government at an appropriate valuation.
- All monetary transactions were to be calculated at 1 shilling 10 pence to the Rupee.

In addition to the controls mentioned in the principal conditions of the contract, the government also retained many supervisory controls over the private companies. The Report of 1859 cited above contains details of the supervisory controls put in place. They were:

> The supervision is exercised by the Government both in this country and in India. An Official Director is appointed, who attends each Board of the Railway Companies in London, and possesses, under the Deed of Contract, a power of veto on all the proceedings of the Directors. This power has never yet been put into force, a circumstance which a Parliamentary Committee on Indian Railways attributed to "the judgment and discretion exercised by the Official Director on all occasions, and to the respect shown to his opinion. The office is filled by Sir James C. Melvill, K.C.B. At the same time, questions involving expenditure, which have not been considered by the local Governments in India, and all matters of importance, are referred to the Secretary of State for India in Council, with whom also the financial arrangements of the Companies are made." (Danvers, 1860, p. 6)

At the field level, supervision was exercised through Consulting Engineers, who had far reaching powers to examine the terms of the construction contracts, the estimates, the direction of the lines, the position of stations and standards of construction.

The model of financing development of railways in India had two notable features. First, the capital required for construction of the railways was not provided by the British government. It was primarily raised in the London market by private entrepreneurs, through shares and debentures. The government of India had agreed to make good only the difference between the actual earnings of a railway company and a 5 per cent return on the capital invested. Hence the capital component would not feature in the books of accounts of the government. Secondly, the interest payout to the companies was financed from the taxes paid by the Indian population. The development of the railways in India was thus financed, at least partly, by the Indians.

Engineering, Management and Legal Issues

After the policy parameters governing the investment and construction of railway lines was decided, the engineering, managerial and legal issues of constructing railway lines and running a railway system had to be addressed.

A decision was taken that one line each would be constructed in the three Presidencies of Calcutta (now Kolkata), Bombay (now Mumbai) and Madras (now

Chennai). The project of the Great Indian Peninsula Railway (GIPR) received great support from the cotton interests of Liverpool, who were keen to develop new sources of supply of raw cotton and a good market for their finished products. Contracts with the GIPR and the East India Company were signed in 1849. An experimental line, 35 miles (56.35 km) long would be constructed by GIPR. Finally, the line was proposed to be extended, linking the GIPR with the other presidencies of India. Surveys for the first section from Bombay to Thana commenced in 1850. Plans and tenders were finalised by September 1850. Construction began in 1851 and was finished early in 1853. The first passenger train on Indian soil ran on 16th April 1853.

Col. Kennedy succeeded Mr. Simms as the Consulting engineer in Calcutta. He developed a plan for an experimental line between Howrah (near Calcutta, on the western side of the Hooghly River) and Pandua, with an extension to the coalfields of Raniganj. The earthwork was planned for laying double tracks in the future. This plan was approved by Lord Dalhousie in 1850. Construction commenced in 1851 and was completed in 1854. The first train on the East Indian Railway ran between Howrah and Hooghly on 15th August 1854. The line was extended to Pandooah by September 1854 and up to Raniganj, which was at the heart of the coalfields, by February 1855 (a distance of 121 miles).

The development of the railways in a distant land that did not have major manufacturing facilities was a gigantic exercise in logistics and project management. All equipment required for construction such as rail tracks, locomotives, coaches, wagons, signals and other equipment had to be imported from England. Secondly, skilled manpower capable of setting up the railways and running it would have to be deputed to India. Thirdly, an administrative apparatus was required for managing and supervising operation of the railways. The management would have to take decisions on a tariff policy for passenger and freight traffic, and the managers would require a legal mandate to operate. These were not easy tasks as the conditions of the country were not well known.

Challenges Faced in Construction of Railway Lines

Once construction began, issues, perhaps not envisaged earlier, surfaced. The import of materials from England was a complicated exercise in trade. The report for 1859 observes:

> As the balance of trade between this country and India is always on the side of India, the natural limit to the conveyance of dead weight from this country is regulated by the trade from India. Ships go out from hence for return cargoes. If that natural limit is exceeded, and there are too many ships in the Indian ports to secure remunerative freights for the voyage home, a rise necessarily takes place in the freights to India, and

> the enhanced price falls upon the Railway Companies. In other words, the cost of constructing the works is increased. (Danvers, 1860, p. 29)

After importing the construction materials, there was the challenge of transporting these materials to the worksites. The report of 1859 gives the details of the various methods used to ensure that the pace of construction of railway lines did not falter. It states:

> But when the difficulty of conveying the materials to India is got over, a more formidable one presents itself there. With the great lengths of line which materials are in course of construction it is impossible, without incurring great delay, to lay down the rails upon what is termed the telescopic principle, i.e., by leading them from a certain point over the line, as it is finished, and laying them down by degrees. If this course had been followed with regard to the East Indian line, the opening of any section in the upper portion would have been delayed long after the earth-works were ready to receive the rails, and the line between Allahabad and Cawnpore would never have been available for troops during the military operations in Oude. The means of transport are, however, very deficient, and great risk and expense is incurred in conveying materials, whether by land or river. So much has this been felt on the East Indian Railway, that the Directors have provided a fleet of tug steamers, with barges, to take their materials up the river. The Great Indian Peninsula Railway have also great difficulties to contend against in conveying the materials for the Deccan lines across the Ghats; likewise the Sind Company, in having to send their materials for the Punjab Railway a distance of from 670 to 900 miles from the Port of Kurrachee (Karachi, now in Pakistan). (Danvers, 1860, p. 129)

For every mile of railway line constructed, 125 tons of materials were required, and if the materials for buildings, siding lines and other facilities were included, the requirement would go up to 250 tons per mile. The report for 1859 provides the following data:

Table 1.2: Import of Materials for Railway Construction 1854–59

Year	Tons of materials Imported
Up to 1854	77,200
1855	111,642
1856	126,835
1857	123,103
1858	147,844
1859	208,280
Total	794,904

Source: Danvers, 1860, p. 28.

Based on calculation of 250 tons per mile, the material sent out to India would be sufficient for

In year	For miles
1855	446
1856	507
1857	492
1858	591
1859	833
Total	2869

Source: Danvers, 1860, p. 28.

Formation of Companies to Run the Railways

With the establishment of the Guaranteed railway system, a number of companies entered the field, and construction in several parts of the country commenced. Lord Dalhousie had been a great proponent of developing the railway along important trunk routes. Three main routes which had been proposed were Calcutta-Delhi, with an extension to the North-West frontier area, Bombay-Delhi and Madras-to the west coast. Contracts between the East India Company and the East Indian Railways were finalised to construct the line from the east to the north and with GIPR for a line between Bombay and north India and another line from Bombay to Raichur. The Madras Railway Company was constituted in 1853 and between December 1855 and August 1858, contracts for the construction of trunk lines from Madras towards the west coast of India along with branch lines to the northwest towards Bombay were finalised. The other important trunk line company was the Bombay Baroda and Central India Railway. It signed a contract for a line from Surat to Ahmedabad in 1859.

In the southern part of India, the Great Southern of India Company was formed in 1857. It planned to construct lines in the extreme southern part of the peninsula from Negapatnam to Trichinopoly and also two lines towards Erode and Tuticorin. A contract for the first section was signed in 1858. The Great Southern originally constructed lines on the specifications of Standard gauge. Later, in 1873, the company was merged with the Carnatic Railway, the new name being South Indian Railway. After the merger, the lines were converted to metre gauge specifications and covered an extensive area of south India.

Some lines were developed by companies without guarantees. Railway lines were also constructed by the Princely states of India.

For the movement of coal, the lines emanating from the East Indian Railway were most important as coal mining was confined initially to the area around Raniganj in Bengal. Later, the coal mines in Jharia, the Central Provinces, Warrora, and the princely states of Rewa and Hyderabad came up and were joined to the railway network for the distribution of coal.[7]

Legislations to Regulate Railway Operations

The running of a railway system in India required legal sanction. An enactment was made in 1854. The laws adopted were mostly borrowed from the model of the railways in Britain and were applicable only to the areas under British rule at that time. The issues covered were regarding the responsibility of the railways as common carriers of traffic, and rules for booking and handling of luggage, passengers etc. Several areas, such as safety, protection of the customers against undue preference etc. remained uncovered. An example of this is found in the Report to the Secretary of State in Council on Railways in India for 1876–77. It mentions:

> On the Oudh and Rohilkund, damage was caused by the sparks from an engine, and an action was brought against the Company to recover the loss. Judgement was given in favour of the plaintiffs by the Assistant Commissioner before whom the case was tried, and confirmed by the Commissioner of the District, on the ground that the Company possessed no legislative power to use locomotives. Strange though this reason may appear, it seems that there was ground for it. In order that, in future, all doubts may be removed, it has been suggested that the new Railway Bill about to be introduced into the Legislative Council for consolidating all existing Acts relating to Indian Railways should contain a clause by which the power to use locomotives on railways should be distinctly given. (Danvers, 1877, p. 15)

Issues arising from time to time were addressed through Government resolutions. In 1867, it was decided that laws for defining the responsibilities of public servants and penalties for misdemeanour needed to be defined. A short act was passed in 1867. A more comprehensive legislation was being considered and was sought to be discussed. However, the Government's right to legislate for privately owned railways was questioned. Consequently, the enactment of a comprehensive legislation was kept pending. In 1870 and 1871, two short Acts covering areas such as reporting of accidents and cattle trespass were passed. At this time the Government was considering the introduction of State-owned railways and hence further legislation was again postponed. The applicability of the existing laws to all railways, whether or not under British rule, was announced.

---

[7] Please see map of railway lines and coalfields at Appendix 1.

An Act was passed in 1879 to take over the East Indian Railway by the Government. The Act related only to the EIR and its relationship with the Government. With the operation of the railways by the State it was required that certain issues like the periodical inspections to ascertain the quality of management and the protection of customers be enacted. In 1883 a short Act (Act IV of 1883) was passed, which authorised the Governor-General in Council to initiate steps for the protection of the travelling public and for periodic inspections of the working of the railways. It was laid down that prior to the opening of any line for passenger traffic, the line would mandatorily be inspected, whether it was under British territory or not.

As the level of traffic increased, disputes among railway companies on interchange of traffic and preferential rates and fares increased. A draft bill was prepared in 1884 and put out for discussion. The debate on this bill lasted five long years. In the meanwhile, the 'Railway and Canal Traffic Act' was passed in England in 1888. This was a comprehensive piece of legislation and opinion in England regarding the type of laws required for India, was moulded by the provisions of this Act. The Boards of the guaranteed railways had raised several issues regarding the provisions of the draft of 1884. A Select Committee was appointed to address these issues. The Committee took the view that instead of addressing the issues of each company piecemeal, a comprehensive piece of legislation was required that would be applicable to all railway companies. The Indian Railway Act was finally passed in 1890. The Act applied to all railways including those belonging either wholly or partially to Indian states. Sanyal observes:

> An important feature of the Act was its applicability to railways belonging wholly or partially to Indian states, or those passing through their territory, as well as to the railways in British India. In many cases such lines formed part of through routes and it was evident that civil and criminal jurisdiction for damage or offences under the Act must lie with the Government of India. After considerable negotiations with almost every Indian State this end was finally achieved.
>
> The general tenor of railway legislation in India has been to follow the example of Great Britain, and the Act of 1890 which was passed into law on 21st March as Act IX of the year was no exception. In fact, some of the chapters and clauses were taken almost verbatim from the Railway and Canal Traffic Act of 1888. The law came into operation on 1st of May 1890. (Sanyal, p. 175)

Impact of Operation of Multiple Railway Companies

Construction of railway lines required large investments. Private entrepreneurs opened lines to operate in areas that suited them. Consequently, several railway companies under different managements were opened in India. Over the years, this policy gave rise to multiple issues regarding uniform standards of construction of railway lines, cooperation between the companies for through running of trains, common tariff policies, agreements regarding operational procedures and supervision of railway companies by government agencies. However, the British government adhered to its policy of encouraging the expansion of the railway network through participation of several entrepreneurs. By 1890, the railway companies under different types of management were:

1. State lines operated by companies such as the East Indian Railway (EIR had been taken over by the government in 1879), Patna-Gaya Railway, Bengal Nagpur Railway.
2. State lines operated by the State such as the Oudh-Rohilkhand Railway, North Western Railway, Eastern Bengal Railway.
3. Lines operated by guaranteed companies such as Great Indian Peninsula Railway (GIPR), Bombay Baroda and Central Railway (BBCR), the Madras Railway.
4. Lines owned by Native States and worked by private companies such as the Nizam's Guaranteed State, Gaikwar's Patlad.
5. Lines owned by Native states and worked by State agencies such as Rajpura-Bhatinda Railways. (Khosla, p. 187)

The need for a developing a cohesive railway system to achieve optimum output was thus compromised.

Administrative Supervision of Railway companies

The British administration had always maintained that strict supervision and control would be exercised on the railway systems in India. With so many management systems, it was necessary to articulate some policies for exercising control. The Administration Report on Railways in India 1881 clarifies the methodology of the control mechanism exercised by the British administration:

> 'The whole system of Railways in India is under the control of the Indian Administration Government. In return for the State aid afforded to the old Guaranteed Companies, the Indian Government exercises this control over each Company by means of officers termed "Consulting Engineers to Government," posted at Bombay for the Great Indian Peninsula and Bombay, Baroda and Central India Railways; "Madras for the Madras and South Indian Railways; at Calcutta for the East Indian and Eastern Bengal Railways; at Lahore for the Sind, Punjab and Delhi Railway; and at Lucknow for the Oudh and Rohilkhand Railway. The Consulting Engineers at Madras and Bombay are under the orders of the Governments of those two Presidencies; those at Calcutta, Lucknow, and Lahore are under immediate orders of the Government of India.

> State Railways are classed under three heads: – I. Imperial. II. Provincial. III. Native States. Imperial Railways are constructed from Imperial funds, and will be generally under the control of the Director General of Railways. Provincial Railways are constructed from funds for the interest on which the Provincial Government has accepted all responsibility. These are controlled by the Local Governments and Administrations, under the general supervision of the Government of India. Class III comprises those lines which have been constructed on the financial responsibility of the Native rulers in Native States. whose territory they lie. These are in most cases controlled by the Consulting Engineers to Government' (Trevor, 1882, p. 207).

Standards of Construction of Railway Lines

An important decision of the British government was the laying down of uniform standards for the construction of railways soon after the decision to launch railways was taken. Sanyal (pp. 38–9) observes:

> Standard dimensions of roadway and roiling stock had been definitely fixed, as early as 1856 by the consulting engineers of the railway companies, with the approval Government, and these were rigidly adhered to. India gained through the unhappy experiences of other countries. and the benefits accruing from this early decision cannot too much be emphasised. Some of the principal dimensions then determined may be of interest. These were:
>
> Minimum clear width between two tracks ... 6 ft.
>
> Minimum distance of Platform wall from rail 2 ft. 6 in.
>
> Minimum clear height for all openings above rail, in centre ... 14 ft. 6 in. ...
>
> Extreme width of body of coaches 8 ft. 6 in.
>
> Maximum length between centre of wheels 11ft.
>
> In later years these dimensions have been reviewed and separate standards have been fixed for railways of smaller gauges. It may be noted that the loading gauge in India has never been sufficiently liberal in proportion to the wide standard gauge for the railway, and much of the potential capacity of the line has therefore been left neglected.

Issues in the Management and Development of the Railways

A. Deviations from Standards of Construction

Despite the laying down of standards of construction and the imposition of controls, the system of supervision by the government still provided considerable freedom to the individual railways. For example, in practice, each company decided the standard of track suitable for its traffic, which was not the original idea. This concession regarding track standards had long term repercussions on traffic movement when the railway systems got connected. Some companies like the EIR and GIPR decided on Broad Gauge (5' 6") lines, while several others opted for metre Gauge lines (one metre distance between the rails). A network with different gauges was certainly not ideal for good mobility. Break of gauge transhipment led to delays in movement. Lord Dalhousie had warned about this possibility and the need to guard against it.

'The Indian Railways were beset with the gauge problem in their infancy.' In 1851, Lord Dalhousie had written:

> The British Legislature fell into mischievous error permitting the introduction of two gauges in the United Kingdom ... The Government of India has the power, and no doubt will carefully provide that, however, widely the railway system may be extended in this Empire in the time to come, these great evils should be averted."
>
> But as fate would have it, the evil of multiple gauges could not be averted in India. There were certain compulsions: the limitation of funds, insufficient traffic, and strategic considerations. But it is a curious fact of history that such factors did not ultimately play any part in the adoption of the standard gauge, 4 feet 8 inches, in Great Britain, the fountain head of the railway knowhow for India. (Khosla, 1988, p. 68)

B. Control on Tariffs

The controls exercised on the tariff policy were ambivalent and the lack of uniformity became a serious issue later on. The report of Julian Danvers (1860) mentions:

> With regard to the regulation of fares, they are, in the first instance, fixed Fares and rates, with the approval of Government, and alterations in them can only be made by the Railway Companies with the concurrence of the same authority. In the event of the profits exceeding ten per cent., the Government can order a reduction in the rates, but not to such an extent as to bring the net receipts below ten per cent. upon the capital expended.
>
> The Railway Companies are also bound, under the contracts, to convey the Mails and Post Office servants free of charge, to take Military Officers in first class carriages at second class fares and soldiers when on duty in second class carriages at the lowest fares; also, horses, guns, waggons, and military stores, & c., at the lowest rate for the time being chargeable for the carriage of such animals, goods etc. (Danvers, 1860, pp. 6–7)

Though the tariff was fixed with the concurrence of the government, in later years the government refused to interfere when it was found that exorbitant tariff rates was leading to loss of traffic. Further, the companies were given a clear mandate regarding the carriage of government materials at concessional rates.

Multiple railway companies slowly developed, each working in its own domain and having its own tariff policy. Consumers moving freight traffic across the jurisdictions of two or more railways had to pay separate rates, as determined by each company, there being no common rates for through traffic. The break of gauge and the system of multiple tariffs would become vexatious issues later and the issues took a long time to resolve.

C. Ramifications of the Financial Model for Development of Railways

The contract between the State and the private companies regarding the provision of guaranteed return on capital invested in the construction of railways had several grey areas. For example, there was no mention of a maximum amount of capital on which the guarantee would operate. Secondly, the exchange rate with the Indian Rupee was fixed a 1 shilling 10 pence, without any variation clause. These features led to unexpected consequences. Assured of guaranteed returns, some contractors were quite profligate in their use of resources for the construction of lines and stations. Economic historian Daniel Thorner has observed:

> Initially, the costs of construction of the railways were very high. Since the companies had a guarantee of 5 per cent interest, they had little incentive to economy. Building went ahead both carelessly and lavishly. Where works were defective, they were simply rebuilt. Stations were erected in a grand style, scarcely suited to India's impoverished economy. From the beginning luxury coaches were provided for upper-class passengers. (Thorner, 1955, p. 206)

The government had a right to refuse extravagant expenditure. However, this impeded the speed of work. The communications between the contractors executing the projects and the government were far from perfect. Frequently, the railway companies found it convenient to report information regarding expenditures after the work was completed. However, despite the aggressiveness of the contractors, progress was perceived to be slow. By 1857, only 300 miles of railway track had been constructed. The First War of Indian Independence (1857), and its immediate aftermath, led to the further slowing down of construction of lines. In 1858, the Queen's Proclamation took away the control from the hands of the East India Company, and now the railway companies had to deal directly with the Imperial Government. A Committee of the House of Commons was set up in 1858 to enquire into the reasons for the poor progress in the construction of lines. The Committee submitted a detailed report which mentioned that given the constraints of working at a location far away from England, the progress of construction was not inadequate and was, in fact, comparable to that of some English lines.

> They classified the causes of delays into four distinct heads, viz.,
>
> 1st. Those arising from Government supervision at home and in India.
>
> 2nd. Those incidental to the execution of extensive and complicated public works, under such circumstances, in a distant country.

> 3rd. Those produced by political causes, such as insurrection and mutiny.
>
> 4th. Those arising from the natural difficulties which the face of the country presents. (Danvers, 1860, p. 7)

The Committee endorsed the Government's decision to permit private capital to be invested in the construction of the railways and also felt that the 'Guarantee system' was required to attract private capital. Supervision and control of the Government over the entire process was also supported. However, the Committee opined that some reforms in the methods of working were required, and suggested that the following changes be brought about:

- Clear delineation of duties and responsibilities to prevent evasion of responsibility.
- Discretionary powers to be entrusted to men of proven merit and vision.
- Adherence to the spirit of the contracts signed with the private entities. (Danvers, 1860)

One of the reasons for the slow progress in construction cited by the private companies in charge of construction was the delay in clearances of expenditure from the Finance department. As the emphasis of the government was on rapid progress of construction and not on economy of expenditure, a change in the system of financial concurrence of expenditure was introduced.

> When the British Parliament ordered an inquiry into the progress of railway construction in India the first of what later turned out to be a long series of Parliamentary and governmental inquiries into the functioning of India's railways-the railway companies had the opportunity for which they were looking for. They painted a black picture of the government harassment to which they had allegedly been subjected. The Parliamentary Committee hearkened to the companies and rebuked the Government of India. The result was that after 1858 the costs incurred in the process of railway construction were checked only by a post-audit system. (Thorner, 1955, p. 205)

The 1860s witnessed a boom in the construction of railway lines, with major British contractors also entering the market. Between 1857 and 1869, it is estimated that 150 million pounds sterling was invested in India by Britain, most of which came to the railways. The huge inflow of funds led to the rapid expansion of railway network. However, the accelerated pace of construction created a new problem. Most of the railway companies were not earning a 5 per cent return on their investment and looked to the government to make good their shortfall, which the government was obliged to do under the terms of the contract. Daniel Thorner observes,

> Except for the E.I.R. from Calcutta to Delhi-which for long stretches passed through a railway engineer's paradise: the level plain of the Ganges Valley above Allahabad-the railways for many decades did not pay their way. For two generations after 1850 the railways, instead of contributing to government revenues, acted as a drain on government finances. (Thorner, 1955, p. 206)

Only East Indian Railways continued to earn profits above 5 per cent. This was largely due to the growing traffic in coal movement.

D. Review of Government Policy for Financing Railways

As the railway network expanded, the financial pressure on the government continued to increase. Faced with the predicament of ballooning expenditure, the government took two major decisions in 1869–70. First, it was decided that any 'additional' railways in India would be owned, built and managed by the government. Secondly, the contracts with the existing companies would be re-negotiated. The new contracts did not make major changes to the existing conditions. Some of the changes introduced were: (a) the exchange rate was increased from 1 s 10 d to 2 shillings. (b) land was granted free in perpetuity, but the State could acquire it after 20 years had elapsed and after any ten year period thereafter. (c) the companies would have to abide by any new legislation regarding railways made after the year of the contract. (d) the government would scrutinise thoroughly the estimates for construction before agreeing to the guarantee. (e) the guaranteed return was reduced from 5 per cent to 4 per cent.

After the conditions of the new contract had been finalised, the Secretary of State took a surprising decision concerning the old, guaranteed railways. He made an offer to the companies stating that they would not have to pay any of the old dues arising out of the advances made by the State for the guaranteed interest. All liabilities on this account would be wiped out. In return, the Government would receive, in perpetuity, 50 per cent of surplus net profits. This amazing decision was taken without any discussion with the Government of India. Clearly, this offer was not attractive to railways which were running at a profit and was targeted only at those incurring losses. The East Indian Railway, which was showing some profits, refused to accept the offer. Railways such as the Great Indian Peninsula Railways, Madras Railway, Bombay Baroda and Central India Railway, Sindh Punjab and Delhi Railway, the Carnatic Railways and the Great Southern of India Railway accepted the offer. The additional concession made for the GIPR, Madras and BBCR was that the Government waived its right to purchase the railway after 25 years. Obviously, the objective was to bolster the financial position of these railway companies.

The government of India protested strongly against this unilateral decision as it bailed out the Railway companies and put the Government of India at a loss. Sanyal observes:

> The protest reached England too late to affect the decision of the Secretary of State. By that time the policy of State construction and management had been accepted and put into operation. In view of this, one cannot understand why the Secretary of State took such steps as were considered injurious by the Government of India.' The loss to the State had been a very material gain to the shareholders and in losing the opportunity of reducing the high and then unnecessary rate of guaranteed interest of five per cent a fault of omission was committed which it is difficult to extenuate. (Sanyal, 1930, p. 70)

The Secretary of State assured the Government of India that in future their views would be sought first.

E. Construction of lines by the State

The construction of railway lines by the State began in real earnest. The engineers of the government had a point to prove and some State lines were constructed at costs much lower than that incurred by private enterprise. However, the experiment of construction of railways by the government was short lived due to some unforeseen circumstances. The 1870s saw the worst series of famines in a century hitting India. At the same time, the London financial market went into a depression. The Anglo-Afghan (1878) war also drained the state's finances. These three factors led to the government deciding that the additional expenditure of building the railways was best left to the private entrepreneurs.

A fresh look at the pattern of investment was required. A Select Committee was appointed by the Government to examine the issue of railway communications in India. The Committee's report recommended that there was a strong case for rapid expansion of the railway network in India. However, each line should be generally self-supporting. The government would provide finance for some protective lines which were required for famine relief. The Public Works Department of the Government of India should not be overburdened with monetary demands and some finance should be made available from England if required. The recommendations were communicated to the Governor General of India in 1884.

A new arrangement was entered into with EIR, which was acquired by the government in 1879. Under this regime, 80 per cent of the old shareholders were paid off and the ones remaining formed a new company retaining the old name. They were entrusted with the management and operation of the company. The guaranteed return was 4 per cent. Thus, a new model of government ownership and private management emerged. The new model became the benchmark till 1924. One significant development was that from 1900 onwards the railway companies started earning 4 per cent or more return on their investment.

F. The imperial government had perhaps realised that it was prudent to keep railway companies under the control of the State. Several railway companies were progressively acquired by the State in the subsequent years, and the drawbacks of earlier contracts was sought to be rectified. One example of this was the reduction in the rate of guaranteed payment. The railway companies that were acquired were:

- The Eastern Bengal Railway (EBR) in 1884. The lines of the Northern Bengal, Calcutta and South Eastern Railway were amalgamated with the EBR and worked by the State.
- The Scind Punjab and Delhi Railway was taken over in 1885. The railway was combined with the Punjab-Northern and Indus Valley state lines to form the North Western Railway. This railway was very important from the strategic perspective and was worked by the State.
- The Oudh and Rohilkhand railway was acquired in 1889 and worked directly by the State.
- The South Indian railway was taken over by the State in 1890, but the old management of the company continued to operate it.
- The same method was followed for the GIPR in 1890.
- The Indian Midland railways was amalgamated with GIPR and the old management continued its operation.

Thus, with the exception of BBCR and the Southern Railways, all the old guaranteed railways came under state control by the turn of the century (Sanyal, 1930, p. 195).

We now turn to the growth of coal production and development of the railways in various areas.

Increase in Coal Production and Expansion of the Rail Network in Eastern India

The output of the collieries in the Raniganj area had started increasing and the railway connection to the Raniganj coalfield provided a huge impetus to the mining of coal as its delivery to the destination was assured. By 1860 nearly 50 collieries were working in the Raniganj field and the average annual output was 7,808,586 maunds or 321,268 tons approx. an increase of 2.2 times from 1850. The Raniganj coalfield was the only field producing large amounts of coal at that time. More areas would emerge soon. Data on the coal output of each province is available only from 1878 onwards.

Between 1855 and 1856, railway lines were laid to connect various collieries in the Raniganj area. The railway line from Andal to Babisol was opened in 1861. A line from Andal to Sonachara was opened in 1863 and a connection from Raniganj to Asansol was also established in the same year. The line from Asansol to Barakar was completed in 1865. Connection to the railway routes proved to be a boon for the collieries. Some mines like Nimcha and Parasia, which had been closed down, were reopened. Coal mines which were near the rail track were provided with a connection to the rail network. The cost of the connecting siding had to be borne by the colliery owner. Mines located far away from the rail track were compelled to carry the coal in bullock carts to the loading point. Some prosperous coal companies such as Apcar and Co. invested in a private line to their coal mines (1881).

In 1864, there was a huge subsidence in the Raniganj area and a devastating fire broke out. The need was felt to map the coal deposits accurately. An intensive study was conducted and in 1881, 'Economic Geology of India' was published. During the nineteenth century, Raniganj continued to be the dominant coalfield in terms of production.

The impact of the railway on the development of the coal industry in India was noted by The Review of the Trade of British India with other Countries for the year 1878–79 It states:

> Coal mining in India is rapidly attaining considerable importance. The commencement of this industry appears to date back to 1820, when a mine ·was opened in the Raniganj district in Bengal. For twenty years no new mine seems to have been opened and then only three. mines were opened down to 1854. In that year the commencement of the East Indian Railway line, which was laid to run through the coal-bearing regions of the Damuda (Damodar) basin, gave an impetus to the mining industry and new pits were opened in large numbers: 2 in 1854, 3 in 1857, 3 in 1859, 3 in 1860, 2 in 1861, 1 in 1865, 2 in 1868, 1 in 1869, 1 in 1870, 2 in 1871, 1 in 1872, 3 in 1873, 7 in 1874, 5 in 1875, 3 in 1876, 5 in 1877. All these were in Bengal in the Raniganj and neighbouring districts, which contain now altogether 56 mines, at work. In the Central Provinces also the coal-fields of Narsinghpur and Chanda have been utilised for the purposes of the Great Indian Peninsular Railway. The total output of coal in India, in the year 1878 was 1,015,21.0 tons. The whole quantity imported in 1878–79 was under 480,000 tons, being considerably under half the Indian production. It is clear therefore that Indian

> coal already plays an important part in the industrial economy of the country, and there is no doubt that that part will increase in importance. Bengal coal is now used on the East Indian Railway, in the steamer employed in the river and coasting traffic, in the cotton, jute, and other mills in Calcutta and its vicinity, and for such purposes there will be a constantly increasing demand. The coal in the fields of the Central Provinces has no present prospect of being consumed in such a variety of ways, the remoteness of the fields from the coast and the absence of navigable rivers in those tracts restricting the area of consumption. As yet it is mainly used on the Great Indian Peninsular Railway, but hereafter it will probably be largely in demand for cotton mills as the numbers of these increase. Extensive deposits of good coal as yet little worked occur in Northern Assam. The completion of the projected railway lines in. that province will offer a good opening for the profitable working of these fields, and in time the Assam coal-fields will no doubt be as vigorously utilised as those of Bengal. (O'Conor, 1879, p. 22)

Methods of Coal Mining

At the initial stages of mining, methods followed were rather rudimentary. Coal was extracted from the outcrops through shallow digging and removal of earth and stones. When deeper depths had to be reached, an incline was created and the coal that was mined was put in a basket which was hauled up through a pully arrangement known as a Gin. In India, the pulleys were hand operated. In England and Europe, horses were used. When the use of steam engines spread to the coal mining areas, steam power was used to haul up the coal. Later, shaft mining and the method of lowering cages into the shafts started.

Mining coal from underground mines was a difficult technical exercise that required specialised knowledge and skills. There was a danger of inundation by water and formation of gas pockets in the underground mines. The pillar and board system of mining which was adopted also required technical skills without which the roofs of the mines could collapse. Indeed, there were several accidents in the Raniganj and later in the Jharia area.

A.B. Ghosh quotes S. Heslop's Presidential address to the Mining, Geological and Metallurgical Institute of India:

> S. Heslop in his Presidential Address to the MGMII[8], described the conditions of mining in the 19th century in the following words: When I arrived in India over 20 years ago, among other fresh impressions, I was struck with the shallowness of the seams, their number and closeness to each other as compared to that of Home Mining. At that time 300 ft. was looked upon as a considerable depth. In some cases, the old fashioned Gin was still in use while it showed signs of having previously been extensively used. I was specially impressed too with the smallness of pillars that generally prevailed in the first working and especially of shaft pillars which seemed to me quite inadequate. Extensive areas have been lost by thrust or by fire in the absence of adequate provision of isolation.

---

[8] MGMII stands for the Mining Geological and Metallurgical Institute of India. It was set up in 1906.

> "Quarrying was a favourite form of work. This generally is a most ruinous system for a colliery causing as it does constant and heavy inlets of water entailing permanent extra cost for pumping as long as the colliery or property lasts. Evidence of this can be seen in long lines of quarries along the outcrop of valuable seams". (Ghosh, 1977, p. 46)

Later, the methods of mining improved to enhance the pace of production to match the rising demand. Labourers were recruited freely and people from various parts of the country could be found at any one mine. One observer had noted that twenty different dialects of language were spoken by the workers of one mine. However, the working conditions of the miners were not very satisfactory.

Table 1.3: Coal Production 1878–1900

Production of Coal in each Province in India: data in Thousand tons											
Year	Burma	Assam	Bihar	Orissa	Bengal Incl. Bihar & Orissa	Punjab	NWFP*	Baluch-istan	Central Provinces	Madras	Total
Average 1878–80					946				41		987
Av. 1881–85		12			1110				103		1225
Av. 1886–90		105			1411	16		5	137		1674
Av. 1891–95	8	165			2064	69		19	134		2460
Av. 1896–1900	12	201			3763	83		18	151		4228

*NWFP is North West Frontier Province and other coal fields
Source: Ghosh, 1977, p. 248.

It is clear from the data that in the initial years of the development of the railways, the only major coal producing area was Bengal. We now turn to the growth of the rail network to evacuate the coal produced and distribute it all over the country.

Expansion of East Indian Railway (EIR) Network

The EIR network extended up to Barakar and a bridge across the river was only completed in 1889. Lines from Andal to Ekra and Baraboni were built in 1894 and the Andal-Gourandi branch line was constructed in 1895.

The attention turned to a line from Burdwan to Rajmahal along the route taken by the river Ganges as this was a prosperous and thickly populated area where commerce was mainly riverine and road bound, which could be diverted to the railway. The railway line towards Rajmahal was constructed and opened in October 1860. Rajmahal to Bhagalpur was opened in November 1861 the intention was to take the line to Allahabad and then on to Delhi, which was the destination in view of the policy makers. The line via Bhagalpur-Kiul-Danapur to Mughalsarai was commissioned in 1862. The bridge on the river Sone was completed in 1862 and the route from Calcutta to Benaras was declared open in 1863 (609miles). The Rajmahal coalfields, which had large deposits, had been producing small amounts of coal from 1858 onwards. This production inexplicably stopped after 1863 and resumed again in 1890.

The region beyond Sone Nagar was under the jurisdiction of Chief Engineer of the north-west division of the EIR and construction had been proceeding apace from the north-west to connect the line moving northwards form the east. Allahabad to Agra via Kanpur was opened in April 1862. *The bridge over the Ganges at Naini (near Allahabad, now renamed as Prayagraj) was completed in 1865 and by August 1865, a continuous route from Calcutta to Agra was established.* The line up to Ghaziabad, which was the junction point of EIR and the Delhi Lahore Railway, had been completed in April 1864. The Delhi route was then taken as a branch line as the route via Agra-Saharanpur-Ambala to Ferozepur was considered to be the main route. *The bridge on the Jamuna River adjoining Delhi was completed in 1866 and the route from Calcutta to Delhi became functional.*

It was now possible to move coal from Bengal to various destinations in north India. The movement from Raniganj coalfield to north Bihar via Sitarampur-Jhajha-Patna also became possible with the commissioning of the Sitarampur-Luckiserai line in 1872.[9]

Expansion of Railway Network to other Coal bearing areas

The Bengal Nagpur Railway (BNR), headquartered at Calcutta, had been incorporated in 1887 and construction of railway lines proceeded very rapidly. The construction of lines initially started from the Nagpur end. The connection between Nagpur to Raipur was completed in 1888 and extended to Bilaspur in 1889. At the eastern end, the line from Purulia to Asansol was completed in 1889 and by February 1891, BNR opened the line from Nagpur to Asansol, thereby connecting the BNR network with the EIR network. The pace of construction of railway lines was remarkable. The line from Nagpur to Asansol traversed through the coal and mineral rich areas of Chhattisgarh adjoining Raipur, Bilaspur, Korba and Raigarh.

---

9 Please see map of Indian Railways showing the lines near the coalfields and years in which they were commissioned at Appendix 2.

The line connecting Bilaspur and Katni was opened in March 1891. This line skirted the Korea Rewa coalfields. The line from Anuppur to Bisrampur, which connected the coal mines of the Korea Rewa field to the main network was opened later in 1929.

The availability of railway transportation was a boon for these coalfields as movement of coal to north and northwestern India via Katni and movement to the east towards Asansol and Calcutta became possible. The advantage of railway transportation is evident from the expansion of the Umaria coalfield (Korea-Rewa field) which started production in 1884. By 1903, it was producing and despatching 2 lakh tons of coal.

Construction of a line along the eastern coast of India had been surveyed in 1888–90. The 800 kilometres long East Coast line was constructed between 1893 and 1896 and opened to traffic. The Sini-Kharagpur and the Kolaghat-Kharagpur-Cuttack connections were completed by 1898–99. The connection between Howrah, the starting point of EIR and Cuttack via Kharagpur was completed in 1900. Thus, Howrah became the starting point of both EIR and BNR. The Kharagpur-Midnapur line was opened in 1901. By 1900, BNR was a vast railway network. However, the railway was not yet a major player in the coal transportation market.

In Bihar, the entire area from Gomia to Daltonganj and beyond up to the valley of the Sone River near Dehri on Sone is blessed with large coal deposits. Coal was mined at Rajhara, near Daltonganj around 1842. Earlier, this coal used to be sent in small boats down the Koel River. A line from Sone East Bank to Daltonganj was opened in 1902. This provided a ready outlet to the coal for supply towards north India. As the Patna-Gaya line had been commissioned in 1879 the coal traffic found its way via Gaya and Patna to north Bihar too.

In the Central Provinces, Mohpani (Pench Kanhan coalfield) was the first mine to be opened in 1862. The railway link to the mine was provided in 1870. By 1900, the mine was producing 40,000 tons of coal. The mine was acquired by the GIPR in 1904 and continued to provide coal for use by GIPR.

Mines at Warora (Wardha coalfield), which was further to the south, were opened in 1874. The Wardha Valley Railway started from the Wardha station on the Nagpur branch of the GIPR. It was built to exploit the coal reserves in Warora. Construction was started in 1871–72 and completed in 1877. The mines supplied coal to the GIPR.

Further to the south, coal had been identified in Singareni by Dr. William King in 1872. The Nizam's Railway was commissioned in 1874 Production from Singareni started in 1887 and reached a level of 4.7 lakh tons by the year 1900. The railway connection between Dornakal and Singareni was provided in February 1889.

The Geological Survey of India, which had been carrying out detailed surveys of the coal deposits, had surveyed the central and southern part of the country between 1860 and 1880. Some coal deposits had been identified in the central India from the early part of the nineteenth century. The large coal deposits in central India are divided into three parts, the Central India Coalfields (CIC), the Korba coalfields and the Mand Raigarh coalfields.

The CIC has eight coalfields or coal producing areas which are: (The years in which the coal bearing area had been identified is mentioned in parenthesis):

Korar, Umaria (1857), Johilla, Sohagpur (1830), Chirimiri (1885), Sonhat (1883), Jhilmili (1872) and Bishrampur (1848).

The Sohagpur area was first identified by Capt. Franklin in 1830. The identification of the Gondwana-Rewa Basin, which covers the central part of CIC happened in 1846 and the Umaria basin was identified in 1857.

These coal bearing areas were later serviced by the Anuppur-Bisrampur line, which was constructed in 1928.

The presence of the Korba coalfield, which is adjacent to the Hasdeo river (presently in the state of Chhattisgarh), was known from 1838. However, systematic mapping of the coalfield was completed only in 1886–87. The coal from Korba was inferior grade and not considered suitable for use. The development of this huge coalfield took place much later, when uses for the inferior grade coal were found.

The Mand-Raigarh field (Chhattisgarh) was identified by Blankford in 1870 and exploratory drilling was done in 1886–87. This coalfield is adjoining the Mand river. The coal in this area was also not of very high quality and was not suitable for use in contemporary machines. The exploitation of the reserves occurred later.

The coal deposits in the Jharia area of Bihar (now Jharkhand) had been surveyed in 1839 by one Lieutenant Harryngton, who mentioned that large coal deposits were available. Three more surveys were done between 1866, 1887 and 1890, the last by T. H. Ward on behalf of the East Indian Railway (EIR). All three reports confirmed the existence of large deposits of high-grade coal. The report of T. H. Ward mentioned that the field contained 804 million tons of good quality coal. The prospect of good quality coal for their locomotives prompted EIR to extend the railway line to the coal deposit areas at Katrasgarh (near Gomoh) and also lay two branch lines to Kusunda and Patherdih. These lines were completed in 1895. Many coal mining companies took leases and the output of coal increased by leaps and bounds from a small base of 1500 tons in 1894. There was a flood of applications for mining leases as the EIR extended a railway line to the mining areas and evacuation of coal became assured. By 1901, the Jharia field was producing 2 million tons of coal.

Other Minor Coalfields

Assam: Production of coal in Assam started in a small way in the 1880s, with output averaging only 12,000 tons between 1881 and 1885. However, the production increased rapidly to reach 2 lakh tons by the turn of the century. The report to the Administration on Railways in India for 1877 mentions that 110 miles of rail track were sanctioned for construction in Assam. A contract for the development of the Assam-Bengal Railway was entered into in 1892 and by 1902, it had a track length of 589 miles. The coal was not used much outside Assam. The second railway company in Assam was the Assam-Behar railway which had two sections, the Tirhoot section and the Assam-Behar section. The latter connected it to the Northern Bengal State Railway. The development of the coalfields in Assam was limited as mining conditions were difficult and the coal had high sulphur content.

Punjab: Another minor coalfield was in Punjab, where there were two locations, the Dandot group and the Makerwal group. The Dandot area was worked by the North Western railway. This production did not sustain for very long. Production from the Makerwal group was better. The total production of Punjab was an average of 16,000 tons between 1881 and 1885 and reached 68,000 tons only in 1901. The coal was of poor quality and like Assam had high sulphur content. The coalfields were not served directly by the railways and perhaps as the output was low, the railways had no interest in laying lines to the mines. The coal had to be transported to the railhead, after which, it is recorded that railway wagons were readily available.

Baluchistan: The third coalfield of note in the northwest was Baluchistan, where Kalat was the main producing area. which produced only 25,000 tons in 1901. The coal mines were located at a high altitude and bringing them down to the railway area posed a big problem. The coal was evacuated by the North Western railway.

A map showing the major coalfields and the adjoining railway lines for coal movement is placed at Appendix 1.

Development of Other Major Railway Lines and Impact on Overall Movement

As mentioned earlier, the Great Indian Peninsula Railway (GIPR) had the distinction of running the first ever train in India in April 1853. The line from Bombay to Kalyan was completed in May 1854, as a double line, which was a surprising decision given that it was a new line, but indicative of the traffic anticipated to flow in the near future. The plan was to extend a line eastward towards Nagpur and Calcutta and another line to the southeast via Pune towards Madras.

The line from Kalyan to Nagpur via Jalgaon and Bhusawal was completed in 1867. This line passed through the district that produced the largest cotton crop in India, and it was an important strategic objective for the mills of Lancashire. (Khosla, 37)

The opening of the Suez Canal in 1869 provided a fillip to international trade. The GIPR's line towards Calcutta via Jabalpur was completed in 1870. Naini to Jabalpur had been completed by EIR in 1867 and hence by 1870, the Bombay-Calcutta connection via Naini was established. The connection of the EIR and the GIPR's network at Jabalpur meant that Calcutta, Bombay, Delhi and Lahore (now in Pakistan) were now connected. Demand for rail transport increased sharply.

The Bombay Baroda and Central Railway Company (BBCR), which had been established in 1852, had advocated a line from Bombay via Surat and Baroda to Ahmedabad. This line was completed in 1870. The headquarters of the BBCR was at Churchgate, in Bombay.

The line from Bombay to Madras was completed in March 1871.

By 1 January 1881, 9325 miles of lines had been open to traffic of which 2932 miles were State Railways, 297 miles belonged to Native States, 1,504 miles to East Indian Railway (which had been acquired by the State in 1879) and 4,592 miles to Guaranteed lines. The length of railway tracks in England and Wales as on 31 December 1879 was 12,547 miles. The progress of construction in India was commendable indeed.

Coal Production

The total coal production in India was 4.75 million tons in 1900. Railway lines were laid in all areas where coal mining had commenced or was expected to commence. There was good business sense in this for the railways, as coal was crucially required for extending railway operation and diverse sources of coal were likely to reduce the price at which the coal was procured at locomotive depots spread all across the subcontinent. The coal available in the country, including the import of coal and the export of coal from India is shown in table 1.4.

Table 1.4: Production and Import/Export of Coal 1878–1900 (data in lakh tons)

	Imports	Indian Production	Export of Indian coal	Available Supply of Indian Coal	Total Available Supply
Average 1878–80	5.6	9.90	0.005		
Average 1881–85	6.8	12.30	Not available		

	Imports	Indian Production	Export of Indian coal	Available Supply of Indian Coal	Total Available Supply
Average 1886–90	8	17.60	0.2		
Average 1891–95	7.1	27.60	0.4	27.2	34.3
Average 1896–1900	3.3	47.50	3.1	44.4	47.7

Source: Excerpt from Ghosh, 1977, p. 258.

It is clear from the data that as the production of indigenous coal increased, the import of coal slowly reduced and Indian coal started being exported.

Evolution of Tariff Policy

When deciding the source of supply and the mode of transportation, a consumer compares the costs of each alternative. Prices (tariff) charged by the railways depends on its tariff policy, which is conditioned by its business philosophy, the costs incurred in transportation and its perception about customer response to tariff levels. The level of technology and management skills impacts the efficiency of operations, and this also influences the tariff policy. In the case of India, the conditions of the contracts between the government and the railway companies, the hesitation of the railway companies to cooperate with each other, and the high costs of operation of railways influenced the shaping of the tariff policy considerably.

Coal was the basic fuel used by all railway companies and its landed cost at the locomotive shed was an important ingredient in their cost of operation. With the expansion of the railway network, locomotive sheds and industries spread across the country demanded coal. High railway tariffs prompted users at distant locations to look for alternative sources of fuel. The evolution of the tariff policy of the railways in India thus had a great impact on the pattern of movement of indigenous coal by rail. The manner in which the policies changed and their impact on the distribution of coal is an interesting facet of history.

Phases in Evolution of Tariff Policy

After the introduction of the railways in India, the Government felt that it required some time to assess the nature of the market. Hence, the initial decision of the government regarding the tariff structure was that each railway company would determine its own rates, with the approval of the Government, and that the optimum rating pattern would emerge after careful experiments had been conducted. The Administrative Report on the Railways in India for the year 1859 stated:

> In considering this question, the Government is influenced by the two fold desire to produce as remunerative a traffic as possible, and to confer as much convenience and benefit upon the population of the country, and as many facilities for its trade, as are compatible with the extent of profits contemplated in the clause of the contracts relating to the question of fares. The problem is a difficult one, and can only be solved by careful experiments. These have been and are now being, tried, and modifications in the tariffs have, from time to time, been made, as circumstances seemed to require. (Danvers, 1860, p. 41)

However, in a clear departure from stated policy, it was mandated that there would be concessional rates for carriage of military personnel and materials and that carriage of Mail and Post Office staff would be free of charge. The Report of 1859 stated:

> The Railway Companies are also bound, under the contracts, to convey the Mails and Post Office servants free of charge, to take Military Officers in first class carriages at second class fares and soldiers when on duty in second class carriages at the lowest fares; also horses, guns, waggons, and military stores, &c., at the lowest rate for the time being chargeable for the carriage of such animals, goods etc. (Danvers, 1860, p. 7)

This was the beginning of the enunciation of tariff policies by the government which would go through several iterations towards becoming consumer friendly. A multi-ownership railway network would function most efficiently if uniform operational and tariff policies could be implemented across the entire network. Unfortunately, the individual companies showed little inclination towards mutual cooperation, except when it suited their business interests. Due to contractual stipulations, the government hesitated to dictate tariff policies to the companies, except when it was in strategic interest of the empire.

The tariff policy also had to be calibrated keeping in view the capacity of the railways to carry traffic. On several occasions, reduction if tariff led to a surge of traffic, which the railways could not handle. Thus, the issue of tariffs and the improvement in operational efficiency both had to be addressed. The evolution of the tariff policies in the nineteenth century can be broadly divided into two periods: 1855 to 1875, 1876 to 1902. The issues of operational efficiency and costs of operations were addressed by the railway companies in their own ways. A cohesive policy was not in place. The status of technology and operational parameters obtaining at that time shall be addressed later.

The assurance of guaranteed returns to the companies on capital invested became a drain on imperial resources and it was this financial drain that prompted some changes in policy after a few years. Weak attempts were made periodically by the government to evolve systems for enhancing cooperation amongst the companies, but these met with limited success. Only in the 1880s did the government show a strong desire to resolve the issue of inter railway cooperation.

1855–1875

The Government's decision to allow the railway companies to decide their own tariffs led to different rates being quoted for the same commodity. Rates for goods traffic were divided into six classes. The difference in the rates charged by railway companies is shown below:

Table 1.5: Goods Tariff on three Major railway Companies 1854–1856

	East Indian Railway (EIR)	Great Indian Peninsula Railway (GIPR)	Madras Railway (MAS)
Year →	**1854**	**1856**	**1856**
1st Class	9 pies* per ton per mile	10 p per ton per mile	6.75 p per ton per mile
2nd class	13.5 p per ton per mile	14 p per ton per mile	13.5 p per ton per mile
3rd Class	18 p per ton per mile	18 p per ton per mile	20.5 p per ton per mile
4th Class	27 p per ton per mile	20 p per ton per mile	No classes beyond 3rd
5th Class	44 p per ton per mile	20 p per ton per mile	
Special class for **Coal**	7 p per ton per mile	30 p per ton per mile	

Source: Administrative Reports of various years. *12 pies = 1 Anna and 16 Annas= 1 Rupee.

Though the EIR quoted a special rate for coal which was lower than the lowest (1st Class) rate, it was still quite high and would have a serious impact on the cost of fuel for industries located far away from the coalfields. As events would show in later years, there was scope for considerable reduction in the rates.

Alternative modes of transport were not very well developed in India at that time. This allowed the railway companies to operate like quasi-monopolies. The primary objective of the rating policies of the railway companies was not always carriage of the maximum amount of freight traffic and earning an acceptable level of profit. In fact, the actions of some railway companies showed that they would prefer to carry less traffic at higher rates and earn greater profits. *For example, in 1864 the government observed that the revenue of some railways had risen, while the traffic carried had actually reduced*! The news sparked off a debate on the tariff policy. The Government Director of Indian Railway Companies in England felt that the rates had been fixed too high by the railway companies and that a reduction in rates would lead to greater aggregate revenue. The issue was who would determine the specific rates. Changes could not be forced easily as the clauses of the contracts with the railway companies did not permit the Government to take unilateral decisions regarding tariffs.

In 1865, an opinion in England, which had gained some traction, was that rail tariff should be lowered to bring its services within the reach of all people without consideration of the financial implications of the reduction in fares and freight. The Government of India also felt that lowering of tariff could lead to higher revenues. It observed:

> The people in India are now taxed to pay the guaranteed interest. For their protection the Government exercises a control over the railway companies, with the twofold object of securing such a system of good management as shall provide all the legitimate advantages of railway communication for the country at large, as well as such profits as shall release the Government from payment of the guaranteed interest; and in the second place, of affording the best means of encouraging capital and enterprise in India by affording an example of success in works which have been undertaken .... It must not be thought, however, that high profits and high fares are synonymous; on the contrary, low fares, that is to say low, compared with those in Europe, are perfectly compatible with large remunerative receipts. (Quoted in Ghose, 1918, p. 6)

One reason for keeping tariff rates high was, perhaps, the implicit knowledge that the capacity to carry traffic was rather limited. In 1866 it was found that even with the existing tariff, the traffic offering was so high that the railways were not able to carry it due to shortage of wagons and locomotives. The EIR and GIPR responded to this crisis by raising the rates of freight further. The increase was met by strenuous protests. After enquiry, the Government decided that the increase in tariff had happened under special circumstances and did not pursue the matter further. The tariff question was examined in depth, and it was decided by the Government of India that while the fixation of rates would be left to the local administrations, the Government would specify the maximum rates which could be charged. However, the Government retained in its hand matters pertaining to the fares for lowest class of passengers, and tariff for foodgrains and coal. The understanding was that the railways would charge a rate for transportation which would ensure that maximum number of passengers that could be carried by the railways actually did access rail services. The same would hold for freight services as well.

With expansion of the rail network, the consumption of coal by the railway locomotives increased rapidly and the movement of coal by the railways had to keep pace with the consumption. In the interest of the railways, the Government felt that the EIR and GIPR should plan for free flow of traffic between the two railways. A meeting between the two railways was held and though there was some agreement on the movement of traffic, there was no unanimity on the question of freight rates. Differential rates of tariff continued. The data for 1870 is presented in Table 1.6.

Table 1.6: Goods Rates in Annas and Paise per Ton Per Mile in 1870

Railway	1st Class		2nd Class		3rd Class		4th Class		5th Class		6th Class		Special Class
	Annas	P	As	P	As	P	As	P	As	P	As	P	Special Rate
EIR	0	8	1	2	1	6	1	10	2	4	None		7pies for distance of over 300 miles
GIPR	0	8	0	10	1	2	1	3	2	0	4	8	
Madras	0	8	1	0	1	2	1	6	2	0	4	0	
BBCR	0	8	0	10	1	2	1	8	2	4	3	4	
Eastern Bengal	0	8	1	2	1	6	2	4	4	8	--------		
Oudh & Rohilkhand	0	10	1	2	1	6	2	4	4	8	----------		

Source: Ghose, 1918, p. 13.

Growth of Coal Traffic

Despite the imperfections in the system, the level of traffic increased considerably. Within 16 years of its opening, EIR was moving 1.2 million tons of traffic, with 23 per cent being coal. GIPR had also reached a level of almost a million tons. However, most railway companies were incurring losses, and a thorough review of the tariff and costs of operations was required.

The amount of coal and other traffic carried by each railway is presented in table 1.7:

Table 1.7: Movement of Coal and other minerals and Total traffic in 1870

Guaranteed Railways	Miles open to Traffic	Tons of coal & coke	Tons of other minerals	Traffic Other than Minerals	Total all Commodities (in Tons)
EIR Main Line	1131	269,486	15,262	885,909	1,170,657 (Coal 23%)
EIR Jubbulpore Line	224	390		69,057	69,447
GIPR	1258	2,240	429,874	540,465	972,579
Madras	783	709	40,368	303,042	344,119
BBCR	312	5396	11,368	244,796	261,560
Scinde, Punjab & Delhi	666	282	1,458	279,040	280,780

(Continued)

Table 1.7: *(Continued)*

Guaranteed Railways	Miles open to Traffic	Tons of coal & coke	Tons of other minerals	Traffic Other than Minerals	Total all Commodities (in Tons)
Great Southern	168		610	70,809	71,419
Eastern Bengal	113	14,625	5,044	171,500	191,169
Oudh & Rohilkhand	42		477	26,860	27,337
Carnatic	19		10	2,855	2,865
State railways:					--------
Calcutta & South Eastern	28	556	688	21,434	22,678
Khamgaon	8			11,463	11,463
Unguaranteed Railway:					---------
Nulhuttee	28		3,295	6,457	12,821

Source: Excerpt from Ghose, 1918, pp. 14–15.

The data shows that 92 per cent of the coal traffic was moved by EIR.

Impact of High Tariff in India

Due to the high level of tariff in India, the landed cost of imported coal at Bombay was less than that of Indian coal. The construction of the lines of GIPR connecting the EIR, therefore, did not create a major demand for Indian coal from the western part of India. Import of coal from Cardiff to Bombay continued till the end of the nineteenth century. After the development of the coal mines in the Central Provinces and Rewa, some indigenous coal started being used, particularly for use in railway locomotives working in the vicinity of these coal-fields. After some reduction in tariff in 1879, Bengal coal was used in the areas adjoining Jabalpur on the GIPR.

The imperfections in the tariff structure were compounded by the high cost of operations, the overall inefficiency of operations and poor technology. The Government Consulting Engineer in London examined the issue and commented adversely on the high cost of carriage in the railways in India and also on the large disparity in the costs between the railway companies. The costs of carriage of some selected zones for the year 1871–72 may be seen in Table 1.8:

Table 1.8: Cost of Carriage of Freight in Selected Companies 1871–72

	EIR Mainline	EIR Jubbulpore	GIPR	Madras	BBCR
Miles open	1281	223.75	1274	832	349.5
Av. Receipts from each Goods Train per mile	Rs. 5-10-8	Rs. 3-4-0	Rs. 4-9-4	Rs. 3-0-8	Rs. 5-2-0
Av. Charge for carrying one ton of goods (taking all classes together) one mile	As. 0-9.92	As. 0-9.2	As 1-0.72	As. 0-11.6	As. 1-0
Av load per goods train in tons	109	68	69	50	82
Av Cost of carrying one ton one mile	3.248 pies	5.76 pies	7.76 pies	5.36 pies	8 pies
Av. Profit per ton per mile	6.672 pies	3.44 pies	4.96 pies	6.24 pies	4 pies
Av. Number of goods trains running each way per day (assuming all trains are through trains)	2.66	1.13	2.52	1.92	1.54

Source: Excerpts from Ghose, 1918, p. 16.

The Government Consulting Engineer in London having examined the data remarked that there was ample room for improvement in the operating parameters of some of the railways. He found that the wagons were not being loaded to their full capacity and consequently the load carried per train was extremely low. The low tonnage per train was inflating operating costs and also increasing the number of trains required to be run to clear the traffic. The Consulting Engineer suggested the running of mixed (passenger and goods combined) trains to reduce costs. Lower costs would open the door for lower tariffs which could bring in larger volumes of both passenger and freight.

It was no wonder that the railway companies continued to remain a burden for the government. The financial results for 1871–72 showed that a sum of Rs. 1,58,29,000 would be required to make up the deficit in the guaranteed interest payable by the Indian railways. It was also discovered that a large amount of traffic was moving by barges up to distances of 300 miles. The Government felt that the major railway systems had been working for sufficiently long to have a good idea of the transport market and should be capable of taking a call on tariff matters and whatever needed to be done to increase the level of freight loading should be done without delay.

As the railway network continued to increase, and areas got interconnected, the expenditure on fulfilling the guaranteed returns to the railway companies continued to increase. Lord Lawrence, then Viceroy of India (1864–69) advocated that a maximum amount be stipulated for payment of guarantees. He advocated several other radical departures from the existing contracts. The Secretary of State did not agree to these proposals. However, it was decided that new lines would be put in two categories, 'Commercial' and 'Political'. Commercial lines would be funded by private enterprise under the guarantee scheme and would aim to open up districts blessed with mineral reserves and hitherto unconnected by rail. Competing lines ought not be promoted if competition was likely to occur. Feeder lines would be developed by the railways in consultation with the local government. The 'Political' lines would be funded by the government.

The matter of lowering the tariff was once again taken up by the Government of India in 1873 when a firm proposal regarding lower rates was sent to the Secretary of State. The proposal for rates was modified slightly two years later.

Lower Tariffs

In a perverse way, the pressure to lower freight rates got created due to intense food shortages in various parts of the country in 1873–74. The government directed EIR to move grain to the famine affected areas at specially reduced rates, with a promise to make good the difference between the existing rates and the new rates. The effect of reduction in rates was remarkable. There was huge demand for movement and the railways earned handsome profits from movement of food grain. The government kept its promise of making good the difference between the old and new rates, though there was no need to do so. In addition, for the first time, the State received some money above the guaranteed interest.

This was a revealing discovery about the potential of the Indian market and brought home to the railway companies the message that high tariff was, in fact, harmful to the interest of the railways.

1876–1902

Under pressure from the Government of India, the railway companies experimented with several rates, and by 1876–77, the policy of low rates being beneficial for traffic generation had got established. Special rates, even lower than the lowest class were quoted in exceptional circumstances for long distance transportation of staples such as rice, grains, salt and coal. Tariffs for passenger travel were also reduced. These steps undoubtedly benefited the Indian population. The EIR always charged a special rate for coal, for which it enjoyed a special locational advantage.

The 1870s and 1880s witnessed a great surge in the demand for Indian wheat in Britain. The freight tariff in America was lower than that in India and interests in Britain raised the demand for reduction of railway rates in India. Reduction in freight tariff charged by the railways in India was a sure way reducing costs and competing in the international market. When this was done, the results were remarkable, and this was a subject of much rejoicing. The Report to the Administration for 1877–78 reported

> the stimulus which has been given to the grain and seed trade between India and this country may be seen in the fact that, while in the twelve months ending with March 1871 the wheat exported from India to the United Kingdom was 248,522 cwt., and the oil seeds 1,354,023 cwt., in the twelve months ending last March the exports of wheat to this country were 4,337,208 cwt., and of oil seeds 3,740,362 cwt. The exports of wheat from Calcutta alone during the year were 3,404,800 cwt., of which more than half was brought down by the railway. (Danvers, 1877, 28–9)

Table 1.9: The export of grains from India between 1881–82 and 1890–91

Year	Cwt*	Year	Cwt
1881–82	49,926,000	1886–87	51,009000
1882–83	49,926,000	1887–88	44,606,000
1883–84	49,220,000	1888–89	42,416,000
1884–85	39,217,000	1889–90	42,687,000
1885–86	50,425,000	1890–91	51,149,000

*1 Cwt= 0.05 tons
Source: Compiled from various Administrative Reports.

It is noteworthy that the export of wheat, stimulated by lower rail tariff rates, continued at a time when parts of India had experienced devastating famines between 1874 and 1879 and a Famine Commission had been appointed in 1880.

In the report for the same year, Juland Danvers alluded to the beneficial effect of reduction in tariff. He observed:

> I have no hesitation in saying that the recent development which has occurred in the merchandise traffic is due, in a great measure, to the more liberal scale of lower rates which has lately been adopted. Other causes, especially the famine, have contributed to produce this effect, but the chief one is the reduction in the rates for carriage. The policy of moderately low rates for the staples of the country may, I am glad to say, now be regarded as one which has been generally accepted by the Companies, and its encouraging results will probably lead to its further extension. The greater the traffic, the more the rates may, within moderation, be safely lowered; for by good management,

> with a large traffic, full train loads may be secured, and waste of carrying power will be avoided. The railway can then afford to carry at cheaper rates. Thus, one reacts upon the other. Low rates produce traffic and a large traffic proportionately reduces working expenses and increases profits. The two leading Companies, the East Indian and the Great Indian Peninsula, have acknowledged in their reports to the shareholders the success of their policy in lowering rates. (Danvers, 1877, pp. 29–30).

It is worth noting that the report of Danvers praised the administration for reducing tariffs, and alluded to the famines as 'other causes'.

Poor Coordination between Railway Companies and its Impact on Costs and Railway Movement Patterns

Even though the benefits of lower freight rates had been established, cooperation between railway companies, which was essential for improving the quality of service, did not progress significantly. Dovetailing of operational procedures to ensure smooth interchange of wagons between companies, rules and procedures for balancing wagon availability and financial codes for keeping an account of the movements needed to be developed. Efforts to do so were made over the years, with mixed success.

An example of the operational constraints created by the prevalent status of technology and operational systems is evident from the account of Huddleston of EIR. During the famine of 1876 in the Madras and Bombay Presidencies, traffic from the North West and the Punjab moved over EIR for movement via Jubbulpore for destinations on the GIPR railway. Some traffic for Madras moved towards Calcutta for movement by sea. The usual movement of grains towards Calcutta Port for export was also present. This large volume of traffic moving over long distances revealed a shortcoming of the system which had hitherto been hidden. An acute shortage of wagons and locomotives developed. In 'The History of East Indian Railways' G. Huddleston observes

> The papers in India teemed with expressions of disapproval of the East India railway management, because it had not sufficient stock to meet the extraordinary demands made upon it. The facts were that the stock of wagons had amply sufficed to meet the famine requirements of 1873–74, but when it came to sending East Indian Railway wagons hundreds of miles away from the home line to distant Madras, it became impossible to meet all demands. Out of a total stock of 6,600 goods wagons, as many as 1200, or say one-fifth were constantly absent from the line, conveying produce to the Bombay or Madras Presidencies. There would have been an abundant supply of wagons to carry our own traffic but there were not sufficient to carry grain to Madras as well as to Calcutta, and obviously it was beyond the bounds of possibility to meet this exceptional demand. The Board however at once applied for Government sanction to the provision of 1000 more wagons and 50 additional engines at a cost of a quarter of a million of money, and sanction was accorded after some short delay. (Huddleston, 1906, pp. 77–8)

The important issues emanating from the comments of Huddleston are that the there was no system to ensure balancing of wagons between railway companies, and that the availability of rolling stock, i.e. wagons and locomotives, was inadequate to absorb large variations in traffic. To clear the traffic, an increase in the cargo carried per wagon and the number of wagons per train would have been the ideal solution. This did not happen. Instead, the management of the railway companies attempted to keep the distance of movement short so as to keep the wagons within their own domain and utilise the wagons more efficiently. Consequently, the cost of operations of the railways located far away from the coalfields remained high and these railways had to use either imported coal or alternative fuels like wood. Meanwhile, the demand for coal from the expanding railway system continued to rise.

Rising Demand for Coal and Tariff Policy

At the end of December 1876, the Guaranteed and the State railways together owned 1519 locomotives, which went up to 1630 by December 1877. That is, an addition of 111 locomotives in one year (Danvers, 1878, p. 9). This large and rapidly growing fleet required a huge amount of coal. Due to the lack of operational coordination and the prevailing tariff structure, free movement of coal across the country was not possible. The railways were unable to handle all the traffic offered and a number of complaints were registered.

The railway companies that were fortunate to be operating in the coalfields, such as the East Indian Railways and the Eastern Bengal Railways, had a tremendous advantage as the availability of coal was assured and it was cheap due to lower transportation costs. Railway companies such as the GIPR had to depend on imported coal for a long time as the landed cost of Indian coal from Raniganj was higher than that of coal imported from England. The Report for 1877–78 mentions the comparative costs of coal for the GIPR and Madras railways. It reports that for GIPR coal from Mohpani was available at Rs. 9 per ton and that from Warrora at Rs. 5 per ton. However, coal from Raniganj was available at Jubbulpore at Rs. 19 per ton. The landed cost of Indian (Bengal) coal at Madras was Rs. 21 per ton, whereas English coal was available at Rs. 18. Madras Railways continued to use a huge amount of wood, which was also slowly becoming scarce. The rapid increase in the production of coal and some moderation in tariff led to the use of Bengal coal by the GIPR in the areas adjoining Jubbulpore. The report observes: '... it will be necessary to wait until some arrangement can be made by which the cost of bringing the coal by sea from Calcutta to Madras can be reduced' (Danvers, 1878, p. 32). The massive increase in coal costs due to inefficiency in transportation and the tariff policy was to be a source of intense dialogue between the coal companies and the railways in the future. The policies of the Imperial government also played an important role in this exercise.

Incentive for Railway Companies to Own Coal Mines

To control costs and ensure quality, EIR and some other railways invested in opening coal mines which were able to provide cheap coal for railways. The coal of EIR was cheaper than that produced by the other coal mine owners. Any surplus was despatched to adjoining railways such as Oudh and Rohilkhand and also sold in the market. The coal mining companies in Bengal objected to the railways selling cheap coal. The complaints were ignored by the Government. Partly as a result of provision of cheap and good quality coal, the working expenses of EIR continued to be much lower than that for other railways. In 1879 (second half) the expenditure dropped to 31.86 per cent of gross receipts, a very good financial result indeed. The low cost of coal, a major component of the cost, was one of the main reasons why EIR remained a profitable railway.

Availability of balancing traffic[10] of foodgrains moving from north towards the Calcutta Port helped EIR to send surplus coal to railways in the north and north-west. However, movement to the deep south and the west continued to remain difficult as there was no return traffic. It is important to note that the Oudh and Rohilkhand Railways did not require imported coal as it was receiving coal from EIR.

Cost of Coal and Operational Costs

The impact of the cost of coal on the cost of locomotive power per train mile is evident from the calculations of Mr. Rendel, Consulting Engineer, in 1877–78. The report of Mr. Rendel mentioned:

Table 1.10: Cost of Locomotive Power per Train Mile 1877–78

Railway	Cost in Pence*
EIR Main Line	8.11
EIR Jubbulpore	11.06
Madras	19.4
BBCR	13.36
Sind Punjab & Sind	16.07

[10] Balancing Traffic: For efficient railway operations, cargo movement in both directions is ideal. If a wagon moves from east to north and returns to the east in an empty condition, the railway earns revenue only in one direction. Balancing traffic, here, refers to the return cargo of foodgrain from north to the east.

Railway	Cost in Pence*
South Indian	14.9
Eastern Bengal	12.83
Oudh & Rohilkhand	13.59
Rajputana state	19.14

*{1 pence = 8 Indian Pies}
Source: Danvers, 1878, 25.

Commenting on the difference in costs due to haulage distances, the Administration report on the Railways in India for the year 1880–81 stated:

> Owing therefore to its partial distribution and to the few places where it is as yet worked, the Railways of the Punjab and Madras have to import their coal from long distances, and consequently at a high cost. Coal which is worth Rs. 3 a ton delivered into wagons at Giridi, Bengal, costs Rs. 30 a ton by the time that it reaches Lahore. Madras finds it cheaper to use patent fuel imported from England than to depend on Indian coal. The total quantity of English coal imported into India during the year was 683,768 tons (coke and patent fuel included) valued at Rs. 123,998,52. (Trevor, 1882, p. 8)

Some estimates put the difference in operating costs, due to the high cost of transportation, as high as 7 to 8 per cent (Danvers, 1878, p. 25).

In the case of GIPR, one of the largest railroads at that time, the use of coal was 73 per cent English coal, 11 per cent of Mohpani and about 8 per cent each of Bengal and Warora coal. It had been assessed that in terms of quality if English coal were taken as 100, Bengal coal would be 95, Mohpani 75 and Warora 70. There was, therefore, good reason to try to get good quality indigenous coal to the distant consumption centres through appropriate tariff regulations and improvement in operations. At an all-India level, the use of imported coal even in 1884–85 continued to be 31 per cent of a total of 6,34,146 tons, while coke was 12,805 tons, patent fuel 18,657 tons and wood as high as 2,16,443 tons. The ratio of imported to total consumption remained virtually the same in 1887 (30.6 per cent). This position changed slowly over the years due to changes in tariff structure, improvement in operations, movement of coal by rail-cum-sea route and a rapid increase in the production of coal in India.

Growth in Coal Production, Transportation and Reduction in Tariff

Despite the imperfections of the system, continued injection of capital, expansion of network and addition to rolling stock created new areas of demand and overall movement of freight traffic, particularly coal continued to increase steadily.

Coal carried by the railways increased from 403,632 tons in 1872 to 673,178 tons in 1877, i.e. a growth of 1.7 times in five years. Coal loading by EIR alone had increased from 295,852 tons to 520,262 tons during the same period, i.e. by 76 per cent. (Danvers,1878, p. 32). With increase in demand for coal, the shortage of wagons and locomotives and the operational issues mentioned earlier continued to plague the movement of traffic. The Report to the Administration for 1876–77 recorded:

> Largely as the traffic has increased, it might have been still greater if more rolling stock had been available. The want of locomotives and wagons has been a great check, and I am afraid that goods have, in consequence, sometimes, been damaged by delay and exposure. The Agent of the Oudh and Rohilkund Railway recently observed that three times the amount of traffic might have been taken on that line if they had possessed the means of carrying it. On other lines it has been more or less the same. The stations in the Punjab and Delhi, and on the East Indian and Great Indian Peninsula, have frequently been blocked with grain and other goods, because the means of carrying them away failed. At Patna and Benares a steamboat service came to the aid of the East Indian Railway, and took some of the grain to the Kooshtea station of the Eastern Bengal. (Danvers, 1877, p. 29)

On the EIR, the movement of coal from Raniganj both in the down and up directions[11] was far from satisfactory. One probable reason was that all coal mines were not connected to the railway network. EIR, therefore, took the initiative of offering second hand rails to the mine owners to lay the tracks for coal sidings and connect them to the rail network. In October 1880, EIR also reduced the tariff of coal for more than 300 miles distance from 1/5th of pie per maund per mile to 1/6th of a pie per maund per mile. This was done with the hope of creating some demand from the mills of North India. In 1881, sale of coal produced in railway coal mines to outsiders was stopped.

The overall picture was that the production of coal had increased significantly. There was potential for greater coal production, which would be available for transportation by rail. However, the railway system was unable to carry it as the utilisation of the rolling stock was poor and the cost of carriage was high due to operational inefficiency and a skewed tariff structure. Import of coal on large scale was taking place even though sufficient coal was available in India.

Export of coal from England suited British interests as coal surplus to domestic requirements was being produced. Increased coal production and its transportation in India would generate capital formation and employment, which would spur economic growth. For India's benefit, a change was needed if India were

[11] Up direction refers to movement away from Calcutta to the north and down refers to movement towards Calcutta.

to move to an upward trajectory of coal production and transportation. Would the impetus for change be initiated by the British government or would it be forced by circumstances?

Impetus for change in tariff structure

A great impetus for change in the tariff structure came with the opening of the of the Rajputana-Malwa Railway in 1881. This railway had a junction with the Bombay-Baroda line at Ahmedabad. Earlier, the route from Bombay to Delhi was via Jubbulpore, a distance of 1234 miles. At one stroke the distance between Bombay and Delhi was reduced by 345 miles. Grain producing centres in north India were now closer to Bombay than Calcutta. Traffic from north India which earlier moved to Calcutta, began moving towards Bombay. EIR protested against this, but the Secretary of State disagreed and decided that competition should be allowed to prevail, as in the long run it would lead to reduction of tariff. A new era of freight tariff rates began. The opening of the Cawnpore (Kanpur)-Achnera Railway in 1884 also created newer routes of travel and a relook at tariff rates.

Given the pattern of operations, areas of shortages developed, which were met through imports as in the case of coal for the western and southern parts of India. The management issue which once again came to the fore was whether the railways ought to be operated as individual companies pursuing their own objectives or whether they should be run as a cohesive unit to achieve economies of scale and provide better service to the Indian population. The Government of the day continued to make weak attempts to achieve some cohesion in working systems, but with limited success. Some efforts for rationalisation of tariff policy were also made as we shall presently see.

Attempts at Inter Railway Coordination

In an attempt to bring some cohesion in the working of railway companies, a major conference of was held in 1880 and a set of rules was drawn up. The Report for 1881 records:

> This Conference met at Calcutta on the 6th January 1880 and was attended by delegates from every Guaranteed Railway, and a sufficient number from State lines. The following important business was transacted: –
>
> (1) A Code of general Rules for all Indian Railways was framed under Section 8 of the Indian Railway Act of 1879: This Code, with some slight modifications, received the sanction of the Governor General in Council, with effect from the 1st October 1880 and as far can be gathered from a few months, experience, its rules appear to· work smoothly.

(2) A general system for recording shunting and other miscellaneous locomotive service was passed, and has been generally adopted, by which the train and engine mileage given in the half-yearly accounts, are based on the same principles for all lines.

(3) Difficulty having been experienced as regards the interchange of stock in working Rule XVII passed by the Conference of 1879, an amendment of that rule was passed. (Trevor, 1881, p. 5)

Other rules and procedures for introduction of uniform systems in all railways in areas such as: (a) continuous brakes in trains on all systems, (b) recording of interchange of rolling stock, (c) recording and maintenance of statistics, (d) uniform goods classification, were discussed and adopted. The Railway Act of 1879 was later repealed and replaced with the Indian Railway Act of 1890.

Some reforms in the administrative structure were also implemented at various stages to improve coordination among railway companies. In 1879, the post of Director General, Railways had been created and the administration was now under the Railway Branch of the Public Works Department. A Director Traffic was appointed to oversee the traffic related issues. Further modifications in the structure of administration of Indian Railways occurred in the course of time. In 1897, the post of Director General Railways was abolished and replaced with Secretary to the Government of India, Public Works Department, Railway Branch.

Reduction in Tariff

In 1883, the Government issued a circular laying down principles of tariff fixation which stated that the concepts of 'cost of service' and 'what the traffic can bear' should normally be the guidelines for deciding the minimum and maximum rates. Tapering rates for long distances was also suggested. Competing lines would remain free to offer competitive rates so long as reckless undercutting did not occur. Some moderation of tariff occurred, which had an impact on the movement of traffic. EIR witnessed a surge in wheat traffic for Calcutta Port. In the first half of 1883, the terminal at Howrah became choked with wheat for export moving in from Cawnpore (now Kanpur), Beneras and Patna and other stations. The capacity of the EIR was fully stretched. During that time, for the EIR, the earnings from wheat were more than that from coal, the figures being Rs. 31 lacs for wheat and 30 lakhs for coal. (Huddleston, 1906, 173). Import of coal continued to remain quite high. The very next year, owing to fall in the price of wheat in England, the demand for its export reduced suddenly. Fortunately, the demand for coal was growing both internally and for export and rapid changes were witnessed from 1889 onwards.

The complete implementation of the proposed tariff policy of 1883 was a complex exercise and several difficulties were faced in the fixation of local and through rates[12]. The Government realised that the policy of minimum interference with the working of the railways required a review. A conference of traffic officers and representatives of the trade was organised in 1884 where some general principles were agreed to. However, the GIPR did not agree to proposals of tariff simplification.

Further Attempts at Tariff Reduction and Inter railway Cooperation

In the interest of the customers, the Government, through a resolution had suggested in 1887 that the railway companies work in a manner that they were all a part of a single management. The consumer faced difficulties in calculations as each railway quoted a different rate. This, at last, was a step in the right direction. However, this suggestion was rejected in the Railway Conference of 1888. The event highlights the attitude of the railway companies towards their customers.

The government realised that some guidelines were required to control the competition between the railways such that the interests of the public were protected and reckless competition among railway companies did not lead to financial instability. A decision had been taken in 1887 to define the maximum and minimum rates for goods traffic for each class. The railway companies were given freedom to decide the tariff within the range defined by policy. They were urged to cooperate to afford facilities of through rates for the benefit of the customers. The companies raised several objections to the proposed tariff structure, pointing out that it left them little flexibility. The rates were reviewed and revised in 1891. The new proposed structure for freight was as shown below:

Table 1.11: Proposed tariff structure for freight in 1891

Goods Rates per Maund per Mile in Pies in 1891		
Class	**Maximum**	**Minimum**
Special class	1/3 pies or 8.9 pies/ton/mile	1/10 or 2.7 pie/ton/mile* Applicable for Coal {added by author}
1st class	1/3 pies or 8.9 pies/ton/mile	1/6 or 4.5 pies/ton/mile
2nd class	½ pies or 13.5 pies/ton/mile	1/6 or 4.5 pies/ton/mile

(Continued)

[12] Through Rates: Refers to one rate being charged from origin to destination. In case of local rates, each railway charged a rate for its own jurisdiction. 'Through rates' were important for consignments crossing boundaries of several railway companies.

Table 1.11: *(Continued)*

Goods Rates per Maund per Mile in Pies in 1891		
Class	Maximum	Minimum
3rd Class	2/3 pies or 18 pies/ton/mile	1/6 or 4.5 pies/ton/mile
4th class	5/6 pie or 22.5 pies/ton/mile	1/6 or 4.5 pies/ton/mile
5th class	1 pie or 27 pies/ton/mile	1/6 or 4.5 pies/ton/mile

*One ton= 27 maunds (Sanyal 1930, 183)

All railways did not accept these rates. N. Sanyal observes:

> Some of the railways accepted the new schedule, while the Great Indian Peninsula, Bombay Baroda and Central India (broad gauge) and Madras Railways did not readily admit government interference till after the expiry of their first contracts and the acquisition of the lines by the state. The schedule remained in force up to the end of the Great War, with only slight modification in July 1910 by which the special and first classes were amalgamated, thereby bringing down the minimum for the lowest class to 1/10 pie. (Sanyal, 1930, p. 183)

One aspect, which was repeatedly emphasised by the government, was that a railway company should not show undue preference to any individual or administration. The Act of 1890 had a specific provision, {Section 42(2)}, relating to undue preference. However, there was no administrative mechanism to adjudicate on specific cases and hence, the provisions were not effectively implemented. It is important to note that the Railway Act of 1890 also did not touch upon the issue of rates and fares as these were under the ambit of separate contracts with the railway companies.

Some administrators in England realised the importance of streamlining the tariff policy. The Report on the Trade of British India for the year 1888–89, under the section Raw Materials and Unmanufactured Articles, made the following remarks about the export of coal to India and the importance of the tariff policy:

> Imports were slightly smaller (833,478 tons) than the unusually large quantity (848,878 tons) imported in the previous year. Bombay takes about three-fourths of the imports. In India in 1888, 1,695,466 tons of coal were raised, the bulk (1,380,594 tons) in Bengal where the quantity of coal imported was only 19,376 tons. If coasting freights were reduced Bengal could supply coal to Burma, Madras, and Bombay.
>
> Coal represents close on half of the total value of imports in this class. (O'Conor, 1889, p. 26)

With steady increase in coal production India and fluctuations in the costs of maritime shipments, the level of importation fluctuated. The report for the next year 1889–90 again highlighted the importance of tariff policy. It stated:

'The imports into Bombay have fallen materially, the Great Indian Peninsula Railway Company having adopted the use of Indian coal to a considerable extent. The Bengal-Nagpur, Indian Midland, and Rajputana-Malwa lines also now consume Indian coal more or less largely.' It continued to record: 'The extinction of the import trade in coal is, however, only a question of time and of greater facility and cheapness of transport in India.' (O'Conor, 1890, p. 21)

Continuing Demands for Tariff Reduction

Demand for reduction in coal tariffs continued and some reduction in tariff did occur. As in the past, it had a telling impact on the pattern of railway movement.

The British India Steam Navigation Company (having large interests in sea going vessels) wanted to develop coal depots at several ports for storing Bengal coal to replace the Welsh coal used earlier. The mill owners of Cawnpore were clamouring for lower rates of transportation. The Government was also keen to secure cheaper rates for coal for locomotives. The intense pressure led to the announcement of certain concessions. For example, in 1889, a rebate of 16 per cent was offered on the prevailing tariff for export coal and a rebate of 10 per cent was offered on rubble or slack coal. (Huddleston, 1906, 139). An additional rebate of 10 per cent for export coal was introduced in 1895. The changes provided a boost to coal movement. *However, the noteworthy point was that the tariff modifications were mainly addressed at improving exports of Indian coal via Calcutta Port. This management decision was a compromise as the operational systems did not permit long distance coal movement and moving coal within EIR over a short distance to the port was a superior tactical solution.*

Reduction in Rates and Movement of Coal via Calcutta Port

The Kidderpore Dock had originally been set up in 1892 for handling general merchandise. The rebate in freight provided a boost to the export of coal. A lot of coal traffic started moving to the port. By 1893, export trade via Calcutta had reached 250,000 tons. The increase in traffic created congestion and highlighted the need to develop coal handling terminals. Additional jetties were set up for handling coal. Sometime later, jetties with mechanised arrangements for handling coal were added. The Bengal Nagpur Railway proposed the creation of another terminal at Luff Point. This proposal, however, did not fructify. The Jubilee Bridge, over the Ganges between Bandel and Naihati, which had been constructed in 1887, became an important route for carrying coal to the docks. The movement of coal to north was also growing owing to demand from railways and mills at Cawnpore (Kanpur).

With greater movement to Calcutta port, coal exports from India continued to increase and the expectations about the future were very optimistic. In 1894 Sir Strachey in an address to the shareholders of the East Indian Company declared that:

> 'There is no possible reason,' {he remarked,} 'why the whole of the coal now exported from England, whether required on land or for consumption at sea east of Aden, should not be replaced by Indian coal.' (Huddleston, 1906, p. 162)

The issue of further modification of rates was referred to Sir Strachey and General Williams, Deputy Government Director for Indian Guaranteed Railways. The final decision regarding coal tariff was:

(a) For all stations up to 400 miles, 0.15 pie per maund per mile (4.05 pie per ton per mile)
(b) For all distance beyond 400 miles, first 400 miles according to clause (a) and beyond 400 miles at 0.10 pie per maund per mile (2.7 pie per ton per mile). *'These rates were subject to a scale of rebates for large consignments, and certain rules were detailed as to routing and so forth.'* (Huddleston, 1906, p. 152–3)

The proposal was accepted by the Government and were adopted by many railway companies. Huddleston records:

> The general effect of the new arrangement was to give a substantial reduction in the rates for all distances, amounting to about 15 per cent, and this required a corresponding increase of traffic to maintain the revenue at its former level, but at the time no uneasiness was felt, for, as the Chairman remarked, the growth of the coal traffic leaves no room for doubting the early realization of the requisite increase and gives reasonable ground for expecting still further and more satisfactory expansion in the future. (Huddleston, 1906, pp. 153–4)

The expectations of the Government were realised. The coal traffic increased dramatically on EIR. The freight earning of EIR from coal were:

1891: Rs. 63 lakhs,
1896: Rs. 97 lakhs,
1901: Rs. 180 lakhs.

Greater export of coal through Calcutta port also resulted in Bengal coal reaching Bombay by ships. This brought a visible shift in the consumption pattern of locomotive coal on GIPR and BBCR. In the case of BBCR, the consumption of imported coal reduced from 22,477 tons in 1897 to a negligible amount by 1901.

At the same time the use of Indian coal increased from 46,057 tons in 1897 to 77,916 tons in 1901. Similarly, for GIPR, the drop in the case of imported coal was from 13,674 tons in 1897 to nil by 1900 and 1901, and the corresponding increase in consumption of indigenous coal was from 2,73,237 tons in 1897 to 3,81,380 tons in 1901.

The EIR thrived on moving coal over short distances, particularly to Calcutta port and industries in the Calcutta area. This was suited to keeping most of the wagons within its own railway system and reaping the benefits of the concessions for port bound traffic announced by the government. The growth of coal traffic on EIR is shown below:

Table 1.12: The growth in coal traffic on EIR 1889–1905

Year	Total Coal Traffic in tons	Moving Up direction towards north (in tons)	Moving Down direction towards Calcutta (in tons)	Per cent of Total for Down direction	Exported (in Tons)	Per cent of Down Traffic Exported
1889	1,404,711	303,910	1,100,801	78.4	Not available	
1894	2,144,382	466,768	1,677,614	78.2	297,000	17.7
1899	3,897,596	630,544	3,267,052	83.8	1,136,000	34.8
1905	6,142,264	1,260,740	4,881,524	79.5	2,767,000	56.7

(Huddleston, 1906, p. 166) [Percentages added by Author]

The data shows that the despatches by rail from the Bengal coalfields grew at a compound rate of 9.7 per cent between 1889 and 1905 and that almost 80 per cent of the coal moved eastwards towards Calcutta and the Calcutta Port. Also, the percentage of coal exported continued to increase steadily. Coal was exported to neighbouring countries and also moved to Indian ports at Bombay and Karachi.

Opening of the Jharia Coalfield

Extension of the line from Barakar towards Jharia was sanctioned in 1892 and partly completed in 1894. Huddleston records 'On the 20th May 1894 trains began running as far as Ghootrya, some seven miles beyond Barrakur, the first train carrying 100 tons of coal and 50 passengers.' (Huddleston, 1906, p. 147)

The partial opening of the Jharia and Topsi branches in Raniganj led to a further spurt in the coal traffic. There was a huge demand for new colliery sidings, wagons and locomotives. Terminal capacities were inadequate and so was the ability of the railway marshalling yards to handle the traffic. The trade complained bitterly about the inability of the railways. Responding to this criticism, Sir Strachey pointed out the initiatives which the railways had taken to help the trade and to the enormous growth in the value of the shares of the coal companies.

The increase in production of all coal from all coalfields between 1885 and 1906 is shown in Table 1.13:

Table 1.13: Production of Coal in Tons 1885–1906

Coal-field	Bengal	Central Provin-ces	Assam	Central India	Nizam's Territory	Total including other minor fields	Indian Coal Con-sumed by railways	Indian Coal moved to Indian Ports	Coal exported to for-eign ports	Coal im-ported into India	Per cent of Indian pro-duc-tion con-sumed by rail-ways
Year											
1885	1123700	119116	43707	7698	0	1,294,221	486,716	162,276 for 1885	310000 Average 1895–1900	819302	37.6
1901	5487585	191,516	254,100	164,362	421,218	6,635,727	1,956,631	1,157,892		191627	29.4
1906	8095303	92848	285,490	170,292	467,924	9,261,714	2,878,281	1,830,793		226365	31.1

Source: Report of Railway Board for 1906, 1907, Appendix 28, p. 102

The data shows that production in the country increased from 1.3 million tons in 1885 to 9.3 million tons by 1906, a very high rate of growth. Bengal continued to produce more than 89 per cent of the coal in the country, the growth in other fields being much smaller in comparison. The rapid increase in total production and the spatial skew in the production pattern imposed a serious load for transportation on the railway companies in eastern India, particularly the EIR and BNR, which were moving most of the coal. Unless there was balancing traffic in the return direction, movement to distant destinations created the issue of return of wagons in time. The EIR therefore continued to prefer movement of coal to the Calcutta port.[13]

[13] A map of the major coalfields of India and the adjoining railway routes as of 1903 is placed in Appendix 1. Only the railway routes important for coal movement have been shown on the map.

Coal Movement Patterns

A study of the annual reports named 'Review of the Trade of India' between 1890–91 and 1901–02 (published by the Finance and Commerce department of the Government of India), shows that the trends observed in earlier years were persisting:

a) The production of coal in India was increasing steadily.
b) The importation of coal into India from England was mainly for Bombay, Sind and Madras as the cost of imported coal at these destinations was less than Indian coal.
c) A considerable amount of Indian coal was moving to Bombay and Madras via the Calcutta Port. After the construction of the East Coast line in 1896, coal from Bengal and Singareni coalfield started gaining access into Madras. However, Bombay and Karachi continued to depend on imported coal, though not necessarily for railway use.
d) In addition to the coastal movement to Madras and Bombay, Indian coal was exported to several countries. Under the section 'Exports' the Report of the Trade of India for 1900–01 makes a specific mention about the coal trade and capacity constraints of the railways:

> This trade was actively stimulated last year by the extremely high price to which English coal was raised. The production exceeded six million tons, and 541,445 tons were exported, the coal being shipped as usual mainly to Colombo, but going last year further afield than ever before, to Suez and the east coast of Africa, to Java and to Sumatra. It also displaced a considerable quantity of English coal in India, as stated under the head of imports. A still larger trade would probably have been recorded if the carriage of coal from the mines to Calcutta had not been impeded by the want of railway trucks. (O'Conor, 1901, p. 23)

This was a reassertion of the statement of Huddleston that the movement of coal to the Calcutta Port was becoming a problem as the railways found it difficult to handle the volumes of wheat and coal together. The railway transportation issue was a serious constraint on the Government's active effort to encourage exports by offering a rebate in freight rates and reduced port charges for export. Surprisingly, there was no parallel action to promote coal movement to interior parts of the country, or to augment the capacity of Calcutta Port. The movement pattern that had evolved suited the government's overall interests and the non-fulfilment of the requirement of coal by the industries in the hinterland was overlooked.

The table presented below gives a clear idea of the trend of production, imports, coastal movement and exports as well as usage of coal by the railways. The data has been derived by the author from the information available at Appendix 29 of the Administrative Report for 1901.

Table 1.14: Production and Use of Coal 1885–1901

Year	Production	To Indian Ports	Export Outside	Total Imports	Used by Rlys	Per cent used by Railways	Coastal as movement % Of Production	Imports as % of Indian Production
1885	1294221	NA stands for Not available	500	819302	486716	37.6		63.3
1886	1388487	NA	199	740134	470075	33.9		53.3
1887	1564063	NA	315	829159	488774	31.3		53.0
1888	1708903	NA	15796	806239	551770	32.3		47.2
1889	1946172	NA	39972	769204	715240	37.3		39.5
1890	2168521	NA	26336	653582	654829	30.2		30.1
1891	2328577	NA	4515	743413	797142	34.2		31.9
1892	2537696	NA	15725	651497	885492	34.9		25.7
1893	2562001	NA	52302	634385	924900	36.1		24.8
1894	2823907	143813	154282	732155	1062748	37.6	5.1	25.9
1895	3540019	162276	211407	789133	1119621	31.6	4.6	22.3
1896	3683698	389842	191030	617632	1182051	32.1	10.6	16.8
1897	4066294	731742	390979	257273	1328120	32.7	18.0	6.3
1898	4068196	737689	490290	331285	1423463	35.0	18.1	8.1
1899	5093260	672311	467306	518505	1561821	30.7	13.2	10.2
1900	6118692	1030709	711874	135649	1867185	30.5	16.8	2.2
1901	6657573	1157892	845953	351738	1965530	29.5	17.4	5.3

Source: Brereton, 1902, p. 168 [Percentages inserted by Author].

Production and Consumption of Coal

The data presented above shows that the production of coal in India had grown at a compound annual growth rate of 10.8 per cent between 1885 and 1901. The consumption by the railways had also grown at a compound rate of 9.1 per cent clearly showing the mutual dependence of the two industries. Secondly, the incidence of coastal movement for centres in India had grown eight times between 1894 and 1901. Similarly, the export of coal had also increased from a mere 500 tons in 1885 to 845953 tons in 1901. At the same time, the import of coal from all sources had reduced from a level of 53 per cent of Indian production to 5.3 per cent of India's production and in absolute terms from 0.8 million tons in 1885 to 0.3 million tons in 1901. Even after factoring in the wide fluctuations in the level of imports due to factors such as the price of coal in England and other countries, the rates of international freight, the demand for coal in India and so on, the import of some coal into India continued till well into the twentieth century. However, the input was miniscule compared to the overall production of India and was the result of comparative advantages of sea freight and concessions granted by exporting centres. The quality of coal was also an important factor.

The coal consumed by industries other than the railways can be derived from table 1.14. If the production and imports are added to arrive at total availability of coal in the country and exports and railway consumption are deducted from total availability, we get a reasonable assessment of consumption by other indigenous consumers.

This consumption grew at a CAGR of 6.1 per cent between 1885 and 1901, indicating a steady growth in the coal consumption by other sectors of the economy. Industry wise data for that period is not available.

The coal industry in India continued to complain about the high tariff rates of railways and the lack of adequate supply of wagons. The continuous growth of consumption of indigenous coal does not fully support this contention. The movement of coal to Bombay and Sind by rail remained an issue. The lack of pan India operational systems and the absence of balancing traffic from Bombay towards Calcutta remained the main hurdles. There was no gainsaying that this aspect required urgent attention as was pointed out by the Administrative Report for 1901, which, noting that the prices of English coal had dropped, observed:

> English coal has again entered into competition with Indian coal in some of the markets, Bombay especially, and the imports of English coal and patent fuel during the year have increased from 91,710 tons to 272,630 tons, and of coal from other countries, from 43,939 tons to 79,108 tons. The quantity of Indian coal consumed by railways increased from 1,867,185 tons to 1,965,530 tons and there has been an increased demand for coal for private factories and for domestic consumption. Notwithstanding, therefore, the competition with imported fuel, the prospects of an increase in the coal trade are hopeful. As affecting the railways as carriers, the large quantity of coal carried by sea to places in India which can be reached by railway, amounting as it does to 1,157,892 tons, deserves attention. (Brereton, 1902, pp. 8–9)

With the increase in coal production and rail movement, it would have been expected that the Government would invest more in development of railways and industry. This, however, did not happen as the existing fiscal and trade policies suited imperial interests.[14]

Trade and Fiscal Policy

The major industries in India were cotton in the western part of the country and jute in Bengal. The tea industry was developing. Development of other industries in India remained muted. Industrial progress, which could be expected of a country with large coal production and a big railway network, did not take place. One of the main reasons for this was the unwillingness of the British government to protect Indian industries against international competition.

In the nineteenth century, the dominant policy of the Government of India was one of free trade. There was no import duty to protect any Indian industry. This was contrary to the worldwide trend of protection, particularly against British goods. India was a large importer of British manufactured goods, and the exports of India were divided between England, mainland Europe and USA. The free trade with USA and continental Europe enabled India to have a trade surplus with those countries with whom Britain normally had a trade deficit. Financially, this was rewarding for the Imperial government. Thus, both the industrial interests and Imperial interests benefitted from the free trade arrangement.

The period between 1890–91 and 1897–98 was financially adverse for the government whose losses were more than the profits. The prevailing internal and external situation made the balancing of the budget very difficult. Most of the railway companies continued to report losses till 1900. Other issues such as the impact of famines and income from opium trade also exerted a financial pressure on the government.

The losses in the railways were partly attributable to the old guarantee system wherein the government had to bear the entire losses of the losing railway systems and received only a part of the profits of the profitable systems. As Bagchi observes, 'there was a tendency of all paying systems to inflate their losses and for all losing systems to keep their ways unchanged.' (Bagchi, 1972). The second reason was that much of the railway network in Northwestern India had been built at the end of the nineteenth century for strategic reasons and was financially not remunerative. The third reason, as we have observed, was the lack of cooperation between railway companies, poor technology and the inefficient operational practices.

---

14 Fiscal Policy of the Government: Amiya Bagchi: Private Investment in India 1900–1939: Chapter 2.

It was no surprise that the government, already stressed for funds would accord low priority to expenditure on railways. The situation improved after 1898, and between that year to 1913–14, surpluses were reported for all years except one. There was an overall buoyancy in the world economy and trade thrived. Railway companies also turned the corner after 1901 and losses were no longer reported.

Providing adequate freight transportation services to fulfil the demands of a large country was an extremely challenging task. The private railway companies, content to operate in their own domains neglected the need to upgrade operational procedures and technology and the imperial government also failed to take any cogent initiative. The review of 1873 had highlighted several deficiencies in the operational practices and status of technology. However, not much had changed. A review of the status of railway technology at the end of the nineteenth century emphasises the dismal state of affairs.

Status of Technology on Railways 1890–1901

Freight Wagons

With the benefit of hindsight, we can say that it was not surprising that constraints were faced for long distance transportation as the standards of operation and rolling stock had not developed much sophistication at that time. In History of Indian Railways, G.S. Khosla observes:

> It will strain the imagination of most people to learn that at one time goods and passenger vehicles of the Indian railways carried a coupling device at one end only. How railwaymen in the nineteenth century managed to put vehicles together to form a train must have been a feat worthy of the respect of their present-day successors. In 1890, the East Indian and the Madras Railways had not fitted even their passenger vehicles with couplings at both ends. The goods stock of most of the railways had couplings at one end only. One of the reasons for carrying on with one coupling was economy in expenditure, though an extra coupling then cost Rs. 22 only. Some railways like the G1P and the BB & Cl joined up good vehicles with side chains, not using screw couplings at all. Some others like the BNR took the position that they experienced no inconvenience working with one coupling only. The Public Works Department of the Government of India, of which the railways formed a branch, was not quite sure whether it had the legal authority to force guaranteed companies to incur the extra expenditure.(Khosla, 1988, p. 299)

The report of the Consulting Engineer of the railways in the 1870s had flagged the poor carrying capacity of the freight wagons and the low gross load per train. Unfortunately, the situation did not improve very much thereafter. The report to the Administration for 1901 Appendices 32 and 33 provides details for various railway companies regarding the carrying capacity of freight wagons, the number of wagons per train and the average weight of freight carried per train. The data is very revealing as it shows that: (a) the standards of rolling stock used varied in terms of the weight of the empty wagon (tare) and their carrying capacity and (b) there was no uniformity between companies in the number of wagons per train.

The following data pertaining to wagons highlights the issues (excerpts pertaining to data for major railway systems on Board Gauge have been shown):

Table 1.15: Actual load of freight trains against an ideal load of 500 tons per freight train for period 1897 to 1901

	Carrying capacity of open wagons			AVERAGE LOAD PER GOODS VEHICLE IN TONS			AVERAGE LOAD PER TRAIN IN TONS			AV NUMBER OF VEHICLES PER TRAIN		
Railway Companies	EIR	GIPR	BBCR	EIR	GIPR	BBCR	EIR	GIPR	BBCR	EIR	GIPR	BBCR
YEAR ⇩												
1897				7.00	4.95	5.40	203.61	103.29	186.87	29.08	20.86	34.62
1898				7.12	6.03	5.78	199.20	141.33	212.34	27.97	23.46	36.68
1899				7.14	5.03	5.33	198.67	140.41	207.59	27.81	23.03	38.92
1900				7.12	5.38	4.93	196.11	133.78	199.55	27.51	24.85	40.15
1901	14.82	14.53	14.23	7.45	5.52	6.31	203.12	143.72	250.75	27.26	26.05	39.75

Source: Brereton, 1902, Appendices 32, 33.

The wide variations in the data reveals the disparity in standards of operation. In the case of all three major railways operating on broad gauge, the average load per vehicle was half of the carrying capacity. The number of vehicles per train also varied widely. Improvement in these parameters would enable an immediate increase in the throughput of cargo.

Braking Systems

By 1901, all three railway companies named in table 1.15 had more than four decades of experience managing freight operations. It is extremely surprising that they would be running trains with half the cargo that could be carried. It is possible that the brake power of the trains and the system of signalling and interlocking did not inspire confidence among the officers responsible for freight operations. The braking system of the wagons was not modern. Continuous brakes[15] had not been introduced in many areas. On the EIR, the premier freight railway, only 8 per cent of the wagons were fitted with continuous brakes at the end of 1901 (Brereton, 1902, Appendix 35). Heavier wagons would require more powerful locomotives, which was also an area of concern. These could be reasons why a sub optimal load of train was preferred so as to avoid accidents.

Locomotives

The poor performance of the locomotives had long been a source of concern. In 1880, it had been observed that new steam locomotives were unable to haul a load of 600 tons at speeds greater than 13 to 15 miles per hour. Further, the average load of a goods train was 175 tons as against the stipulated weight of 400–450 tons for destinations beyond Mughalsarai and 600–700 tons for destinations below Asansol (Huddleston, 1906, 165,174).

Several issues were faced in the management of steam locomotives. First was the uncertainty of coal supply, particularly for railways situated far from the coalfields. Secondly, steam locomotive sheds received coal from multiple sources. The coal received from various sources had different characteristics and the quality varied considerably. The use of this blended coal created problems for the engine crew, who had the task of maintaining a uniform temperature in the boiler of the engine.

In the case of sourcing of coal for locomotives, many Indian coal producers had alleged that the railway companies preferred to source coal from companies owned by the British.

Most of the locomotives used in India were imported from England. The Imperial Government did not encourage the development of railway industries in India. It is arguable that had industries been set up in India, it would have been possible to produce assets at lower costs and to design them to Indian conditions.

Expertise in engineering was available in India. The first college for engineering had been started in Roorkee in north India in 1847. It was renamed as the Thomason College of Civil Engineering in 1854. The first engineering college in Bengal was the Civil Engineering College of 1856, with the avowed purpose of producing engineers for the Public Works department. This college, later shifted to Howrah and was renamed the Howrah Engineering College. It started a course in Mechanical Engineering too from 1880 onwards. However, the pool of engineering talent available was not utilised.

---

15 Continuous brakes: Refers to the braking system where the brakes of all wagons are connected via a pipe to the locomotive. When the locomotive driver applies the brakes, the braking system of all wagons of the train get activated together.

Signalling Systems:

The systems of signalling, interlocking of signals, use of block instruments for obtaining line clear were developing and had not proliferated. In the case of EIR, the predominant coal loading railway, the situation in 1889 is best described in the words of G. Huddleston, who was the Chief Superintendent of the EIR. He wrote:

> When General Strachey visited India in 1889, he found that the train service was exceedingly slow. What was described as the "fast train" took no less than 37 hours to cover the distance of 954 miles between Howrah and Delhi, that is to say, it trundled along at a through speed of little more than 25 miles an hour; while consignments of goods occupied weeks in transit where they should have taken days.
>
> Everything in the way of progress seemed to have been neglected, nothing was up-to date. The stations were not interlocked; the out-door signals and the train signalling apparatus were of the most primitive kind; passenger carriages were illuminated with vegetable oil lamps, which only served to make darkness visible, and not a single engine or vehicle was fitted with a vacuum brake. In addition to this, the conditions of working were risky, if not dangerous, for over the greater portion of the line "following trains" were allowed, and it was only over a comparatively short section of double line that the "absolute block" system was in force. With such a state of affairs there was obviously a crying need for remedy. (Huddleston, 1906, 176)

Use of the Absolute Block System[16] for running of trains was expanded gradually at later stages. This system of signalling requires the interlocking of points and signals and the use of 'block instruments' for granting permission for a train to approach a station or for despatching a train to another station. On the EIR at the end of 1901, only 75 out of 340 stations were equipped with interlocking systems and 30 with block instruments (Brereton, 1902, Appendix 37). At the all-India level, by the end of 1901, 763 stations out 3147 (24.5 per cent) were provided with block instruments and interlocking. Improved methods of signalling were introduced gradually.

---

[16] Absolute Block System of working trains: It is a system in which the section between two stations is called a 'Block Section' and only one train can remain at a time in the Block Section. The movement of trains is controlled through a 'block instrument' present at stations. The permission to run a train from one station to the other can happen only with the cooperation of two station masters operating block instruments. The points at the station are 'interlocked' with the signals such that unless the permission to start a train has been granted, and the points set and locked, the signal would not operate. This is called 'interlocking' of points and signals.

Safety

The record on safety was not flattering. In 1900, a total of 6558 accidents were reported of which 233 were categorised as 'serious' in terms of the provisions of the Indian Railway Act of 1890. There was, perhaps, good reason for the managers to be cautious about the load of the trains and their speeds.

Expansion of railway Network

In 1900 India had 24,752 miles of railway tracks. Still, many areas were without railways. With improvement in the economic scenario after 1900, there was a demand from the mercantile community for greater investment in railways. After the turn of the century, another report in 1903, focussed on the specific weaknesses of the system in terms of technology and tariffs and also made specific suggestions for improvement.

The approach of the British government towards railways in India did not exhibit any consistent philosophy of service towards the indigenous population. There appeared to be no long-term vision or policy for the development of the railways as an instrument for industrial progress. The primary focus remained the protection of strategic defence interests and maritime commerce to keep the Indian and British economies enmeshed. The railway companies were allowed to operate independently, following some basic parameters. The policies of the government evolved on the basis addressing specific issues, as they arose.

The perils of non-cooperation between the railway companies had been amply demonstrated during the years from 1855 to the end of the century. The British government was slowly veering towards the idea that the freedom of private railway companies needed to be controlled. To this end, a large number of companies had been progressively taken over by the government. The task of welding the companies into a cohesive whole and upgradation of technology required proactive actions from the government that would come some years later.

Despite their shortcomings, the railways and the coal industry had come a long way since 1855. Their mutual cooperation had ensured a steady growth in coal movement and support to the economy. The level of operational efficiency and the tariff regime had undergone several modifications and were more user friendly. By the beginning of the twentieth century, the coal industry and the railways had established a strong foothold in India and the level of coal production and transportation by railways achieved within a span of less than fifty years was indeed commendable. Development of the coal mines and the railways were proceeding hand in hand. Though there were short term issues of mismatch of supply and demand, there was also close cooperation between the two industries.

The future would see both industries scaling new heights, which could have been achieved earlier if more favourable administrative policies had been adopted.

As Daniel Thorner observes,

> It would appear that the very economic changes which the railways made possible in India were retarded by the way in which the railways were built and the way they were run. A different type of railway policy might have brought India much further along the path of modernization. (Thorner, 1955, p. 216)

1902–1947: Growth amidst challenges

The period 1902–1947 is distinctly different from the earlier period as several internal and external factors combined to give this period in the history of the railways and coal industry a different flavour. A period of economic prosperity after 1898 increased demand for domestic and international trade. Investment and production increased, and with it, the demand for rail transport. These factors modified the philosophy of the British government towards railways in India. Reforms, which could have been initiated earlier, were now implemented slowly to make the administrative apparatus of the railways more centralised. The Railway Board was created in 1905 for coordinating the working of the railway companies and enunciating policies. There was a major reform in the tariff structure which provided relief to the consumers and increased demand for coal transportation. Investment in the railways also increased. The expansion of the railway network continued unabated and route milage increased from 26,955 miles in 1905 to 40,524 miles in 1947, a growth of 50 per cent. Some industries received support from the government.

The process of transformation from a fragmented group of railway companies to a cohesive organisation was slow. Old issues regarding management of operations, upgradation of technology and cooperation between railway companies remained. However, with the efforts of the Railway Board, the level of cohesiveness of the railways as an all-India organisation slowly increased.

The production of coal in India grew rapidly in the first half of the twentieth century to keep pace with the rising demand. A number of controls on coal production and distribution were imposed during the first and the second World Wars. There were more than seven hundred collieries in India by the 1940s. They were all privately owned and the industry was characterised by lack of coordination and cohesion amongst the mining companies. Only a small percentage of the miners were trained, the rest being recruited from the local population, many times by contractors appointed by the mining companies. The level of mechanisation remained very low as compared to Europe and America as did the output per person. The existence of many small and uneconomic mines remained a problem. Several committees were appointed to examine the problems facing the industry. Implementation of some suggestions such as the creation of a Coal Grading Board proved beneficial. The Indian Coal Mines Committee of 1946 also made a number of recommendations to improve the situation which included interference by the State in certain matters.

The Indian National Congress had been set up in 1885 and the demands of the nationalist leaders for a greater share of Indians in decision making was gathering momentum. The railway was one of the prime areas of their concern as there was a feeling that the Government's policies pertaining to the railways and coal industry were not conducive to the interests of Indians. The partition of Bengal in 1905 and its subsequent annulment in 1911, inflamed passions further. As the struggle for political freedom continued to gather momentum, certain concessions were made to the Indian public by the Imperial government. The separation of the railway finances from the general budget in 1924 was a significant historical event in the evolution of the railways. A separate budget put the railway policies on a firmer footing as it now had freedom to decide allocation of finances. The two World Wars and the great Depression of the 1930s left their imprint on government policies and affected the coal and railway industries severely, though in different ways. The interplay of all these factors created a complex tapestry of policies and movement patterns which we now turn to.

Administrative Changes

Changes in the administrative structure of the railways had been attempted on several occasions in the nineteenth century. A number of railway companies had been gradually acquired by the State. Despite the changes, the administrative structure of the railways at the beginning of the twentieth century was quite amorphous and not conducive to progress in the direction of a cohesive organisation. In his book Development of Railways in India, N. Sanyal describes the administrative structure in the following manner:

> From time to time altered systems were tried. and finally, by the end of 1902 the following classification based upon ownership and management came to be adopted:
>
> I. State Lines worked by Companies. II. State Lines worked by the State. III. Lines owned by Companies guaranteed under old contracts. IV. Lines owned by Companies

> guaranteed under new contracts. V. District Board Lines. VI. Assisted Companies' Lines. VII. Native State Lines worked by Companies. VIII. Native State Lines worked by State Railway Agency. – IX. Lines owned and worked by Native States. X. Lines in foreign territory. The classification was thus made more scientific and the old nomenclature of Provincial State and Central State railways was given up. At the close of the year 1902, these railways were worked by 33 separate administrations. including 24 companies operating 17,754 miles. 4 Government Agents for 6,000 miles, and 5 Native States managing 2,184 miles. (Sanyal, 1930, p. 189)

This was clearly quite an administrative soup!

In 1903, an expert from England, Mr. Thomas Robertson examined the working of the railways in India and commented on the status of the administrative and controlling mechanisms prevalent at that time. He found that the existing railway companies could be divided into two broad classes, those for which the Government had financial liability and those for which it *did not* have financial responsibility. The first group covered 20,474 miles of rail track and the second 5462 miles. The supervision of the latter group was confined to investigations of accidents and some supervisory inspections to ascertain the level of safety and public convenience. The first group, i.e. the group for which the Government had responsibility, consisted of railways run by the state and those run by companies under contracts. For the lines run directly by the state, the actual working was supervised by line Managers, who had extensive powers for control of internal administration and their work was supervised by the Government of India. Independent inspectors were appointed by the Government to conduct inspections regarding safety and public convenience and also enquire into accidents.

In the case of railways run by companies under contract, the chain of command was more complicated and shared between England and India. In the case of England, control over the company within the contractual terms, was exercised by the Secretary of State in Council. The Secretary of State also appointed a Government Director to the boards of all companies. The Director possessed a plenary veto power. A consulting Engineer, who was not a government servant, was appointed to provide inputs and advice on technical matters to the Secretary of State.

In India, control was exercised at several levels and in several areas. The structure was as follows:

The Railway Branch was part of the Public Works Department. The Governor General in Council controlled the management and expenditure through this department. The Railway Branch consisted of: (a) Member of the Viceroy's in Council charge of Public Works, (b) Twelve officers who were: 1 Secretary,

3 Deputy Secretaries (for Traffic, Construction and Accounts), 4 Under Secretaries and 4 Assistant Secretaries. Here too seven Consulting Engineers were appointed to the seven circles and they were the representatives of the Government for the railways in different areas. The Consulting Engineers were also the Railway Secretaries to the local governments and were assisted by one deputy each in Bombay, Madras and Burma. The Consulting Engineers supervised the upkeep and general management of all departments of the railways under their jurisdictions. They also conducted inspections under the Railway Act of 1890.

A Government Examiner of Accounts was appointed in each of the seven circles to exercise close supervision on the expenditure in construction and management.

Mr. Robertson found the administrative structure unsatisfactory and recommended changes in the administrative set up including the setting up of a Railway Board as a central controlling authority to enunciate policy and effect more cohesive working of the companies. The suggestion was accepted and the Railway Board Act was passed in March 1905 to set up the Railway Board. In the same year Government appointed a Tariff Simplification Committee.

Major Changes in Tariff Structure

The issue of railway rates was also examined by Mr. Robertson along with Mr. Priestley in 1903. They compared the rates in India with those in the USA and found the rates in India to be very high, particularly as there was considerable amount of long-distance traffic. Tapering rates were recommended for both local and through traffic. The two experts also recommended that, as suggested by the Government earlier, the railway companies should act in a manner that they belonged to one administration. S.C. Ghose records Mr. Robertson's recommendation as:

> the reduction in passenger fares should be from 18 to 40 per cent., in general merchandise from 30 to 60 per cent., and in coal from 40 to 60 per cent., and also pointed out that such low rates were obtainable on American Railways. He also observed that reductions were particularly needed for long distance traffic and that in this respect the application of telescopic and sliding scales of rates should be on the through distance of all the railways from the place of origin to destination, instead of the traffic being charged at the local rates of each railway. (Ghose, 1918, p. 140)

In August 1905, the Railway Board issued a circular revising the tariff for haulage of freight. The circular reduced the tariff considerably and also laid down detailed conditions for its application. The circular stated:

> In Government of India letter, No. 517 R T, dated the 8th July 1897, it was ruled that the rates quoted in the Schedules to Government of India Circular No 8 Railway, dated the 4th May 1895, were maximum rates, the minimum, rate on railways for which a minimum has been prescribed, being 1/10th pie per maund per mile.
>
> The Railway Board consider that this minimum restricts trade in places distant from the coal-fields, and they accordingly authorise, subject to the conditions enumerated below, the adoption of the following minimum rates:
>
> Per Maund Per Mile
>
> —For distances up to 300 miles: 1/10 pie or 0 .10
>
> Plus, for any distance in excess of 300 miles and up to .500 miles inclusive: 1/15th pie or 0.066
>
> Plus for any distance m excess of 500 miles. 1/20th pie or 0. 05
>
> Condition 1 —That the rate shall be calculated on the through distance between the station of origin and the station of destination of the consignment
>
> Condition 2 —That when there are two or more routes to destination from the colliery where the traffic originates the railway or railways forming the longer route may calculate charges on the same mileage as the railway or railways forming the shorter route.
>
> Condition 3 —That coal for the use of foreign railways is charged at the same rates and under the same conditions as coal earned for the public
>
> Condition 4 —That the rates charged are divided between the railways over which the traffic is carried in proportion to the mileage of each, provided that if the distance the coal is carried over any railway is less than 25 miles, the mileage of that railway in dividing the freight shall be reckoned as 25 miles.
>
> Condition 5 —That these rates shall be subject to revision at the end of three years from the 1st of September 1905. (Ghose, 1918, p. 372)

Two other very important decisions were taken by the Railway Board that year. The first was to lay down

> '... revised form of agreement for extensions of railways into private premises' and also a decision that wagon bodies and frames could be manufactured by Indian firms (Railway Board, 1907, Appendices 44,46)

The reduction in rates actually occurred only in November 1906 as the EIR and BNR wanted more time to add requisite wagons to their fleets. Secondly, the EIR had planned to open the Grand Chord for traffic by the end of 1906. This would reduce the distances to be traversed for destinations in north India, and hence there would be a change in costs.

The following was the revised scales of rates for coal introduced in November 1906:

— Consignments in full wagon loads

For all distances up to 75 miles inclusive: 0.14 pie per maund per mile

Plus for any distances in excess of 75 miles up to 200 miles inclusive: 0.12 pie per maund per mile

Plus for any distance in excess of 200 miles and up to 500 miles: 0.06 pie per maund per mile

Plus for any distance in excess of 500 miles: 0.05 pie per maund per mile

(Ghose, 1918, p. 372)

There were two major reductions in tariff rates in 1902 and 1906. The rates for transportation to some selected destinations from the Jharia coalfields are shown below:

Table 2.1: Rates for Transportation per Ton of Coal from Jharia Coalfields

	1901 (In Rupees, Annas and Pies)	**1902 (In Rupees, Annas and Pies)**	**1907 (In Rupees, Annas and Pies)**
Patna	4-15-0	4-2-0	3-9-0
Benares	8-1-0	6-2-0	4-2-0
Kanpur	11-1-0	8-15-0	5-15-0
Delhi	14-14-0	12-5-0	7-15-0
Lahore	19-5-0	16-9-0	9-13-0
Bombay	21-4-0	21-7-0	11-4-0
Karachi	27-13-0	25-2-0	12-10-0

(Ghose, 1918, p. 373)

This was huge reduction in rates. As Ghose observes, *'The rates to Lahore, Bombay and Karachi from the Jherria coal field in 1907 were reduced by 41, 48 and 50 per cent, respectively from the rates in force in 1902.' (Ghose, 1918, p. 373)*

The Tariff Simplification Committee set up in 1905, submitted its report in 1909. It suggested a general classification which was approved by the Indian Railway Conference Association[17] and the Railway Board and was to be

[17] Indian Railway Conference Association (IRCA) set up in 1902 to streamline and collate the rules regarding booking of traffic, interchange of wagons between railway companies and so on. The role was expanded later on.

implemented from 1910. However, it was found that the process of simplification and generalisation of tariffs was leading to an increase in the maximum rates that could be charged for some commodities. There was public agitation against this and the Railway Board issued an order stating that the maximum rates that could be charged for any commodity by a railway could not exceed the maximum rates which had been in force earlier.

The Committee re-examined their proposals and submitted a revised report which led to the reduction in number of classifications of commodities and also prescribed certain minimum weight conditions to be used in through booking of goods traffic on the railways.

The reduction in tariff rates led to a keen competition among the railway companies to garner traffic. A number of agreements for routing traffic were also entered into for mutual advantage. *Thus, financial allurements led to increase in cooperation among the railway companies.*

Growth in Coal Production and New Railway Lines

The most significant development of coal production in the early twentieth century was the emergence of Jharia coalfield as a major producer of coal. The production from Bihar (which included Orissa up to 1932) averaged 2.3 million tons between 1900 and 1905, with the preponderant share coming from Jharia. The average for 1906–10 shot up to 6.79 million tons, while the production from Bengal averaged 3.5 million tons for the same period.

The railways responded by improving the connectivity of the coalfields by building new lines to Katrasgarh and Patherdih, which were in the heart of the Jharia coalfield. The rising star of the Jharia coalfields was noticed by the Bengal Nagpur Railway too and a railway line from Midnapur to Bhojudih, an area under the Jharia coalfield, was proposed by BNR. The EIR objected to this, probably fearing competition from an adjoining railway system. The matter was enquired into by Mr. Weightman, who ruled in favour of construction of the line. The line from Midnapur to Gomoh via Bhojudih was constructed in 1904. EIR completed the construction of the Grand Chord (GC), connecting Dhanbad directly with Koderma and Gaya in 1907. This new line, which connected Raniganj, Asansol, Dhanbad and Gomoh and proceeded towards Delhi as a shorter alternate route from Calcutta to Delhi via Gaya, created a direct route for coal movement towards the north and provided a fillip to the mining activity in the Jharia area. The commissioning of the Grand chord line led to a virtual rush for developing coal mines in the Jharia area. By the year 1908, 50 mining companies were working in the Jharia area. The number of joint stock companies registered for coal production gives an index of the 'coal rush' after the opening of the GC. Up to 1906, about 5 new companies used to be added each year. Between 1906 and 1909, the number increased from 48 to 122 and the paid-up capital increased from 2.3 crores Rupees to 5.3 crores[18]. Later, in 1929, Dr. Cyril Fox, in a paper submitted to the Geological, Mining and Metallurgical Institute, stated that the whole future of the coalfield depended on railway transportation. European companies started taking interest in India. Raniganj and Jharia were the main coal producers, with 529 out of 583 mines (91 per cent) being located in the Raniganj and Jharia fields in 1907–08.

Jharia had favourable mining conditions and the coal was of very high quality. As the coal production from Jharia increased rapidly, the coal mine owners in the Raniganj field, sensing intense competition, reacted in two ways. Some mine owners developed the best mines to produce high grade coal comparable to Jharia coal, while others attempted to reduce costs by resorting to the cheapest mining methods. This proved to be counterproductive and a spate of accidents and mine fires were recorded. The Government had been observing the poor safety record of the coal mines for some time. The first Indian Mines Act had been promulgated in 1901. In 1902, the Department of Mines was created, with a Chief Inspector and three inspectors. The Electricity Act and Explosives Act were also made applicable to the mines a few years later. The years 1906–08 were the 'coal rush' years and output increased rapidly. However, there was a fall in output during 1909–11. The production increased from 1912 onwards. In 1914, the total production was about 16.5 million tons, of which Jharia contributed 9.5 million tons and Raniganj 5 million.

Uneconomic Mines

During the period of the 'coal rush' of 1907–08 in Jharia, a number of small companies entered the coal mining business and started operating small mines. As mentioned earlier with regard to Raniganj, the Permanent Settlement of 1793 had vested the title of the land in the Zamindars. By the end of the nineteenth century, most of the land available in the Jharia area had been leased out. With growing demand, the leased land began to be handed over in the form of subleases to new miners. Over time, a breed of middlemen and intermediaries emerged, dealing in the trade of land between the Zamindar and the final beneficiary. A large percentage of the mines were small and unprepared to face the vicissitudes that would confront them in later years. As in the case of Raniganj,

[18] One crore is equal to 10 million. So, 5.3 crores is equal to 53 million Rupees.

the issue of small mines became a serious problem and the issue of fragmented coal holdings was flagged by expert committees in later years. The small mine owners did not invest in modern technology, their productivity was poor, the labour was exploited and, in times of distress, they resorted to unsafe mining practices. The effort to amalgamate the small mines into economically viable holdings continued even in the 1950s and 1960s.

Rising Coal Production

The coal industry took full advantage of the reduced transportation costs after 1906 and increased the level of production to earn handsome profits. There was sufficient demand for coal both within the country and abroad. The increased demand triggered an increase in the price of Bengal coal from Rs. 3.8.0 per ton in 1905 to 4.10 in 1906 and Rs. 6.12.0 in 1909. The sudden and sharp rise in prices curtailed internal demand. Cotton mills in Ahmedabad started using wood instead of coal. Industries in North India also reduced the use of Bengal coal. Import of English coal to the western coast increased. The export of coal was also affected with Indian coal being substituted with coal from Australia and South Africa. The loss of market share led to some unscrupulous miners to resort to supply of lower grade coal to control prices. This was a tragic development as it led to a loss of confidence in the quality of coal from Bengal.

The production picked up from 1910 and the output between 1910 and 1914 increased from 120 lakh tons to 165 lakh tons. Consumption also increased from 118 to 163 lakh tons. Import of coal increased during this period, especially from South Africa, on the back of some concessions granted by their government on exports. The demand for coal remained buoyant and the price of Bengal coal increased from Rs. 6.8.0 per ton in 1913 to Rs. 7.5.0 in 1914. The trend of coal production is presented in Table 2.2.

Table 2.2: Trend in coal production, exports and imports (1878–1920) (in lakh tons)

	Net Availability of Foreign Coal	Indian Production	Export of Indian coal	Net Indian Coal	Total Imp+ Indian
Average 1878–80	5.6	9.90	0.005		
Average 1881–85	6.8	12.30	NA		
Average 1886–90	8.0	17.60	0.2		

(Continued)

Table 2.2: (*Continued*)

	Net Availability of Foreign Coal	Indian Production	Export of Indian coal	Net Indian Coal	Total Imp+ Indian
Average 1891–95	7.1	27.60	0.4	27.2	34.3
Average 1896–1900	3.3	47.50	3.1	44.4	47.7
Average 1901–05	2.1	76.30	5.7	70.6	72.7
1906	2.3	97.80	10.0	87.8	90.1
1907	3.0	111.50	6.6	104.9	107.9
1908	3.9	127.70	6.6	121.1	125.0
1909	4.9	118.70	5.6	113.1	118.0
1910	3.2	120.50	9.9	110.6	113.8
Average 1906–10	3.4	115.20	7.8	107.4	110.8
1911	3.2	127.20	8.6	118.6	121.8
1912	5.6	147.10	9.0	138.1	143.7
1913	6.5	162.10	7.6	154.6	161
1914	4.2	164.60	5.8	158.8	163
1915	1.9	171.00	7.5	163.5	165.4
Average 1911–15	4.3	154.40	7.7	146.7	151
1916–20	0.4	193.60	6.2	187.4	187.8

[Ghosh, 1977, p. 258] (two columns, Imports of Foreign coal and re-exports of foreign coal, have been omitted as re-exports were very small)

New Mining Areas

The Bokaro and Karanpura fields had been surveyed in 1866–67. However, data regarding coal production from the fields is not available for the nineteenth century. Production started in Bokaro from 1915 and increased rapidly from 1,90,000 tons in 1916 to over 2 million tons by 1928. In the case of the Karanpura coalfield, production started in 1925 and rapidly reached 4.24 lakh tons by 1935. The railway line from Gomia via Barkakana, Barwadih to Daltonganj was constructed in phases and the connection between Gomoh and Daltonganj was established in 1929. It joined the Calcutta-Delhi route at Sone Nagar. Thus, the Raniganj, Jharia and Karanpura fields were now all connected to the trunk route of the railways to north India and via Jabalpur to the GIPR network which extended up to Bombay.[19]

Reduction in use of Imported Coal by Railways

With the increase in production of indigenous coal, the percentage of imported coal used by the railways continued to diminish and dropped to a level of about one per cent of the total coal available in the country. The Report for 1906 records the total use of coal by the railways as follows:

Table 2.3: Consumption of coal and wood by Railways in India 1902–06 (Data in Tons)

	Indian Coal	Imported Coal	Wood**	Total Coal	Imported coal as percentage of Total Coal	Wood as % of coal
1902	2,091,992	21,459	402,442	2,113,451	1.02%	19.04%
1903	2,203,882	17,696	497,185	2,221,578	0.80%	22.38%
1904	2,417,841	17,432	395,297	2,435,273	0.72%	16.23%
1905	2,668,424	18,235	253,093	2,687,659	0.68%	9.60%
1906	2,878,281	37,289	248,224	2,915,570	1.28%	8.51%

(Railway Board, 1907, Appendix 27, pp. 98–101) *(Percentages inserted by author)*
*{** for wood, the conversion ratio of Wood to coal is: 2.5 tons of wood to 1 ton of coal and for oil it is 0.55 tons of oil = 1 ton of coal}*

The dominance of indigenous coal is clear. However, the surprising feature is the substantial use of wood even up to 1906. The railway companies using large quantities of wood were Madras, North western and BBCR. In all cases the cost per ton of wood, including the freight, was much less than indigenous coal, as wood was available locally. For example, in the case of North Western Railway, the cost per ton of wood was Rs. 5 to 5.5 whereas the cost of Bengal coal was Rs. 12 to Rs.14.58 per ton. However, there was a clear declining trend even in the case of wood. Some railways like GIPR had tried the use of oil instead of coal. The experiment was not successful.

Cost Control: Ownership of Coal Mines by Railway Companies and Impact on Coal Market

We have noted earlier that EIR had its own coal mines. To have assured supply of coal as also to control costs, other railway companies had also opened their own coal mines. The railway companies owned the following seven collieries:

19 A map showing the important railway lines adjoining the coalfields and the year of construction is placed at Appendix 2. The map shows the status for the year 1939.

Table 2.4: Collieries owned by Railway Companies

Name of Colliery	Owned by	Production in Tons in 1906
Kuhurbari & Serampore	East Indian Railway	623979
Warora	State	33,327
Mohpani	Great Indian Peninsula Railway	27,503
Dandot	North Western State Railway	43,661
Khost	North Western State Railway	32,500
Haranpur Pressed Fuel Factory	North Western State Railway	6,541

(Railway Board, 1907, Appendix 29 p. 103)

The total production of these collieries accounted for 27 per cent of the total coal consumed by the railways in the country. The total coal consumed by the railways in 1906 was about 29.15 lakh tons (including imported coal), which was approximately 30 per cent of the coal produced in the country.

The predominant position of the East Indian Railway as a producer of coal had an impact on the price of coal in the market. The cost of production of the railways was less than that of other miners and railway was also the largest buyer of coal. When the railways purchased coal from the market, they offered a lower price to the miners. As the quantity likely to be purchased was large, many large mining companies offered coal to the railways at a slightly lower price than the market to secure a large order. This hurt the smaller mining companies as the market price got depressed. There was also an allegation that the larger mining firms owned by the British and the railway companies connived to lower the market price for coal and hurt the smaller Indian owned companies. This, however, cannot be proved. The issue continued to be represented against, and the grievance continued to be aired for a long time. Years later, it found prominent mention in the Report of the Indian Coalfields Committee of 1946 (popularly known as the Mahindra Committee Report, after its Chairman Mr. K. C. Mahindra).[20] The report observed that the railway companies were entitled to have their own coal mines to ensure steady supply of good quality coal. However, the railways were by far the largest user of coal and a very large producer as well. This dual role gave the railway companies an opportunity to influence the market. In the overall interest it would be advisable to transfer the railway collieries to another government department. (Report of the Mahindra Committee Vol-1, 1947, pp. 195–6)

[20] This report will henceforth be referred to as the Mahindra Committee Report, as that is how it is known in the available literature.

The increased production of coal imposed a pressure on the railway companies to improve the level of transportation and improve the efficiency of operations. The scrutiny by Robertson, however, threw up a number of issues which required immediate attention.

Efficiency of Train Operations

Speed of Trains, Signalling, Wagon Design, Locomotives

The important areas of railway operations which needed attention were:

- The average speed of goods trains was extremely slow, averaging between 3.7 and 12 miles per hour on some important routes.
- Terminal management was poor. There were delays at the originating station, at intermediate stations for changing of locomotives and crew, at junction stations and yards and finally at the destination terminal first for obtaining room for placement of the wagons and second, for unloading of the consignments. In the case of EIR, a major coal loading railway, speeds as low as 2 to 5 miles per hour had been reported, when the distance to be covered was only 180 miles.
- The methods of loading wagons needed to be modernised.
  - The ordering of the trains needed to be done in a way that maximised the running of through trains which avoided getting into marshalling yards. This required forethought and interaction with the trade.
  - If more through trains could be run and the efficiency of handling consignments at the loading and unloading points improved, considerable increase in speeds could be achieved.
  - Increase in the speeds of freight trains would bring enormous economies in wagon usage and the demand for rolling stock would diminish as 'turn round time' (or 'cycle time', i.e. the time interval between two successive loadings of a wagon)[21] would reduce. The constant demand for procurement of more rolling stock would also be controlled.
  - Mr. Robertson advocated the introduction of superior high-capacity wagon design based on the American model.
  - 80 per cent of the traffic carried by the railways in India was low class bulk traffic and for this a special wagon had to be designed having higher carrying capacity.

---

21 Turn Round Time or Cycle Time: The time interval between two successive loadings of a wagon. A low turn round time shows better mobility in the system and reduces the requirement of wagons required for a given level of traffic.

- The locomotives in India could haul loads only up to 1,000 tons, whereas in the USA, locomotives were hauling loads of 3,000 and 4,000 tons. In addition, the percentage of locomotives under repair was as high as 15 per cent in India, while it was only 8 per cent in the USA.

The findings of Mr. Robertson were on the same lines as that of the report of 1873. Clearly the response of the railway managements and government to the suggestions made in 1873 had been slow. Even after the recommendations of 1903, the resistance to change continued as was found from a review of the data for the period 1907 to 1915. The review showed that the practice of not loading wagons to capacity continued and this resulted in unnecessary increase in the number of trains required to be run. The output of the wagons in terms of wagon miles per wagon day was low. To keep pace with the rising demand, particularly from the coal industry, the railway companies added large number of wagons to their fleet, further depressing the standards of utilisation. Thus, there does not seem to have been much improvement in this area since the 1870s. There were notable differences in the efficiency among the companies. The data shows that the EIR continued to remain one of the most efficient companies and also one with the highest amount of freight movement, thanks to the coalfields in its domain. Some data for selected companies for few years is presented below in Table 2.5 as representing the trend:

Table 2.5: Statistics Showing Efficiency of Train Operation

	BNR	BBCR	EIR	GIPR	NWR	OUDH& ROHILKHAND
% INCREASE IN NUMBER OF WAGONS 1907 TO 1911	36.3	45.1	16.7	20	50.8	14.9
% **DECREASE** IN WORK DONE PER WAGON 1907 TO 1911	*	14.28	+3.77	19.6	22.68	18.18
% INCREASE IN WAGONS 1911 TO 1915	65.59	76.72	63.8	37.7	92.46	37.7
% **DECREASE** IN WORK DONE PER WAGON 1907 TO 1914–15	9.3	14.28	11.37	31.37	45.3	12.12
% INCREASE IN TON MILES[22] 1907 TO 1911	45.03	19.76	33.6	26.9	−1.68	−0.14

22 Ton Miles: Movement of One ton of cargo over one mile = one ton mile. It is the product of the weight of the cargo and the distance it has moved, and is used as a statistical parameter to expresses the transport output.

	BNR	BBCR	EIR	GIPR	NWR	OUDH& ROHILKHAND
% INCREASE IN TON MILES 1907 TO 1914–15	83.3	37.02	68.6	37.4	0.79	5.08
% INCREASE IN MERCHANDISE TRAFFIC 1911 TO 1914–15	21.8	10.2	17.3	6.4	6.13	4.7
% INCREASE IN MERCHANDISE TRAFFIC 1907 TO 1914–15	53.15	25.67	35.02	27.5	13.1	5.4

(Ghose, 1918, p. 530)

It is apparent from the data that the sharp increase in number of wagons led to a drop in the work done per wagon. BNR and EIR are the only two railways which show some parity between the increase in the number of wagons and the increase in ton miles.

The poor utilisation of available wagon capacity aggravated the perceived shortage of wagons, as their ability to carry cargo was not fully utilised. The data presented below reveals the state of affairs. It is important to note that the carrying capacities of the wagons of each railway also continued to be different, as it had been in the nineteenth century. The lack of uniformity in the standards of technology and operational management reinforced the lack of cohesion between the railway companies. The issue was addressed much later by the Railway Board.

Table 2.6 shows the data for utilisation of wagon capacity for some major freight loading railways in 1915–16:

Table 2.6: Utilisation of wagon Capacity

Railway	Carrying Capacity of Wagons in 1915–16		Average Load per loaded vehicle excluding empties	
	Covered	Open	1st half	2nd Half
BNR	16.23	17.77	12.42	12.77
BBCR	18.86	19.17	11.23	10.94
EIR	18.16	16.74	13.93	14.01
GIPR	18.32	16.43	10.76	11.92
NWR	21.32	17.63	10.76	10.33

(Ghose, 1918, p. 540)

The practice of running trains with sub-optimal number of wagons per train also persisted.

Table 2.7: Number of Wagons per Train

Average number of loaded wagons to a freight train in 1915–16 as against ideal of 50 wagons per train		
	First Half of year	**Second Half of year**
BNR	32.15	33.30
BBCR	36.24	37.23
EIR	35.64	37.39
GIPR	27.58	27.84
NWR	34.49	32.81

(Ghose, 1918, p. 542)

Hence during the period of more than four decades between 1873 and 1917, substantial improvement in the area of wagon utilisation had not been achieved. This was a failure of the management system of the railways, and it naturally had its impact on tariff policy as the ability to carry traffic got compromised. With more efficient operations, lower freight rates could have been offered.

Need for Larger Wagons

In an echo of the logic of Robertson in 1903, a paper presented before the Royal Society of Arts in 1919, H. Kelway-Bamber, argued forcefully in favour of introduction of high-capacity wagons in India. The design of the wagons used on the broad-gauge railways, which continued to be four wheeled flat bottom and top open type, had evolved from 1895 onwards. The paper by Kelway-Bamber noted that the average carrying capacity of wagons on Indian railways was about 18 tons and would soon increase to 20 tons. The production and consumption of coal was increasing rapidly. With the present wagon design, the requirement of wagons for coal transportation would increase by three times up to 1930 and by five times up to 1950. The increased number of trains would stretch the available line capacity. It was only by increasing the payload per wagon to 60 tons, (such wagons were already in use in the US railroads), could the wagon requirement and proliferation of number of trains be kept under check. Unfortunately, this advice went unheeded at that time. [Kelway-Bamber, 1919, p. 156].

Locomotives

The lack of uniformity of coal quality was a constant source of concern for the locomotive sheds. This problem continued over the years and as late as 1947, the Indian Railway Enquiry Committee reported,

> it is not unusual now to find a shed with coal from 30 or more different collieries on hand at the same time. Coal from different collieries has different properties and engine crews have to change their firing technique[23].... Therefore, the supply from different collieries to the same shed at the same time has greatly increased the difficulties of the engine crews. (Benjamin, 2014, pp. 653–8)

Steam locomotives were mainly imported from England. Some were manufactured in India as well. The Byculla workshop of GIPR had manufactured a locomotive as early as 1865. The Ajmer workshop of BBCR produced as many as 400 locomotives between 1896 and 1941, while the Jamalpur workshop of EIR manufactured 217 locomotives between 1885 and 1923. However, as N. Benjamin observes in his paper cited above: '*But the progress was tardy because of the pressure of repair and maintenance work, problems in training the staff, cheaper imported locomotives and Government antipathy.*'

After 1923, when the government was considering granting protection to Indian industries, the Tata Locomotive Engineering Company requested for protection and permission to manufacture locomotives in India. This was not accepted by the Indian Tariff Board. (Bagchi, 1972). The manufacture of locomotives in India in a big way did not take off till after 1947. The issue of improvement in the design of locomotives got addressed gradually as the payload of wagons and total weight of a train increased.

The Railway Board took the initiative of trying to standardise the designs of locomotives and wagons and the report of the Railway Board for the year 1929–30 mentioned:

> At the close of the year about 150 of the new Indian Railway Standard Locomotives were in service on Class I broad and metre gauge Railways. Reports received on the working of these engines are very satisfactory and the anticipated reduction as compared with the original British Engineering Standards Association standard engines in maintenance costs and fuel consumption is becoming apparent. (Railway Board, 1930, p. 54).

Similar initiatives were also taken for the standardisation of designs of wagons and passenger coaches and also stores materials.

Signalling

The situation regarding signalling and safety improved steadily. By 1906, when the History of the EIR was published, Huddleston had recorded a vastly improved situation.

> At the present time the absolute block system is in force throughout the entire length of the line; all coaching vehicles are fitted with vacuum automatic brakes; goods vehicles are

[23] Firing technique: The method of firing or feeding coal into the boiler of the steam locomotive, which was usually done manually with the help of shovels.

> being so fitted and their carrying capacity has been materially increased; the majority of stations are either interlocked or are being interlocked; the signalling has been greatly improved and the train service has been very much accelerated. The mail train, with a load equal to eighteen heavy coaches, now runs from Howrah to Delhi in 28 hours, and lighter trains have been run over the same distance in very little more than 24 hours. Such speeds would have been impossible even five years ago, for it took a long time to carry out the many improvements required, to enable the staff in India to work up to such results. (Huddleston, 1906, pp. 177–8).

There had undoubtedly been appreciable progress. However, the account of Huddleston was perhaps referring to a particular route and not to whole EIR system. According to the Report to the Administration for 1906, on EIR out of 414 stations, only 217 were interlocked and block instruments were provided in 255 stations (Railway Board, 1907, Appendix 26).

In 1906, new rules were framed for design and inspection of signalling and interlocking equipment. These rules were to be followed by the manufacturers and inspectors checking the instruments would also use these rules as guide. As a result of the introduction of new signalling systems, the General Rules for operation of trains had to be modified. A Committee was appointed for this purpose and the new rules were introduced from 1 July 1907.

By 1918, 43 per cent of the stations on the entire railway system had been provided with interlocking devices. The progress continued steadily thereafter, and the level of mobility increased progressively. The Report for 1928–29 mentions that strenuous efforts to standardise signalling equipment was in progress. It recorded:

> The Signal and Interlocking Standards Committee met twice during the year under review. They held their third session from the 14th to 25th May 1928 at Simla, and their fourth session in November 1928 at the Great Indian Peninsula Railway Offices, Bombay. The more important subjects considered were (1) the examining of different types of token Instruments, (2) standard drawings of signal fittings, (3) a catechism and rules for the design and inspection of signalling and interlocking, for inclusion in the "Rules for the Opening of a railway, etc.," and (4) the preparation of a manual of instructions for the maintenance and installation of signalling and interlocking and standard forms for use in connection therewith. The standard drawings of signal fittings and the manual of instruction, etc., prepared by the committee have been approved by the Railway Board and are being printed for distribution to railways. (Railway Board, 1929, p. 9).

Investment in the Railways and Industry: Impact on Railways

As mentioned earlier, the period after 1900 up to 1913 was good for trade. The railway companies also started reporting surpluses. After Robertson's report in

1903 and the formation of the Railway Board in 1905, the Government decided to examine the feasibility of increasing expenditure on the railways. The expenditure for purchase of railway wagons increased and this provided an impetus to firms such as Burn & Co. and Jessop & Co. to set up railway wagon building divisions.

The government had appointed the Mackay Committee to examine the financing and administration of the railways in India. The Mackay Committee (1908) recommended an annual expenditure of 12.5 million pounds (Rs. 187.5 million) annually for the foreseeable future for railway. The actual expenditure was much less. However, the infusion of fresh capital led to the creation of new assets and increase in transportation capacity.

Table 2.8: Capital Expenditure on Railways in India

The capital programmes on Indian railways (Rs. Million)			
Year	**Investment in Rs. Million**	**Year**	**Investment in Rs. Million**
1908–09	150	1915–16	120
1909–10	150	1916–17	45
1910–11	163	1917–18	54
1911–12	142.5	1918–19	63
1912–13	135	1919–20	265.5
1913–14	180	1920–21	219.8
1914–15	180	1921–22	178.2

(Bagchi, 1972, p. 39)

Bagchi observes that from the published data it is difficult to make out exactly how much the Indian firms benefited from the capital investment as the level of imports fluctuated considerably. The Indian firms, however, did benefit from the orders of construction, including those for bridge and girder work. Only a fraction of the money spent on the railways benefitted Indians as the firms in Calcutta, Bombay, Cawnpore, Madras and Muzaffarpur were almost entire controlled by the British. In addition, very little part of the investment was spent in India, with the best part being spent on imported equipment.

There were only two major industries in India, jute and cotton. The jute industry was based in Bengal and cotton in Bombay and Ahmedabad. The cotton industry benefitted from the development of the railway network. Import of cotton piece goods and cotton twist and yarn increased substantially both in the western and eastern ports between 1901 and 1914. The increase in local demand led to expansion of capacity of some of the mills. In the case of the jute industry, there was great expansion during the period 1901–14. The paper industry was adversely affected as it did not adopt the latest technological changes.

The Indian economy remained open for trade, which thrived. Imports were mainly from Britain and there were low import duties on a few commodities. Exports were of raw materials and foodgrains to many countries, which earned precious foreign exchange for Britain. During the period 1900–13, India's exports and imports increased by more than 100 per cent. There was also substantial inflow of foreign capital at this time. This was mainly on public account, for investment in the railway and other social capital. [Bagchi Chapter 3, page 73]

The period before WW-1 saw two pioneering industries being established in India. Bengal Iron and Steel had started manufacturing pig iron at the end of the nineteenth century. However, they were unable to manufacture steel. The Tata Iron and Steel Company (TISCO) started manufacturing steel from 1912. They received help from the government in the form of land grants and orders for supply of steel. The manufacture of steel created demand for movement by rail of iron ore, limestone and coking coal[24].

Thus, the years between 1900 and 1913 were very hopeful from India's industrial development perspective. Though the government was not keen to commit itself to any large-scale enterprise, there was some investment in industry by British residents in India. All this came to an end with the WW-1, and the hiatus continued up to 1920. Investment in railways also dried up. The focus was only of keeping the railways going. Jute and cotton industries made windfall gains due to increase in prices.

Trends in Production and Policies for Movement of Coal up to 1918

Despite the cooling off in the investment climate due to the War, the demand and movement of coal continued to increase. The total loading of all commodities in the railways in India in 1915–16 was 64.14 million tons of which coal was 19 million tons or about 30 per cent. The importance of coal in the overall freight basket of the railways had been increasing steadily with both Raniganj and Jharia fields increasing their outputs. The movement via the Grand Chord line opened in 1907 provided the additional impetus. The profile of the freight loading from 1905 to 1915–16 was as follows:

---

[24] Coking coal, also known as metallurgical coal, is a grade of coal suitable for production of good quality coke, which is required for manufacture of steel.

Table 2.9: Coal Movement by Rail in India

Year	Total freight in Million tons	Coal in million tons	Percentage of Coal to Total
1905	40.78	10.20	25.55
1910	50.23	13.91	27.69
1913–14	62.54	17.12	27.48
1915–16	64.14	19.04	29.72

Source: Kelway-Bamber, 1919.

The share of revenue from coal had also increased steadily and stood at 17.56 per cent of the total in 1915–16. The share in revenue was much lower than the share in traffic would warrant. This was because coal was carried at a low rate of tariff.

Equity in Supply of Wagons for Coal

Despite the increase in the level of coal production and transportation, the supply of railway wagons for loading coal continued to be a sore issue, especially with smaller coal mine owners, who alleged that the railways favoured the large mine owners as full trains could be loaded from their sidings. The demand of coal from railways and the need for bunkering coal for ships were the primary demands and some insinuations of favouritism by the railways in wagon allotment in favour of these two consumer groups can also be found in the literature. A.B. Ghosh mentions,

> It may not be a mere coincidence that since 1907 East Indian and Bengal Nagpur Railways began placing rake-load of wagons on the sidings of large collieries and distributing the balance of the available wagons among all collieries on the basis of their contribution to the total output, larger collieries sharing also in this proportionate distribution. Continuous representation by the Indian colliery owners brought about the abolition of the unjust rake system between March 1916 and March 1917 after almost a decade. (Ghosh, 1977, p. 227)

The distribution of coal produced was either through direct sale to the customers or through agents who took del credere risk on behalf of their principals. For small collieries, who did not sell directly to the customers, the agents or middlemen acted as important intermediaries to ensure sale of coal and its despatch to the customer. In situations of coal shortage, either due to excess demand or failure of production, the supply to customers through the agents got adversely affected.

Competition between the railway companies also resulted in the use of 'Block Rates', which hurt the interests of the consumers. These 'Block Rates' were levied by adding terminal charges for selected terminals or by charging inflated rates for through goods traffic which originated on another railway and left that railway after covering a small distance. The motive was clearly to make the movement of a particular commodity via a specific route uneconomical. In this manner, the railway companies continued to prioritise their own interests over those of the consumers, introducing another impediment to smooth transportation.

Impact of the First World War

The demand for coal by the railways increased suddenly during the First World War. Most of the high-grade coal was requisitioned by the Government at fixed prices and this coal got priority in railway transportation. Consequently, there was a shortage of coal for non-government users and the prices of this coal soared. The mine owners attempted to increase output by whatever means possible and frequently the private users ended up receiving inferior grade coal. By 1918, the output of coal increased to 21 million tons, with Jharia's share being 11 million tons and Raniganj contributing 6.5 million tons. In 1919, the output of coal increased further to 22.6 million tons.

As we have observed, the railway companies usually preferred to keep the wagons within their own domain, unless a return cargo from another railway was readily available to assure that the wagons would return. During the War, these systems were discarded, and the wagons were loaded whenever available, without any regard to the ownership of the wagon. In the absence of a protocol for wagon sharing, such random movements created a problem as areas of surplus wagon availability and other areas of shortages developed. It was realised that a system of pooling wagons between the railway companies would have to be developed at the earliest opportunity. This work would be done by the Indian Railway Conference Association (IRCA), which had been set up in 1902 as a central organisation to frame rules for keeping track of the wagons moving between two or more railway systems. However, it would not be till 1925, when the pooling system was finally put in place.

The War led to increase in prices of commodities and in wages. It was realised that the existing tariff structure needed to be reviewed. In 1916, the Railway Board permitted a general enhancement of rates. Movement of coal to Bombay by the rail-cum-sea route via the Calcutta Port became difficult as ships were needed for the war effort. The pressure on the railway system increased tremendously due to the addition of this long distance (referred to as 'lead' in railway parlance) traffic. A number of restrictions on traffic movement were introduced. Tariff for coal moved to Bombay was increased in September 1916.

To raise resources for the War, the Government imposed a surcharge of 1 pie per maund on coal and 2 pies per maund on other commodities from April 1917. The proceeds of this surcharge went to the Government and not to the railway companies.

Distribution of Coal during War: Administrative Measures

A system of special supplies had evolved to service essential requirements of important industries. A special mechanism was created to control and regulate coal production and transportation. Some of the powers exercised by the Government were: (a) power to requisition the produce of a coal mine (b) control the opening or re-opening of a coal mine (c) controlling the production and despatch of coal. A Coal Supplies Committee was appointed in December 1916 to control the distribution of wagons and end the system of unequal treatment of miners. The Mining Engineer of Railway Board was the nominated officer for requisitioning coal for the Government. He was later inducted into the Coal Committee, which had also been formed in 1916. The office of the Coal Controller was set up in 1917 and these functions were transferred to that office. The Coal Controller reverted to the system of special supplies when the situation warranted. During this period there were protests regarding allocation of coal which continued unabated. Finally, a Coal Transportation Officer was appointed in 1919. He announced that the system of special supplies would be discontinued from January 1920. However, some special supplies continued under this regime too, through the creation of separate categories. The protests by the coal industry continued and finally in 1922, it was announced that the system of special indents and supplies would be stopped. The quota for each colliery would be determined on the basis of its production. The wagon requirements of the collieries owned by the railways would be provided additionally by the railways. Provisions were also made for supplies of full and half rakes to meet emergency requirements.

Due to a surge in government traffic, both civil and military, certain administrative changes had to be introduced in the railways during the War period. In 1916, a war branch was formed in the Railway Board. However, later that same year it was merged with the Indian Munitions Branch and the Adjutant General's office. A post of a Controller of Traffic was created in 1917 to make the best use of the transportation capacity available. Later, in 1918, the post of a Special Member of the Railway Board was created to oversee and ensure optimum utilisation of available resources. A system of issue of 'Priority Certificates' was instituted to ensure that coal went to the targeted customer. These systems were withdrawn slowly after the end of the War in 1918.

Development of Industries in India after 1918

Due to the expenditure of the war, there was a general increase in import duties and tariff. The expenditure of the government continued to be more than the revenue earned and public debt increased between 1918–19 and 1923–24. The government appointed a Retrenchment Commission in 1922, which recommended drastic cut back in expenditure across the board including that on rehabilitation of railways, which had gone through a very rough patch during the war.

The situation improved from 1923 to 1924, the government was able to generate reasonable surpluses on current account. However, it remained cautious about borrowing.

The government adopted a policy of 'discriminating protection' from 1923. This was not a general policy for industrialisation of India. At that time the terms of trade were turning against the agricultural sector of India as exports of USA and Canada were increasing faster than the exports of India. The decision of the government was to grant protection to those industries which had (a) natural advantages (b) might not develop at all or might develop slowly without protection (c) would eventually be able to face the world competition without tariff protection. The policy resulted in protection to some industries like steel, some branches of mechanical engineering, paper and matches. The steel industry prospered under protection. TISCO achieved an increase in production and was also able to reduce its costs of production substantially, making Indian steel attractive. However, the total purchase of rails dropped substantially between 1922–23 and 1937–38. This was due to lower expenditure by the railways and the refusal of some railway companies to buy rails manufactured in India. The positive feature was that of the steel rails actually purchased by class-1 railway companies, the percentage of steel rails manufactured in India to the total purchase of steel rails increased from 61.17 per cent of the total in the period 1922–23 to 1924–25 to 99.19 per cent in the period 1937–38 to 1939–40. (Bagchi, 1972, pp. 315–16).

Use of Coal by Railways and Other Industries

The railways continued to be by far the largest consumers of coal and the level of consumption naturally increased steadily with the expanding network. Coal consumed by the railways in the year 1890 was 858,407 tons, which increased to 7,440,409 tons by 1928–29, a growth of 8.6 times. By 1940, the railways were consuming 8,630,000 tons of coal which was 31.6 per cent of the production of India. Other industries which emerged as large consumers of coal were iron and steel and brass foundries.

The Indian Coal Statistics reports for 1928 and 1940 provide a glimpse into the development of nascent industries in India. The coal consumption of iron and steel and brass foundries had doubled from 4,294,000 tons in 1928 to 8,890,000 tons in 1940. Consumption by collieries and wastage had also been halved. The other three principal consumers, according to the report of 1928 were 'bunker coal' for ships, jute and the cotton industry. The total consumption by all industries was 22,083,000 tons.

Major Changes in Policy: 1919–1925

The year 1919 was very significant in the history of British India for two reasons. On the 13th of April 1919, a gathering of peaceful protestors at Jallianwala Bagh, an enclosed park in the Punjab, was fired upon ruthlessly by the police under instructions from a British army officer and hundreds of people were killed and injured. This incident led to a series of strident protests in the country and a mounting sentiment against British domination.

The second significant development was the promulgation of the Government of India Act of 1919, which introduced the concept of a bicameral legislature with three quarters of the members being elected through a popular vote. The Legislature exercised control on the expenditure, legislation and also administration. Though the Governor General and through him the Secretary of State had a veto power to overrule the Legislature, the overall tenor of the administration changed in favour of greater autonomy for the legislature and this proved to be a boon for the Railways as the Legislature was in favour of state control of the Railways and centralised authority of decision making. The move towards centralisation of policy making in the railway was gathering momentum.

In November 1920 the Secretary of State appointed the Indian Railway Committee, with William Acworth as its Chairman.

Sanyal records:

> The terms of reference of the Committee included the request to consider, more especially as regards railways owned by the state, the relative advantages, financial and administrative, in the special circumstances of India. of the following methods of management:
>
> (a) direct state management; (b) management through a company domiciled in England with a Board sitting in London; (c) management through a company domiciled in India and with a Board sitting in India; and (d) management through a combination of (b) and (c). The Committee was further invited 'to advise as to the policy to be adopted as and when the existing contracts with the several railway companies can be determined.' (Sanyal, 1930, p. 223)

After examining the issues in detail, the Committee opined that the era of absentee control of railway companies from England should end. At the end of the period of contract of a guaranteed company, the company should be taken over by the State. In this manner the railway companies should come under state control. This was indeed the public opinion in India too. The Committee made detailed recommendations about administrative and financial reforms, and it was stated that these reforms should be executed before the takeover of the companies by the State. These recommendations were endorsed by the Indian Legislative Assembly.

The Acworth Committee found that the Government had not invested sufficiently in the railways. The entire system was in a state of disrepair and the existing method of providing funds for the railways from the general exchequer was unlikely to work as the investments for the railways were insufficient and the amount to be invested was decided after meeting the other constraints of the budget. *The Acworth Committee, therefore, recommended that the budget of the railways should be separated from the general budget.* This would enable the railways to have more control over its planning and investment strategy.

The Government of India appointed a Railway Finance Committee to tender advice regarding the separation of railway finances and the capital expenditure in the near future. In 1922–23, the Inchcape Committee on retrenchment of expenditure recommended the appointment of a Financial Adviser in the Railway Board. The Acworth Committee's recommendations regarding the provision for maintenance repairs and abolition of programme revenue expenditure were endorsed.

In his speech, during debate on separation of Railway Finance in the Legislative Assembly, on 20th September 1924, Sir Charles Innes mentioned:

> In September 1924, the final scheme for separation of railway finance in India was placed before the Legislative Assembly. The evils of the existing system were once more explained, and it was proposed:
>
> (i) to abolish the system of programme revenue voted for a year;
>
> (ii) to establish a scientific Depreciation Fund;
>
> (iii) to build up a Railway Reserve Fund with a view to equalise dividend to the state, to provide for arrears of maintenance, and to write down and write off capital;
>
> (iv) to separate railway finance so as to suit the needs of a commercial undertaking, while ensuring a fixed contribution to government and proper control by the legislature; and
>
> (v) to establish a principle in the financial arrangements, so that the government might not indulge in a concealed way, in raising a tax on transportation by claiming further than their legitimate and stable return from railway investments. (Quoted by Sanyal, 1930, p. 244)

The resolution for separation of railway finance was passed on 20th September 1924. The resolution covered the following areas:

1. The separation of railway finances from the general exchequer.
2. A convention for railways to contribute to general finances.
3. Creation of a Railway Reserve Fund
4. Formation of a Standing Finance Committee and a Central Railway Advisory Council. The members of the Advisory Council would be drawn from the members of the Legislature.
5. Procedure for presentation of the Railway Budget and periodic revisions of the scheme.
6. The House had the authority to terminate the arrangement if it felt that the Government was deviating from its bargain.

The Legislature also recommended the representation of Indians in the railways must be increased at all levels, including the Railway Board and that purchase of stores should slowly shift to Indian sources.

1925: A Year of Landmark Developments

The year 1925 witnessed some landmark events. First, the Administrative Report on the Railways for the year 1924–25 noted that the Railway Budget was introduced for the first time on the 20th February 1925 by the Railway Member in the Legislative Assembly and by the Chief Commissioner of railways in the Council of States. The report also noted with satisfaction that the new procedure generated a positive outlook in the railways. Secondly, the East Indian Railways was taken over by the State on 1 January 1925. During the course of the year the Great Indian Peninsula Railway was also taken over by the State and the Oudh and Rohilkhand Railway was merged with the East Indian Railway.

The third important event was the inauguration on 3 February 1925 of the first line with electric traction in India. This was the New Harbour Branch of the GIP Railway. With this began the era of slow replacement of coal with other modes of traction.

The fourth development was that the system of 'wagon pooling' was announced in 1925. This was very important to ensure the free flow of wagons across railway systems and eliminate wastage of time at transhipment points.[25]

As already noted, the administrative structure of the Railway Board had also undergone a change and was now headed by a Chief Commissioner who was in

[25] In the era of private railways companies, the wagons generally remained within the system. There was no system of pooling the wagons to ensure free flow of traffic. The IRCA introduced a system of pooling with 'Creditor' railways being those which required less wagons than they owned and could send wagons to 'debtor' railways for work. There was financial arrangement to compensate the creditor railways.

charge of technical decisions after receiving advice from his colleagues and the Chief Commissioner was answerable to the Government. Sanyal notes:

> The re-organisation thus brought about led to the present constitution of the central controlling authority in India. The Railway Board thereafter consisted up to 1928–29 of the Chief Commissioner as President, the Financial Commissioner, and two members. the Chief Commissioner being Secretary to the Government of India in the Railway Department. (Sanyal, 1930, p. 250)

Thus, Railway Board became more or less an independent administration under the Government. It remained answerable to the Government, though, on major policy issues and financial matters. The railways started preparing its own plans of works of expenditure within the limitations of its budget constraints. These works were approved by the Government and Legislature before being implemented.

After the series of measures to improve railway working, the railway system was earning a profit and making the following payments to general revenues:

One per cent of the capital at charge plus one fifth of the profit of the penultimate year plus one third of the excess over Rupees three crores remaining with the railways after making this payment. In 1924–25, the railways paid Rs. 6.77 lakhs to general revenues. (Sanyal, 377)

With more freedom for planning and investment, the railway companies expanded infrastructure. On the EIR and BNR, lines important for evacuation of coal were doubled. On EIR, the line between Kusunda and Dhanbad and sections of the Grand Chord line were doubled. On the BNR, the line between Purulia to Kandra was also doubled. The Talcher and Karanpura coalfields areas also witnessed strengthening of railway infrastructure. The line from Kazipet to Ramagundam via Ballarshah was under construction.

The position of the railway network in India in 1939 for facilitating coal evacuation is placed at Appendix 2. Only the major coal movement routes have been shown. The year of completion of some important sections have been mentioned on the map.

Coal Industry: Structure, Production, Prices and Transportation (1919 to 1945)

Structure

The coal industry had three segments. There were captive collieries such as those owned by the railways and steel plants, collieries owned and financed by Managing Agents and privately owned collieries. The captive mines and those run by the Managing Agents were generally well managed and the company had systems of recruitment and training. The criticism against the Managing agents was that they were too keen to earn profits and management decisions were often biased. The privately owned mines were usually small, had poor management systems and colliery labour was recruited mainly from the local population. Their presence at work was erratic and their level of professionalism was poor. These mines were prone to closing operations when the demand was low and often took unnecessary risks to maintain or increase production.

The Government took little or no action to streamline the processes in the coal industry, to develop sound structures and sound mining methods. One of the main problems was that whenever demand increased a number of small mines would be opened. The data relating to the number of mines operating over the period 1920 to 1945, shows the widest variation in the number of mines producing 5,000 ton per year, which is only about 16 tons per day on the basis of 300 working days in a year! The Mahindra Committee observed:

> The widest fluctuation is generally in the number of collieries producing up to 5,000 tons per annum, though there are minor variation in regard to larger mines also; but apart from one tendency to which we shall refer later, these variations are not of very great consequence. The opening of small collieries during periods of prosperity and their closure during bad times both have a most deleterious effect on the proper exploitation of the country's resources. These collieries are generally ill-equipped, and their object is to secure the easiest coal. The result, not infrequently, is that the coal-bearing areas become pock-marked with small shallow workings which may lead to unsound development in the neighbourhood and may, as has happened in the Jharia field, be the cause of disastrous fires. (Mahindra Committee Report Vol-1, 1947, p. 26).

There was also an increase in the number of mines producing more than 50,000 tons per year. This was perhaps due to an effort on the part of mine owners to reduce costs by exploiting economies of scale. The period saw the consolidation of large companies. The number of joint stock companies reduced from 256 in 1920–21 to 243 in 1925–26 but the paid-up capital went up from Rupees 9.37 crores to 12.61 crores. Between 1924 and 1926, and between 1927 and 1930, the production actually increased slightly as demand rose due to the low price of coal.

Mechanisation of Coal Mines

The level of electrification of mines and mechanisation remained low throughout the first half of the twentieth century. In 1925, only 13 per cent of the mines were electrified and this number had gone up to only 16 per cent by 1945. Lack of electrical power was a constraint in using machines. Further, the use of machines required capital investment and training of manpower, which was not a priority area. Machines were first introduced after 1910 and up to 1945 only 9 per cent of the total output was cut by machines. Mechanisation of mining would also require means of mechanised retrieval and despatch by rail or road. To achieve this, a fairly high level of planning and coordination with transport operators would be required, including development of railway sidings at the collieries to despatch the coal. Overt initiatives in this direction were not present except for the large mines. Ghosh also points out that the areas which had already been mined would not be suitable for mechanised mining due to presence of pillars in the mines. All commentators on that period bemoan the poor productivity of coal mines due to lack of mechanisation.

Prices and Production of Coal

During the First World War, the production had increased due to heightened demand. In 1920, the production dropped by 3 million tons as compared to 1919. The drop in production was due to the closure of small uneconomic mines which had opened during the demand surge in War period. Secondly, the export of Indian coal declined, and the balance of trade turned against India in the period 1921 and 1922. The prices of coal from the Bengal and Bihar fields rose for a short while from 1920 before being corrected in 1926 due to an increase in production. There was also an overall reduction in prices following the boom of the War period. The fall in prices continued for almost a decade.

Impact of the Great Depression on Coal Industry

The Great Depression of the 1930s hit the coal industry in two ways. First, the demand was low and the overall production in 1931 dropped by 2 million tons. The production in 1933 was below the level of 1918. Many collieries closed down and prices reduced. The second issue was that some colliery managers tried to combat the falling prices by increasing output through 'slaughter mining', throwing good mining practices to the winds and trying to exploit the best quality coal seams to increase overall sales. This had the effect of lowering prices even further. Despite the falling prices, the percentage of high-grade coal mined both in Raniganj and Jharia continued to increase between 1923 and 1933. This was perhaps a desperate effort to keep the prices from falling further by offering good quality at a low price. The production and marketing strategy of the coal miners during this period reflects the complete lack of cohesion within the trade.

Public expenditure reduced sharply during the period of the Depression. There was little scope for developmental efforts. Bagchi records:

> The curious thing is that people at the top were aware of the needs of India for the purpose of long term economic development. .... The explanation of this hiatus between intellectual understanding and practice would take us outside the scope of this study, but it appears that paralysis of will as far as economic decision making was concerned set in among top British officials long before the transfer of power to the Indians had taken place. (Bagchi, 1972, p. 47)

From 1937, the production level of coal revived and continued up to 1942, supported by increasing demand and a revival of the export trade due to a rebate offered by the railways and a reduction in port terminal charges in 1936. Prices of coal also increased and there was some revival in the industry. Once again, however, there was an increase in the number of small mines to satisfy the increased demand. This was not a healthy development. When the demand for coal increased sharply during the Second World War, the mining industry faced two problems. First, the replacement of plant and equipment had been sadly neglected during the period of Depression and it was impossible to rachet up production suddenly with old equipment which needed repair. Secondly, the War created a demand for employment in several areas and many mines faced a shortage of labour. As the level of mechanisation in mining processes was very low, the shortage of labour became a serious handicap.

Transportation and Distribution of Coal (1919–1945)

Even after the War, the issue of inadequate supply of wagons for several industries and the small mines continued to fester. The Railway Finance Committee of 1922 had been critical of the performance of the railways and had flagged the inadequate availability of railway wagons for coal movement.

The overall wagon availability position had improved by the middle of 1924. Following the report of the Indian Coal Committee of 1925, the post of Coal Transportation Officer was abolished, and the control of wagon distribution reverted to the railways. There are several opinions about the degree to which the railways were able to meet the demands for coal movement.

The Indian Coal Committee of 1925 made some important recommendations regarding the supply of wagons for coal loading. Some salient points were:

a) Wagon supply should be improved in the first half of the year.
b) Supply of wagons should be at regular hours and the allotment of wagons should be based on the availability. The '10-hour system'[26] of wagon supply should be implemented on EIR and BNR (this was a requirement as the process of loading coal was manual and was done during daylight hours only).
c) Number of weighbridges for weighment of coal should be increased.
d) The plans for development of new railway sidings should be cleared expeditiously.

[26] Ten hours system: For manual loading of coal, ten daylight hours need to be provided. This implies that all wagon supplies to colliery sidings must be done before early morning and the loaded wagons withdrawn after ten hours have elapsed.

The Railway Board was not in favour of adoption of the 10-hour or the 12-hour system as it implied that wagons for loading would be supplied at specific times during the day. As the railway operated on a 24 hour basis, artificial impediments would affect mobility adversely. The other issues were addressed satisfactorily.

The wagons supply position was satisfactory between 1925 and 1929. Thereafter, some issues in allotment of wagons arose on the EIR and after an enquiry, a modified system was introduced in which the allotment of wagons was done by the Chief Mining Engineer and Transport Advisory Officer of the Railway Board. A priority list for allotment of wagons was prepared. The order of priority was:

A) Admiralty and shipment coal
B) Loco coal
C) Coal on Government and military account
D) Requirements of public utilities
E) Steel and Iron Works
F) Requirements of coke ovens

The first three categories were monitored by the Chief Mining Engineer and the rest by the Transport Advisory Officer.

There was another committee named the Coal Wagon Supply committee which had the two officers from the Railway Board, one representative each from the EIR and BNR and two representatives each of the principal mining associations. This committee considered applications from consumers to be included in the priority list and the demands of the collieries for allocation of supply quotas.

The tariff for coal movement had been reduced and rationalised considerably over the years. Even then, some issues remained. After the end of the First World War, while the coal production and transportation were improving, the mining fraternity had continued to represent against the inequities of freight tariff for coal. Their grievances had merit as some issues such as charging of through rates for long distance traffic and differential freight rates continued to fester.

The issue of high freight rates for transportation of coal from Bengal and Bihar to western parts of India continued to remain an issue flagged repeatedly. Through rates for movement of coal from Bengal and Bihar coalfields to north India or other distant destinations were not being quoted. Ghosh records:

> In an address given by the IMF* to the Viceroy at Calcutta in December 1922 it was stated that India producing the cheapest coal at the pit's mouth was beaten in her own market by foreign coal, and that "freight on one ton of coal from Natal to Bombay, or

with a little favourable exchange, even from Cardiff to Bombay was lower than freight on one ton of coal from Jharia to Bombay." They had demanded a countervailing duty on South African coal, but the Tariff Board of 1926 did not favour it despite the support given by the Indian Legislature by an overwhelming majority in February 1924.

*IMF stands for Indian Mining Federation (Ghosh, 1977, p. 238)

In January 1932, a 15 per cent surcharge was levied on coal, thereby leading to yet another increase in costs. The coal booked to Kidderpore Docks, Shalimar and Howrah were, however, excluded from the surcharge. Through this action, coastal freight and exports were once again promoted at the cost of domestic movement. After strenuous representations, the tariff was reduced by 2.5 per cent in 1935. However, it again went up again in 1941 for the period March to November. The administration was quite openly in favour of short distance coal movement by rail and movement to distant locations through a combination of rail and sea.

Another practice, that of differential freight rates for different railways, also continued. In 1932, the tariff of EIR and BNR for coal from Bengal and Bihar and GIPR for coal originating from Pench and Chanda Valley areas were as follows:

Table 2.10: Tariff for Coal Transportation Charged by Different Railway Companies

	Coal from Bengal and Bihar Charged by EIR and BNR	**Coal from Pench and Chanda Charged by GIPR**
Distances		
0 to 200 miles	0.15 pie per maund per mile	0.1 pie per maund per mile
Next 200 miles	0.6 pies per maund per mile	
201-500 miles		0.06 pie per maund per mile
All distances beyond	0.5 pie per maund per mile	
Beyond 500 miles		0.045 pie per maund per mile

(Ghosh, 1977, pp. 238–9)

The differential rates made the movement of coal from Raniganj and Jharia to Bombay uncompetitive vis-à-vis the Wardha and Pench Valley coal. The coastal movement also continued. As late as 1928, when the railway network was well developed, the Calcutta Port exported 282,441 tons of coal to Bombay, and 146,940 tons were imported (Indian Coal Statistics, 1928, Table 12 pp. 30) This movement may not have been for railway use only, though. To economise on costs, railways such as the GIPR started blending coal from Bengal with coal from

Central India. Following the representation, the freight for GIPR was enhanced to some extent. Finally in 1937, the two tariffs were brought at par.

The government continued to prefer rail-cum-sea movement to the west and south over all-rail movement as the railways would not be able to undertake long distance coal movement on a sustained basis. The movement of coal to the Calcutta Port had to take place for providing bunker coal for the ships. This was a primary requirement. The next charge was to provide coal for export and the third requirement was movement of coal by the coastal route to Madras, Bombay and Karachi. Coal movement for export was overtly supported by providing special rebates in freight and port handling charges. The Coal Committee of 1925 had proposed the setting up of a Coal Grading Board to certify the quality of coal for export. This had had a salutary effect and restored the confidence of the international market in Indian coal. The moot point was whether India was in a position to export good quality coal, when the distribution system within the country was far from perfect and there were frequent reports of coal shortages.

The coastal movements to Bombay and other cities from Calcutta port continued even after the equalisation of freight rates for Bengal Bihar and coal from the Central Provinces in 1937. Shipping freights was the determining factor. Available data shows that right from 1917 to 1939, even after considerable reduction in railway tariff, the rail-cum-sea route was still cheaper than the all-rail route for both Bombay and Karachi. It was only when the shipping rates increased due to exogenous factors, that the rail route became cheaper. This happened between 1918 and 1920 and after 1939, with the outbreak of the Second World War. The immediate impact of rising shipping rates is shown in the following table from the Mahindra Committee Report:

Table 2.11: Railway and Sea Freights to Different Destinations

	1939 Up to August						1942					
	Rs.	A.	P	Rs.	A.	P	Rs.	A.	P	Rs.	A.	P
	Railway Freight			Sea Freight			Railway Freight			Sea Freight		
Madras	12	7	0	7	14	0	13	12	0	22	3	9
Bombay	12	6	0	9	13	0	14	14	0	32	3	9
Karachi	15	3	6	9	14	0	17	1	0	37	3	9

Notes—1. Railway freights shown are averages of Raniganj and Jharia rates. The Rail-cum-sea rates include net average railway freights to Calcutta in 1939 and 1942 respectively and net Calcutta Port dues. Present sea freights are substantially the same as in 1942.
(Mahindra Committee Report Vol-1, 1947, p. 64)

The figures reveal that the economics of movement remained in favour of the coastal movement even after the introduction of pooling of railway wagons from 1925. The Mahindra Committee commented that it was preferable for coal to move by sea to Bombay and Karachi. When shipping rates increased and coastal movement became uneconomic, the Committee commented:

> We feel therefore that the best solution we can put forward is that all coal for bunkers and coal for the railways in Madras, Bombay and Karachi, so long as transport is short, should continue to be carried by sea and that the railways should endeavour to carry all coal for shore industries. We believe that this is substantially the practice now in respect of Bombay and Karachi, and that additional effort by the railways will really only be necessary in the case of traffic via Waltair; we hope, therefore, that the proposal will prove practicable and that the office of the Coal Commissioner will be able to evolve a formula for the individual ports which will ensure that rail borne coal is not re-shipped as bunkers. We regret that our proposal does not do anything to help the railways or steamship companies at these ports, but if the railways' carrying capacity had been greater or sea freights lower the situation would not have arisen. In making our suggestion that coal for shore industries should not be carried coastwise by sea, we have taken note of the fact that latterly the bulk of the coastwise shipments have been for the railways and bunkers. [Mahindra Committee Report Vol-1, 1947, pp. 64–5]

This was a clear admission of the fact that even in the late 1930s and early 1940s, the railway system was not sufficiently developed to compete with rail-cum-sea movement from Calcutta to Bombay and Karachi unless sea freight increased. The Railway Board had also stated its inability to lower tariff for coal further, as it was already being carried at a rate lower than that of most other commodities. With the rebate in freight for movement to ports and reduction of port handling charges, the rail-cum-sea remained cheaper till shipping freights increased suddenly due to external circumstances.

There was a serious shortage of coal in 1942 and 1943, exacerbated by the shortage of railway wagons due to war time controls imposed by the Government. As had happened during the First World War, the industries which were not in the priority list for allocation of wagons, did not receive their share and the prices of coal purchased by them increased sharply. The War led to a sharp increase in demand for rail transportation. By this time coal constituted 40 per cent of the freight movement of the railways and was the single most important commodity in demand. The movement of coal by the coastal route got impeded as the availability of ships reduced. This imposed an additional burden on the railway system. It became necessary to revert to the system of priorities. A decision was taken to combine the role of the Controller of Coal Distribution and the Transport Advisory Officer in the hands of a single officer, who would regulate supplies and also control their movements. This appointment was effective since March 1942.

The supply of wagons to the coalfields in Bengal and Bihar were affected the most in 1942 and 1943 as priority was accorded to other commodities necessary for the war effort, and also because the coastal movement, which was a large share of the total movement, was replaced by the all-rail movement. However, the supply of wagons to the other coalfields was not very badly affected. It therefore became necessary to take a closer look at the demand and supply position In the Bengal-Bihar area. Expanding on the action taken in this area, the Mahindra Committee recorded:

> The increasing difficulties made a regular and periodic survey of the all-India coal position necessary and also emphasised the need for a more closely-knit organisation for the collection of information about supply and' distribution. It was, therefore, decided to set up a Committee at Calcutta consisting of the Chief Inspector of Mines, the Chief Mining Engineer, and the Controller of Coal Distribution. This Committee was to consider monthly— (a) raisings, despatches, and stock figures generally but with emphasis on railways and other important consumers, (b) new industrial or war demands, and (c) the wagon supply position.
>
> A Committee was also set up in Delhi, consisting of the Chief Commissioner of Railways and Secretaries of the Labour and War Transport Departments, to consider the reports of the Calcutta Committee. (Mahindra Committee Report Vol-1, 1947, pp. 223–4)

The demand for coal during this period was far greater than its availability and even the reduced availability was not freely transportable by the railways due to constraints of competing demands for military movement, reduction of coastal movement and other factors. A system of rationing was inescapable, and this system indeed provided a sense of order and fair play during very difficult times. For the coalfields of Bengal and Bihar a figure of 2,700 wagons per day, equivalent to 20.892 million tons per year, was assessed as probable despatch. Excluding the coalfields of Assam, Punjab and Baluchistan, the rest of the fields would contribute 4.75 million tons, making a total availability of 25.64 million tons per annum. The consumer wise allocation was prepared on this basis after converting the availability to monthly supplies. The coal produced had to be distributed equitably and in some cases the grades of coal to be supplied also had to be altered. Alteration of the grade also altered the price and therefore, the freedom of the consumer to choose the source, the grade and the quantity had to be curbed by the Government. If this harsh decision had not been taken, the price of coal would have increased rapidly, and artificial areas of shortages would have been created. These difficult decisions were taken at the meetings of the Central Priorities Committee in New Delhi.

To step up the production of coal, the Government offered bonuses on production and some tax exemptions. Steps were initiated to recruit labour for the coalfields and mining machinery was sought to be imported on Government account. Simultaneously, the Government devised an elaborate system of control over distribution of coal. The Controller of Coal Distribution was authorised under the Defence of India Rules to control the distribution of coal and regulate the transport and supply of wagons. This required close coordination between several branches and hence, as mentioned earlier, a committee was set up with the Chief Inspector of Mines, Controller of Coal Distribution, and the Chief Mining Engineer of the Railway Board as members. The Committee would monitor the production, quality of coal available and its distribution. Further controls were in the offing. In 1944, the production, prices and distribution were sought to be controlled by the Government through an official order. This was followed by the issue of the Colliery Control Order of December 1945, which gave the Government far reaching powers to control coal production and distribution.

Some of the powers assumed by the Government through the Colliery Control Order (1945) were:

1. The Central Government may constitute a Board to be called the Coal Control Board to advise the Central Government and its officers on all matters connected with the working of this order in general l and clauses 4, 6, 8, 10 and 11 in particular.
2. (Clause 4): The Central Government may, by notification in the Gazette of India, fix the price at which coal may be sold by colliery owners; and any such notification may fix different prices— (i) for different grades of coal and coke and (ii) for different collieries.
   (1) No colliery owner, and no person acting on behalf of a colliery owner, shall sell, agree to sell, or offer to sell coal at a price different from the price fixed in that behalf under clause 4. (2) Where a colliery owner has, whether by himself or by another, entered into an agreement for the sale of coal at a price different from the price fixed in that behalf under clause 4 no coal shall be delivered in pursuance thereof unless the agreement is by mutual consent so revised as to bring the price into conformity with the priced fixed under clause 4.
3. (Clause 6.) (1) Where a colliery owner has signified to the Deputy Coal Commissioner (Distribution) in writing his willingness to sell direct to consumers and an allotment is made by the Deputy Coal Commissioner (Distribution) to a consumer with his consent for such direct sale, the coal shall be delivered to the consumer at the price fixed under clause 4, and no commission or other charges shall be paid in addition, except that where a broker is employed, a brokerage not exceeding six annas per ton may be paid by the colliery owner to the broker., (2) Where a consumer purchases

coal through a del credere agent, such agent shall not, on the sale of such coal, charge or receive from the consumer a margin over the price fixed under clause 4 which exceeds:— (a) four rupees per ton in the case of hard coke, or (b) one rupee eight annas per ton in the case of soft coke or coal; and, if, in any such transaction as aforesaid, a broker is employed or the del credere agent himself serves as a broker, a brokerage not exceeding six annas per ton may be paid by the colliery owner to the broker or, as the case may be, to the del credere agent.

4. (Clause 8): The Central Government may from time to time issue such directions as it thinks fit to any colliery owner regulating the disposal of his stocks of coal or of the expected output of coal in the colliery during any period, including directions as to the person or class or description of persons to whom coal shall or shall not be disposed of, the order of priority to be observed in such disposal, and the stacking of coal on Government account.
5. (Clause 11): The Central Government may issue such directions as it thinks fit to any colliery owner prohibiting or limiting the mining or production of any grade of coal and the colliery owner shall comply with the directions.
6. (Clause 12): No colliery or group of collieries which is or may hereafter be worked as a single mine concern shall be sub-divided and worked in separate parts except with the previous permission of the Central Government and in accordance with such directions as the Central Government may, at the time of granting the permission or subsequently, give to the owner or owners concerned. Excerpts from the (Government of India, Colliery Control Order, 1945)

Clearly, these were extraordinary powers and were required to meet the extraordinary situation at that time. As a result of the intense monitoring and control, coal production increased from an average of 279.4 lakh tons between 1941 and 1945 to 297.7 lakh tons in 1946 and 301.2 lakh tons in 1947.

Coal requirement of the economy continued to increase steadily and after the end of the Second World War, a fresh assessment of coal demand was attempted.

The Mahindra Committee Report provides a detailed assessment of the coal requirement for 1946 and '47 prepared by the Coal Commissioner. The report recorded:

> Estimate of Future Requirements: With the end of the war, it became possible early to estimate the country's immediate future requirements of coal on a peace-time basis. After a careful study of war-time consumption and existing industrial capacity, the following estimate of requirements for 1946 and 1947, to be met from coalfields other than those in Assam, Punjab, Baluchistan, Sind and Kashmir, was prepared by the office of the Coal Commissioner:

Table 2.12: Estimate of Coal Requirement in 1946 by Coal Commissioner

Name of Industry	Coal Required in Tons	Per cent of Total
Bunker and Export	2,400,000	7.4%
Railways	10,800,000	33.5%
Essential Steamer Services	480,000	1.5%
Ports	180,000	0.6%
Municipalities and Water Works	180,000	0.6%
Electric Supply	2,100,000	6.5%
Gas Company	180,000	0.6%
Steel Works (Primary producers):	3,360,000	10.4%
Potteries	240,000	0.7%
Refractories	180,000	0.6%
Copper Corporation	60,000	0.2%
Ordnance Factories	84,000	0.3%
Defence	300,000	0.9%
Cement	1,200,000	3.7%
Woolen Mills	120,000	0.4%
Cotton Mills	2,400,000	7.4%
Ginning & Pressing (Seasonal)	200,000	0.6%
Jute Mills	660,000	2.0%
Engineering Works and Foundries	600,000	1.9%
Paper Mills	480,000	1.5%
Tobacco Curing (Seasonal)	120,000	0.4%
Glass Factories	300,000	0.9%
Chemical Industry	300,000	0.9%
Sugar Mills (Seasonal)	100,000	0.3%
Tea Gardens (Seasonal)	110,000	0.3%
Re-rolling Mills	180,000	0.6%
Provincial miscellaneous requirements (including domestic coal and coke)	2,400,000	7.4%
Coke Ovens	600,000	1.9%
Brick Burning (Seasonal)	1,200,000	3.7%
Miscellaneous	720,000	2.2%
Total	32,234,000	

Source: Coal Commissioner Report Vol-1, 1947, p. 40. Percentages added by author.

The data shows that the total consumption of coal was expected to increase by 1.45 times between 1928 and 1946 registering a compound annual average growth rate of 2.12 per cent over the period. Considering the fact that this covered the period of the Great Depression and the Second World War, the anticipated growth rate was commendable and showed a great amount of reliance on the coal distribution system. The railways continued to consume about a third of the coal produced and remained by far the largest consumer. In a laudatory comment about the functioning of the railways, the Mahindra Committee (1946) recorded:

> The coastwise shipment trade through the Port of Calcutta consisted of about 1 million tons of coal annually, and while this was not a large percentage of the country's requirements of coal, the trade was of very considerable assistance to the country's transportation system as it relieved the railways of the long haul to the seaboard of Southern and Western India. The balance of the country's coal requirements was carried by the railways, generally speaking without difficulty, except during the early months of the year, when the peak production of coal unfortunately coincided with the peak movement of agricultural traffic. This was an annual phenomenon and the railways, despite their best efforts, have proved unable to cope with it; and it is, we think, this particular Annual difficulty which has occasioned the longstanding complaint that the coal industry is handicapped by the inability of the railways to carry all the coal traffic offering. (Mahindra Committee Report Vol-1, 1947, p. 221)

After the War

Some changes were introduced after the end of the war. The Coal Control Board ceased to function after 1945. The Essential Commodities Act was passed in 1946, and the control of coal distribution came under the ambit of this act instead of the Colliery Control Order.

The production of coal in India from 1939 to 1947 was:

Table 2.13: Production of Coal in India 1939–1947

	Million tons		Million tons
1939	27.79	1944	26.12
1940	29.38	1945	28.97
1941	29.46	1946	29.27
1942	29.43	1947	30.07
1943	25.51		

(Planning Commission, 1951, Chapter 27, para 17)

The data shows that despite the War, the coal production had been sustained through the elaborate administrative machinery of the Government and the active cooperation between the railways and the coal industry. The Mahindra Committee recorded:

> The coal control enabled the country to pass through most serious times and to survive. We have stated elsewhere that the majority of the witnesses before us have asked for the continuance of the control system in some form or other until supply and demand are more balanced. (Mahindra committee Report Vol-1, 1947, pp. 224–5)

The Second World War had generated an enormous pressure on the railway system as movement of materials required for the war effort were given priority. To support the war effort many railway workshops were put to work for repair of military equipment. Railway store depots were converted to stores for military materials. Railway lines in several metre gauge areas were uprooted and sent to Africa for laying lines for troop movements. All these had a telling effect on the railways, which nevertheless continued to function with the utmost efficiency possible under the circumstances.

The country did not have sufficient production facilities for basic items like passenger coaches, locomotives and signalling equipment. During the Great Depression and the war period, repairs and overhauls had been postponed. A large percentage of the assets were worn out and in need of repair. After the transfer of power to independent India in 1947, the Government of India had to take some very bold decisions to nurture the railways back into shape.

From the perspective of management, the stark fact was that the British Government always considered the railways to be a means to achieve strategic objectives rather than a pan India organisation that needed to be run with a great degree of cohesion and coordination. The coal industry was treated as a source of energy for the railways and other industries. The high level of cooperation which emerged between coal and railways and helped the growth of both was not actively promoted but happened spontaneously as they were mutually interdependent.

The government of independent India enunciated new policies to provide direction and role to the coal industry and railways as instruments in the development of the nation, ushering in a new structure and new style of management.

1948–1980: A New Beginning: Planned Development

Creating Conditions for Industrial Development: 1948–1980

The three decades immediately after India attained independence in 1947 mark a distinct change in the philosophy of the government of India towards management of the railways and coal industry. The British government had used railways as a tool for strategic control over the country and trade of the empire. Coal was a necessary appendage to keep the railways and some other industries operational. The government of independent India viewed the railways as a national transporter and coal as the most important fuel for supporting the development of major industries. Policy choices regarding administrative structures, management, technology and resource allocation for these two crucial industries altered radically and focused on the expansion of coal production and railway transportation capacity.

Both the industries were not in the best of health at the end of British rule. Despite the acquisition of railway companies by the state and attempts of the Railway Board to develop a pan India cohesive functional system, issues of coordination remained due to the presence of several railway companies. There had been minimal investment in railways during the periods of the Great depression and the Second World War. The coal industry had witnessed a lack of demand in the 1930s followed by a sudden upsurge in demand during the War. It faced a serious problem of shortage of manpower and use of outdated technology.

The task before the government was to develop both the coal industry and railways in a planned manner to facilitate the rapid industrial development of the nation. The administrative, legislative, management and technological issues were methodically planned in stages to facilitate the growth of both industries. We shall cover these stages in some detail as they laid the foundations for later policy initiatives. The areas that were left unaddressed or partially addressed would also be mentioned.

The Government of India, under the leadership of the Prime Minister Pandit Nehru, decided to develop the country in a balanced manner through a detailed planning process. The Five-Year Plans were to be drawn up by the Planning Commission of India in consultation with all stakeholders and the constituent states of the Union. The First Five Year Plan covered the period 1951–56. It is a tribute to Indian planning that the Plans that were formulated were detailed documents spelling out the objectives of the Government and the allocation of resources to meet those targets. In the case of the mineral industry and the railways, the first three five-year Plans laid special emphasis on creation of capacity for production of minerals and their transportation to fuel the industrial growth of the nation. Coal received primary importance as it was the most important fuel for major industries. The groundwork for rapid increase in coal production was laid through necessary legislation and development of new institutions under government control. In the case of the railways too, detailed planning covered areas like creation of line capacity in specific areas, electrification of railway routes, introduction of new locomotives, improvements in signalling and induction of new freight wagons of superior design. The allocation of resources was judiciously targeted, and the development of facilities was carefully monitored. The following sections examine the details of planning for the coal industry and the railways in the first three plans. These documents delineated the legislative, administrative and management actions taken during these years to lay the basis for the industrial development of the nation. In the case of coal, the decade of the '70s saw a radical shift in the policy of the government to catapult the production of coal to a higher growth trajectory. We shall come to that presently.

Railways

The Railways was declared to be directly under the control of the central government. The Industrial Policy resolution of 1948 stated:

> Railways and air transport, arms and ammunition and atomic energy will, however, be developed as Central Government monopolies. Whenever cooperation with private enterprise is necessary, the State will ensure, either through majority participation in the capital or otherwise, that it has the requisite powers to guide the policy and control the operations of the undertakings. (Government of India, 1948)

The coal industry would also be under governmental control.

The partition of the country into Indian and Pakistan in 1947 created serious problems. The new country, Pakistan, was created by carving out areas in the western and eastern extremities of India. In 1947 Indian Railways had 54,833 kilometres of railway track. Due to the partition of the country, a considerable portion of the erstwhile network, workshops, maintenance depots and establishment offices, both in the east and west went under the control of Pakistan. In the northeast the connection of the Indian Railway network to Assam was lost. The earlier connection had been through East Bengal which, after Partition, became part of East Pakistan (now Bangladesh). The Assam Link project was started in 1948 to construct a rail link between Fakiragram and Kishanganj. This project was completed in 1950, the new line traversing through the northern part of the state of West Bengal.

Railway Zones

The first task before the government was to weld the disparate railway units into a cohesive whole. India inherited a number of railway systems, some worked by the State, some by companies and some by the Princely states. In 1948–49 *'there were 21 railways operated by the Government of India and several Princely States, consisting of 13 major systems called Class I Railways and 8 minor systems made up of 4 Class II and 4 Class III railways.' (Khosla, 1988, p. 208).* The railways which were under the Princely states came under the Government of India with the accession of these states to the Indian Union.

The task of reorganisation started in 1951 and its first phase of creation of administrative six zones, namely, the Eastern, Western, Central, Southern, Northern and North-Eastern, was completed in 1952–53. However, within three years it was realised that the Eastern Railway was too large and the erstwhile Bengal Nagpur Railway portion needed to be separated from Eastern Railway. This took place in 1955 and the zone was named South Eastern Railway. In 1958, the North Eastern Railway, another large railway, was broken up to create the Northeast Frontier Railway, for catering to the northeastern region of the country. In 1966, the South-Central Railway was created by taking portions out of the Central and Southern Railways. Thus, there were now nine administrative zones on the Indian Railways. Quite a few more would be added in the twenty-first century as we shall see presently.

Nature of Indian Railways

After the separation of the Railway Finances from the General Finances in 1924, the railway was required to make an annual contribution from its revenues to the general finances of the government. This practice continued after independence, with decisions on the contribution of the railways being taken by the Railway Convention Committee (RCC).[27] The RCC of 1949 pondered on the nature of the railway undertaking and concluded that *the railways should be considered both as a public utility and a commercial concern*. The Indian Railways were called upon to pay an interest of 4 per cent on the capital invested in the railways by the government from general revenues. The interest rate payable would be reviewed every five years by the RCC.

Status of Indian Railways in 1951

The First Five Year Plan document candidly noted in some detail the status of the Indian Railways in 1951 and delineated the magnitude of the task of rehabilitation and refurbishment that lay ahead. It is worth perusing these details for a correct historical perspective of the magnitude of the challenge facing the Indian Railways. The Plan document stated:

> The most serious problem facing the railways today is the task of rehabilitation and provision of adequate equipment. During the last twenty years, railways' assets have been put to intensive and extensive use with little opportunity for rehabilitation.
>
> ... In the first phase of the war, the Indian railways, despite the shortage, had to release wagons, locomotives and track materials for the Middle East.
>
> ... As soon as the hostilities ended, new problems came up in the wake of Partition. The division of the North Western Railway deprived the Indian portion of the majority of workshops and maintenance and repair facilities. Similarly, the division of the Bengal Assam Railway left the Assam Railway without any workshop or a link with rest of the railway system. The loss of the port of Karachi led to the diversion of traffic to Bombay causing a great deal of congestion and creating a transport bottleneck in the Bombay Port. This necessitated the development of a major port at Kandla and the construction of the Kandla-Deesa rail link.
>
> ... The magnitude of the problem of rehabilitation may be judged from the abnormal proportion of the overaged stock. From detailed figures summarised below it will be observed that the arrears of renewals already accumulated by March 31, 1951, amounted to 1,050 locomotives, 5,514 coaching vehicles, and 21,418 wagons, against the normal figures of average annual renewals of 190 locomotives, 650 coaching vehicles and 5,000 wagons.

---

[27] The Railway Convention Committee (RCC) is an ad hoc committee constituted from time to time on a resolution adopted by Lok Sabha and concurred by Rajya Sabha. The first RCC was constituted in 1949. Since 1954, each Lok Sabha has been having an RCC. The committee reviews the rate of dividend payable by the railways to general revenue. It also suggests the level of contribution the railways should make to various funds of the railways such as the Depreciation Reserve Fund, Pension Fund and Development Fund.

The Plan document continued to mention that:

> What has been stated in the previous paragraphs refers only to the mobile equipment. The state of the immobile equipment has been a subject of no less concern. The condition of the track has also deteriorated during the last two decades, during which renewals were carried out only to the minimum extent required for safety in operation, leaving considerable rehabilitation of the track for completion in future. Speed restrictions have had to be continued on hundreds of miles of main lines as track renewals could not be carried out. The primary task of the railways is, thus, to overtake this heavy `accumulation of arrears at as early a date as possible. (Planning Commision,1951, Chapter 31)

Demands on the Railway System

There was great euphoria in the country following independence. Aspirations of the people were on the rise and, along with the aspirations, the demands on the railways for both passenger and freight services. The capacity of the railways to handle traffic was constrained by the factors referred to in the Plan document. The freight carried had increased from 21,786-million-ton miles[28] in 1938–39, to 26,581-ton miles in 1950–51, i.e. at a compound rate of 2 per cent per year for 10 years. The rate of growth of passenger traffic during the same period had been 8.3 per cent. The Plan document candidly noted that this traffic had been handled by using extraordinary steps like retaining in service, and not scrapping, overaged equipment, which were due replacement. Such measures would not have been approved under normal conditions. It was further decided that until additions were received, the overaged stock would continue in service. These were very bold management decisions.

The problem was that the traffic actually moved was not a true indicator of the demand, which was probably for a much higher level of traffic. It was estimated that freight traffic would increase by 10 per cent by the end of the plan period in 1955–56. The rehabilitation programme thus had to consider the twin problems of replacement of deteriorated assets and creation of new capacity.

---

28 Ton Miles: The universally accepted measurement of transport output. One ton transported over a distance of one mile is termed as one ton mile of transport output. Similarly, 100 tons over 100 miles is 10,000 ton miles. There is a further differentiation between net and gross ton miles. The gross ton miles includes the weight of the wagon, whereas net ton miles uses only the weight of the cargo in the wagons.

Future Programme for Railways

As noted earlier, much of the industrial inputs required for the railways was imported. While rails and rail fittings were manufactured by TISCO and the wagon industry produced some wagons, locomotives and other equipment were imported.

The Government faced difficult choices. The paucity of financial resources ruled out large-scale imports. Hence, India needed to produce the locomotives, coaches and wagons necessary for providing transportation for a growing economy. A new electric locomotive manufacturing unit was planned to be set up in Chittaranjan in West Bengal and the Tata Locomotive Engineering Company (TELCO), which had been earlier denied permission to manufacture locomotives by the Imperial government, was provided financial assistance to manufacture diesel locomotives. A plant for manufacturing passenger coaches was planned to be set up in Perambur in present Tamil Nadu.

The capacity of the private sector to produce freight wagons was much less than the requirement. The average production between 1948–49 and 1950–51 had been only 2780 wagons per year. It was estimated that the industry might at best be able to provide 30,000 wagons during the five years of the First Plan period. Import of locomotives, coaches and wagons was inescapable and the government decided to import as many as 600 locomotives, 1294 passenger vehicles and 19143 freight wagons. The level of import was naturally constrained by the funds available and the Plan document noted that the requirement of locomotives was much more than that planned.

Next, was the task of assessing the status of mineral resources, such as coal, which would be critical for the rapid development of the country.

Coal

Assessment of Coal Resources

During the four years after Independence to the beginning of the planning process, the government had laid the foundation of a mineral policy for the country. The Geological Survey of India had been expanded, the Bureau of Mines had been set up to enable coordinated development of mining resources in the country. A Mineral Policy had also been announced.

The heartening news was that the production of coal was adequate to meet the current requirements of the country. The production was mentioned as:

Table 3.1: Production and Export of Coal 1951

	Production 1950 in '000 tons	Production 1951 in '000 tons	Exports in 1950	Exports in 1951
Coal Production in'000 tons	32307	34431	903	1908

(Planning Commission, 1951, Chapter 27, para 5)

Coal was used primarily by the railways, power and steel industries. One of the main issues facing the mining of coal was that reliable estimates of deposits were not available. This was the status though the industry had been in existence from 1820 onwards. It was planned to launch surveys immediately to obtain detailed data on the coal deposits. However, the overall sense was that the deposits of non-coking coal would be sufficient for the present requirements, but the availability of coking coal would be much less than the demand. Conservation of coking coal was critical as it was in short supply and many industries, such as the railways, were using coking coal because of its superior properties, though they really did not need that quality of coal.

Consumption of coal

The railways continued to remain the largest coal user, consuming 10.03 million tons of coal and accounting for 31.1 per cent of the total consumption. Five categories of consumers, the railways, steel and foundries, colliery consumption, steam electric utilities and bunker coal, consumed slightly more than 55 per cent of the coal. The share of steam and electric utilities was only 6.9 per cent, but would increase rapidly in the future.

On the coking coal front the situation was such that the iron and steel industry consumed only 21 per cent of the metallurgical coal produced, while the rest was used for bunker coal, by railways and by other industries. The Report of the Indian Coalfields Committee of 1946 had dwelt on this issue and recommended that railways should slowly eliminate the use of coking coal. In compliance, the Railways had already initiated steps to reduce the use of metallurgical coking coal. The Metallurgical Coal Committee (1949) had examined the issue again and concluded that it would be possible to reduce consumption of metallurgical coal by non-steel users by 10 per cent each year. The same Committee assessed the requirement of coking coal up to 1957–58 as 8 million tons, up from 3.7 million tons in 1949. The colliery consumption was of the order of 1.3 per cent of the total production. This was high and needed to be reduced.

Administrative and Legislative Actions for Increasing Coal Production

Regarding the need for a proper geological survey, the First Plan document noted that

> of the total of about 100 coalfields in India, only a few have been investigated to a depth of 1,000 to 2,000 ft. Though working collieries are found widely spread over all the coalfields the full extent of the reserves of these fields are not known. It is therefore, necessary to have all the fields geologically mapped and the resources estimated by the Geological Survey of India in collaboration with the Bureau of Mines and provision has been made in the Plan in this respect. (Planning Commission, 1951, Chapter 27 para 20)

The Geological Survey of India and the Indian Bureau of Mines would undertake surveys in the following fields: Korba, Rewa, Talcher, Kanhan Valley, Karanpura, Wardha and Godavari Valley.

Coal Production and New Legislations

Production of non-coking coal in 1955 was 38.22 mt which was close to the target of 39 mt. India was able to export about 1.5 mt of non-coking coal. The data from 1950 to 1955 pertaining to production, despatch and exports, as recorded in the Plan document is as follows:

Table 3.2: The Production and Despatch of Coal 1950–55 (Figures in million tons)

Year	Raisings	Despatches	Exports
1950	32.31	26.80	0.950
1951	34.30	29.10	2.731
19.52	36.30	31.00	3.298
1953	35.97	30.60	1.991
1954	36.77	31.94	2.022
1955	38.22	32.96	1.574

Source: Planning Commission, 1956, Chapter 18, para 3.

In 1955, the private sector produced major part of coal, with the public sector (i.e. companies owned by the Government of India) contributing only 4.5 million tons. The Industrial Policy resolution of 1948 had laid down that the new ventures in coal production would be under the ambit of the Government. The only exceptions would be where, in the national interest, the Government desired the participation of the private sector.

The declaration of the Industrial Policy Resolution was formalised through the enactment of two legislations. First, the Parliament repealed the Coal Mines

Safety' (Stowing) Act, 1939, and, in 1952 passed the Coal Mines (Conservation and Safety) Act 1952 which gave the Central Government powers to

> (a) to adopt measures for maintaining safety of coal mines for conservation of coal, (b) to delegate powers to a Coal Board, (c)to levy and collect excise duty on all coal and coke raised or manufactured and despatched and an additional excise duty on all coking coal raised and despatched, (d) to impose and collect import duty on all coal imported, (e) to constitute Committees to advise Government in any matter connected with the administration of the Act. (Ghosh, Volume 2, 1977, 18)

The Essential Commodities Act was passed in 1955 with a view to regulate and control the production, supply and distribution of essential commodities. Coal, being a critical input for the development plans of the nation, featured prominently among the list of commodities under the ambit of the Act.

The third initiative of the Government was the passing of the Mines and Minerals Development and Regulation Act in 1957. The Act clearly mentioned the intention of the Government as at its very outset it stated: 'It is hereby declared that it is expedient in the public interest that the Union should take under its control the regulation of mines and the development of minerals to the extent hereinafter provided'. Hence from that time, the emphasis shifted to creation of mining capacity in the public sector.

In keeping with the spirit of the Industrial Policy Resolutions of 1948 and 1956, the National Coal Development Corporation Ltd. (NCDC) was created by the Government in October 1956. The NCDC was a government owned company which started with 11 collieries earlier owned by the railway companies. It was mandated to increase production from new areas.

Distribution of Coal: Coordination with Railways

The Colliery Control Order of 1945 had placed the distribution of coal under the Coal Controller. The movement of coal required the sanction of the Coal Controller and the issue of sanction was contingent on the details of the name of the consumer, the type of coal, its grade, quantity of movement and the origin and destination of the consignment being available with the Coal Controller's office. Thus, the production and distribution of coal, except for a few exceptions, came under the control of the government.

The Mahindra Committee Report had mentioned about the detailed procedures followed for allocation of coal for industrial use (Mahindra Committee Report, 1947, Appendix 20). A similar policy was adopted by the Coal Controller in consultation with the Ministry of Railways from 1953. The scheme envisaged the preparation of a priority list of industries and a system of sponsorship wherein the demand for coal by all consumers would be backed by an endorsement from a government recognised entity. Consumers were put into two separate categories, (a) Centrally sponsored and (b) state sponsored. The centrally sponsored consumers were defence, railways, power stations, steel plants, cement plants etc. The state sponsored industries were other industries not falling in the Central category. The third feature was that the coal movement would normally, barring few exceptions, adhere to the scheme of 'rationalised movement' as followed by the Ministry of Railways. The intention was to avoid the cross movement of coal, which would be wasteful of transport capacity. The Ministry of Railways followed a scheme named the Preferential Traffic Schedule, (issued under Section 27A of the Indian Railway Act, later became section 71 after amendment of the Act in 1989), which laid down the priorities accorded by railways to movement of various classes of traffic. For example, Military traffic was put in the highest category 'A'. Movement of coal was in priority 'C', with power and other centrally sponsored consumers being accorded higher inter se seniority within category C. (Ghosh, Vol II, 1977 p. 259)

Individual railway freights before Independence were replaced in 1948 by that of uniform rates with a separate structure for coal.

Demand for Coal

The progress of the economy and the planned development of heavy industries led to increase in the demand for coal. The total demand for coal up to the end of the Second Five Year Plan (1961) was estimated as 60 mt, which was 22 million tons more than the production achieved in 1955, an increase of 58 per cent.

The administrative challenge was to open new mines to achieve this ambitious target and also develop railway connectivity to these mines. Many of the new mines would come up in the newly developing coalfields of Korba, Korea-Rewa (Central India Coalfields) and Karanpura.

An organisation named the Coal Production and Development Commissioner was created as the administrative head of the of existing State collieries and new collieries to be established in the State sector. The issues regarding the quality, pricing and distribution of coal would continue to remain under the Coal Controller.

It was decided that of the 22 million tons of additional output to be produced, 12 million would come from Government owned mines and 10 would come from the private sector. The objective of increasing the production of coal from the outlying areas to reduce the load on Raniganj and Jharia fields was very sensible from the perspective of logistics. Most of the coal was produced in West Bengal and Bihar and had to be transported to destinations all over the country. The skew in the production pattern placed a great strain on the railway system. The extension of coal production towards the new areas would reduce logistics cost for consumers located far away from Raniganj and Jharia. The table from the Plan document shows the incremental output in the public sector planned:

Table 3.3: Future Plan for Coal Production 1954–61 (data in million tons)

	Output in 1954	Output in 1960–61	Increase
ASSAM	050	0.50	
WEST BENGAL			
Darjeeling	0.03	0.03	
Raniganj	12.22	18.16	5.94
BIHAR			
Jharia	13.19	16.69	3.50
Karanpura	1.44	6.00	4.56
Bokaro	2.38	2.88	0.50
Giridih	0.6	0.26	
Other small fields in Bihar	0.14	0.14	
MADHYA PRADESH			
Chhindwara and Chanda	2.25	2.25	
Korba		4.00	4.00
Sasti	007	0.07	
Central India Coalfields (CIC)	2.31	5.31	3.66
ORISSA	0.52	0.52	
HYDERABAD			
Singareni	1.43	2.93	1.50
RAJASTHAN			
Bikaner	0.03	0.03	
TOTAL	36.77	59.77	23.0

Source: Planning Commission, 1956, Chapter 18, para 15.

This level of detailed planning, that would enable cooperation between producer and transporter, was a sea change from what had transpired in the period before 1947. The standout feature of this production plan was the growth expected from the Karanpura, Korba and CIC fields, which, hitherto, were not large coal producers. The requirement of coking coal was included in the target of 60 mt, with the production of coking coal being pegged at 14 mt. With new steel plants being planned, the demand of coal from the steel sector would increase from 3.5 mt to 9.73 mt. Requirements of other coking coal users was estimated at 1.68 mt, making a total of 11.41 million tons of clean (washed) coal or 16.5 million tons of raw coal with a yield[29] of 69 per cent. With the demand from the steel sector increasing rapidly, production of coking coal would have to increase and use of this superior grade of coal by railways would have to be reduced very quickly.

To ensure that the steel industry received uniform grade of coal, the Government appointed a Coal Washeries Committee. The experts recommended that coal for the steel sector should preferably be washed and that coal washeries should be set up in the Government sector. Three coal washeries were already available in the private sector at West Bokaro and Jamadoba (belonging to Tata Iron and Steel Company) and Lodna (belonging to Indian Iron and Steel Company, Burnpur). Two washeries in the state sector had already been planned to be located at Kargali for supply to Rourkela and Bhilai steel plants and at Durgapur for the Durgapur steel plant. The matter of pricing of washed coal, which was a value added product would have to be decided at the appropriate time.

There was some time slippage in the establishment of three new washeries, which would now function only during the Third Plan. To optimise the use of coking coal, blending of good quality coking coal with some inferior varieties was started. The Indian Railways had also drawn up a phased plan for reducing the use of coking coal. However, the demand for coking coal did not rise as sharply as anticipated and a small amount remained as surplus at the end of the Second Plan.

The new mines proposed to be set up by NCDC encountered several obstacles in opening up virgin areas and setting up large-scale infrastructure for mining. The production of coal at the end of the Second Five Year Plan reached a level of 54.62 million tonnes against a target of 60 million. The achievement on the production front for the coal industry as a whole was, however, commendable as the production grew by 1.6 times between 1951 and 1961. The Singareni coalfields produced 2.6 million tons against a target of 3 million tons. The private sector exceeded its target producing 45.7 million tons against the target of 44 million tons.

The issue of small and uneconomic collieries had been a drag on the system for a long time. To achieve economy in the cost of production of coal it was proposed to amalgamate a large number of small collieries with larger collieries. A Committee for the Amalgamation of Collieries was appointed by the Government

---

[29] Yield is the percentage of useful coal left after washing a volume of coal. Thus, if 100 tonnes of coal is washed and the useful amount available after washing is 69 tonnes, the yield is 69%.

and it suggested, in the first instance, voluntary amalgamation of 31 uneconomic collieries. During the Second Plan 17 of the 31 could be amalgamated. Further work would continue during the Third Plan.

Development Plan for Railways

Placing emphasis on industrial development, the Second Plan document noted that

> In the past, the dominant considerations in the development of transport and communications in the country were trade and administration; but since the second world war the transport system has been increasingly oriented to serve the needs of industrial development. The second plan will carry this process much further. (Planning Commission, 1956, Chapter 18, Introduction)

With this end in view, the Plan allocated 29 per cent of the outlay for the public sector for transport and communications, of which fully 65 per cent was allocated for the railways.

The Government had stepped up expenditure on rolling stock and line capacity creation during the First Plan. The freight traffic carried by the railways (in terms of tons originating) increased by about 8 per cent between 1953–54 and 1955–56. The demand for transport was, of course, much higher, but the progress was commendable.

Though a large number of locomotives and wagons had been imported, the addition to rolling stock from indigenous industry was also significant. The Chittaranjan Locomotive Works exceeded its production target as did the Tata Engineering and Locomotive Company (TELCO).

The expected addition to rolling stock by 1955–56 was:

Table 3.4: Expected Addition to Rolling Stock

	Indian manufacture	Imports	Total
Locomotives	496	1,093	1,589
Coaches	4,351	486	4,837
Wagons	41,192	20,521	61,713

Source: Planning Commission, 1956, Chapter 21 para 7.

It would be seen that the production of locomotives in India was expected to be only 31 per cent of the total. The position regarding coaches and wagons was much better. In the case of track infrastructure, there was an emphasis on new lines and 454 miles of new lines were under construction in 1955–56.

With the railways likely to remain the largest carrier of freight traffic, the Plan formulated strategies for expansion of railway capacity such that it dovetailed with the programmes for industrial development, particularly for major mineral and manufacturing industries. Improvement in inter-modal coordination was also planned to achieve optimum results from investment. The progress of each sector would be closely reviewed and course correction measure applied when necessary.

Expansion of Railway Capacity

An outstanding feature of the second Plan was the targeting of investment in specific mineral rich areas for serving new industries. It was declared that funds would be allocated for investment in creation of railway capacity for these areas even at the cost of sacrificing investment on passenger traffic. The Plan document declared '*the provision in the plan for new lines is confined to lines required for operational purposes and for the new industrial projects*'. *[Second Five Year Plan, 1956, para 13]*

Railway capacity was sought to be enhanced through introduction of new breed of wagons and locomotives, improvements in signalling and telecommunication and upgradation of track. A view was also expressed that the objective was to run longer, heavier and faster freight trains to utilise the available track capacity optimally. This was an echo of what Kelway Bamber had stated in his paper in 1919. As would be seen later, the focus on longer, heavier and faster freight trains enabled Indian Railways to carry bulk cargo to large industries efficiently and reduce unit costs of operation, but the policy extracted a price in terms of loss of other traffic, which did not require bulk movement.

The Plan provided for converting 1607 miles of single line to double line, and for converting 265 miles of metre gauge track to broad gauge. In addition, a number of minor line capacity enhancement works like provision of additional loops lines (siding lines) at stations and extension of loop lines to accommodate longer trains, were planned. A number of major marshalling yards were also planned for remodelling. In the case of doubling single line tracks, the focus was on the important mineral routes of Eastern and South Eastern Railways such as Bokaro-Barkakana, Andal-Ukhra, Manoharpur-Rourkela, Rourkela-Nagpur, Sini-Gomharria, Rajkharswan-Barajamda, Kharagpur-Tatanagar, Khurda Road-Nergundi and several congested lines on the Northern, Western, Central, Southern and North-Eastern railway systems.

Improvements in signalling systems were planned to improve line capacity utilisation and enhance safety in train operations. Automatic signalling was proposed to be introduced in some highly congested sections. The working of major marshalling yards such as Mughalsarai (now renamed as Deen Dayal Upadhyay Terminal) was planned to be mechanised by introducing speed retarders,[30] and automatic operation of points.

There was a big push for electrification of railway tracks and for introduction of diesel locomotives on non-electrified routes. The Plan provided for electrification of 826 miles of lines in critical freight and passenger growth areas such as Burdwan-Gomoh (Howrah-Burdwan having been electrified earlier), Howrah-Kharagpur and the suburban sections of the Eastern Railway's Sealdah division. Diesel traction was proposed to be introduced between Gomoh and Mughalsarai, which was the main coal route from the east to north and north western India, and Asansol-Rajkharswan, Rajkharswan-Jharsuguda which were principally iron ore routes. Other important routes on the Central, Western and Southern railways would also see the introduction of diesel locomotives. Electrification and dieselisation would lead to higher efficiency of operation through higher speeds and running of longer trains. Most of the steam locomotives were old and had low efficiency. The tractive effort[31] of the new locomotives was much higher than the steam locomotives.

To foster inter-modal coordination, the Government enacted the Road Transport Corporation Act, 1950, creating corporations at the state levels to coordinate with the railways for improving customer satisfaction through integrated operations. An expert committee was also appointed to examine the possibilities of coordination between the railways and coastal shipping.

The final achievement during the Second Plan on the infrastructure front was that 1,300 miles were doubled and 800 miles were electrified. 1,200 miles of new tracks were added. A total of 400 miles of lines which were dismantled during the Second World War were reinstated. This rate of progress was possible due to focussed planning and resource allocation. As we shall see, progress of doubling of tracks in later years was much less, when the need for doubling was very high.

Expectations from the Indian Railways could be realised only through maximising efficiency and achievement of operational economy. The movement of

---

30 Retarders: The task of a large railway marshalling yard, is to sort trains with mixed composition i.e., with wagons destined for various destinations, into a train for a particular destination(s)/direction(s). This is done by placing wagons for particular destinations or particular directions in nominated lines. To speed up the process of segregation, the wagons of train with mixed composition are rolled over a hump and the wagons are put into different lines on the basis of direction of movement. When the wagon is rolling down the hump, its speed is controlled by 'Retarders' which act as brakes.

31 Tractive effort is the force at the rims or outer edges of the driving wheels of a locomotive. Higher tractive effort enables heavier loads to be moved.

important commodities like coal and iron ore would have to be rationalised to eliminate cross movement. Far flung areas such as the north eastern part of the country would have to be served through coordination between railways and riverine transport as many large rivers did not have bridges. The office of a Joint Director, Rail Movement was created for this purpose at the Eastern Railway Headquarters in 1962.

Indian Railways moved 154 million tons of freight in 1960–61 against a revised target of 168 million tons (reduced from 180 earlier) of which 49.5 million tons (32 per cent) was coal. The share of coal would creep up steadily with the setting up of new coal based thermal power stations and other coal consuming industries.[32]

Spatial Distribution of Coal Production and Other Issues

The merit of centralised planning for creation of transportation and coal production capacity in tandem was seen as conscious steps to integrate the production and transportation infrastructure. The continued dependence on Raniganj and Jharia coalfields in eastern India for coal inputs for the steel plants and various other industries spread all over the country created a strain on the railway system. It was obvious that the situation would only aggravate during the Third plan period. Though railway facilities were being created, they would not be sufficient to take care of the surge in the demand for movement from the two main coal producing areas. To mitigate the strain, planners went to the extent of suggesting that short distance movement of coal should take place by road and coal for consumers in west and south should be moved by the rail cum sea route. This was throwback to the days of the Mahindra Committee report (1946), which also advocated movement for Bombay by rail-cum-sea. Here the critical factor was the capacity of the ports to handle the traffic and the rail connectivity to the ports, which would need to be strengthened. The feasibility of oil being used by consumers located far from the coalfields was also to be examined.

Recognising the problem of movement from Raniganj and Jharia, the Third Plan document recorded that

---

[32] The Government of India passed the Standards of Weights and Measure Act in December 1956 and the Act became applicable from 1958. Through this legislation, India migrated to the Metrication of measurements. The currency had been converted to the decimal system in 1957. However, perhaps the changeover took a little time to be implemented and the Plan documents continued to use the nomenclatures of miles and tons even in the Third Five Year Plan.

> On account of a substantial increase in the average lead[33] of traffic, however, the volume of traffic handled by the railways in terms of ton miles in 1960–61 is somewhat more than what was originally provided for in the Second Plan and the railways have recently been working under some strain. Difficulties have been experienced in the movement of coal, particularly from the Bengal-Bihar coalfields. This is partly due to changes in the pattern of coal production and in the plans for supply of raw materials to the steel plants, resulting in longer leads for the railways than were originally anticipated, and partly to a shortfall in some of the railway development programmes, notably wagon procurement. (Planning Commission, 1961, Chapter 28 para 9)

Freight Equalisation Scheme for Railways

Another important reason for the increase in the average lead of movement of railway freight traffic was the 'Freight equalization Scheme'. This scheme was introduced in 1956 and was operational till 1991. The objective was to ensure balanced regional development by providing subsidised transport to resource deficient areas. The scheme provided that a factory could be set up anywhere in India and the transportation cost of raw materials would be subsidised by the Government. States such as West Bengal and Bihar, which had rich mineral deposits and most of the steel manufacturing units, protested vociferously against this scheme. Industries which would have come up in these two states could now be set up anywhere in the country. The natural advantage of the mineral rich states was lost and with it the revenue streams and employment that would have been generated had industries been set up within these states. From the perspective of logistics, this scheme resulted in an artificial inflation of the demand for rail transport. Three and a half to four tonnes of raw materials are required for producing one tonne of steel. Hence, transporting so much raw material across the country to produce steel (and other products) at distant locations also resulted in a colossal wastage of energy used in transportation.

There have been several studies on the Freight Equalisation Scheme. However, most have focused on the level of subsidies the government had to dole out to sustain the scheme. The impact of the scheme on inflating transport demand in areas where line capacity was already under strain has not been adequately addressed. Many years later, answering a question, in the Lok Sabha (Lower House of the Parliament) on 25th March, 1992, the Minister for the Ministry of Planning and Programme Implementation, informed the House that the original justification for the scheme had been to promote balanced industrial development by supporting areas which did not have mineral deposits. Though the scheme fulfilled its objectives in the initial years, later studies showed that

[33] Average lead refers to the average distance moved by the freight consignments.

the increase in real transportation costs more than offset the benefits of balanced development. There were other methods of promoting balanced regional growth through fiscal and credit policies, providing direct transport subsidies and the like (E Parliament Library, 10_III_25031992_p383_p383_t450.pdf)

Rolling Stock

The Indian railways added considerably to their rolling stock to augment transport capacity. In the decade 1951–61, the number of wagons increased by 53 per cent and locomotives by 25 per cent. As the tractive power of the new locomotives was higher the gain was more than proportionate.

Decade of the 1960s

The Third Five Year Plan (1961–66) raised the sights and set the achievement of a 'good life' for every citizen as the ultimate goal of socialist society. It defined the immediate task as laying down the foundation of a self-reliant economic growth. The Third Plan was conceived as 'first stage of a decade or more of intensive development leading to a self-reliant and self-generating economy'.

Unfortunately, this decade witnessed a number of events which affected macroeconomic planning adversely. In October 1962, there was a war with China which lasted for a month and sent shockwaves through the economy. Prime Minister Nehru died in 1964 and was succeeded by Lal Bahadur Shastri. In 1965, an unprovoked attack by Pakistan, led to clashes from April to June and a war from August to September 1965. The two wars led to a sectoral diversion of resources in the economy. Prime Minister Shastri tragically died, while on an official tour to Tashkent, USSR, in January 1966. The Congress Party elected Indira Gandhi, daughter of Pandit Nehru, as the new Prime Minister. The wars and the sudden changes in leadership of the country had repercussions on planning and economic growth. However, the new Prime Minister had a vision for the country, which was implemented in great measure during her tenures.

Planning for Coal and Railways

Demand for coal in 1965–66 was assessed as 97 million tonnes (hereinafter mentioned as mt), which was an increase of more than 42 mt over the actual production of 1961. For the private sector, the additional production during the Second Plan had come from existing mines. The incremental target for the private sector was pegged at 17 mt, the rest coming from the public sector. The task for NCDC was challenging as the investment requirement for this expansion would be large and the learning curve for the organisation would be fairly steep. It was a major challenge for the coal industry and also for the railways which would have to quickly develop transportation facilities for the coal from the new mines.

In 1960, production of coking coal had been 13 mt and that of blendable coal 2 mt. The demand from the steel sector for metallurgical coal at the end of the Third Plan (1965–66) was estimated as 25 million tons and merchant cokeries would require another 2 mt while the railways and other organisations using superior grade coal would require 10 mt.

The steel plants in the public sector were just being set up. The Rourkela steel plant had been set up in 1961 and the Durgapur Steel Plant in 1962. A huge steel plant at Bhilai was planned to be set up at the end of the Third Plan (it was commissioned in 1967). The successful operation of these plants depended crucially on the availability of coking and blendable coal. A coke producing plant had been set up at Durgapur and it planned to use a blend of coking and superior blendable coal.

One problem which emerged was that the production of superior grades of coal was not increasing fast enough. The new areas which were planned to be opened up were not expected to contribute to the basket of high-grade coal. Thus, it was clear that the use of high grade and coking coal would have to be controlled judiciously. The Fuel efficiency Committee of the Coal Council provided some suggestions regarding the types of coal to be supplied to various industries. The growth of the steel industry led to increasing demands for coking coal, which had to be imported later.

Investment Planning for Railways

One feature noted by the Third Plan was that the elasticity of transport demand[34] with respect to National Income was greater than one for both the railways and road transport. That is, if the growth in National Income was 5 per cent, the transport demand would increase by more than 5 per cent. It was also noted that this trend was likely to continue in the future too. The relatively high elasticity of demand had major implications for infrastructure planning for transport sector. As it would be seen later, the investment in development of the railway infrastructure by the Government failed to keep pace with the requirement.

---

[34] Elasticity of demand for freight transport with respect to National Income: The percentage change in transport demand consequent to a percentage change in National Income. If the percentage increase in transport demand is more than the percentage increase in national Income, the demand is called 'elastic'.

At the time of the formulation of the Third Five Year Plan, the Indian Railways was a profit-making organisation which could contribute positively to the funding of the plan for creation of infrastructure. It was imperative that the financial position of the railways was not allowed to deteriorate. The Third Plan recorded,

> In view of the large fresh investments the Indian Railways over the past ten years and proposed for the Third Plan, the capital-at-charge[35] of the railways increased from Rs. 834 crores in 1950–51 to Rs. 1559 crores in 1960–61 and it is expected to rise to Rs. 2313 crores by 1965–66 these matters assume considerable importance. Prima facie, it is desirable that financially the Indian Railways should not take the downward path followed by the railway systems in some other countries. (Planning Commission, 1961, Chapter 28 para 13)

Finalising the investment strategy was not easy. There were numerous demands for new lines, and the choice was to decide between the lines required for major industries and lines in new areas. The Committee on Transport Policy and Coordination (Neogy Committee) noted that in several countries uneconomic lines had been closed down. In India, many of the new lines and lines which had been relaid were not carrying sufficient traffic. The Committee flagged the need to lay down definite criteria for deciding on investment proposals. It recorded:

> where a choice exists between a railway line and a road, careful examination may be required before a decision is taken ... one approach that could be considered is that in respect of lines which on technical studies are found to be of an unremunerative character, and have to be taken up either on strategic grounds or for other social and political considerations, Government or the parties concerned should subsidise the railways directly. (quoted In Planning Commission, 1961, Chapter 28 para 12)

This recommendation of the Neogy Committee was repeated later by some experts, but found few takers.

The traffic loading target for the Indian Railways for Third five Year Plan was set at 245 mt for the terminal year 1965–66, up from 154 Mt in the terminal year of the Second Plan. The share of minerals and major industries would constitute about 60 per cent of the total, with coal being 37 per cent. This pattern would continue in the future too, with other bulk commodities like foodgrains, fertilisers

[35] Capital at Charge is the capital received from the government on which the railway pays dividend.

and petroleum products getting added to the list. Consequently, commodities which were not moved as bulk consignments would progressively get crowded out from the freight basket of the railways. The production target for coal was 97 mt of which the railways would carry 90 mt.

Strengthening Railway Infrastructure: New Assets

The Third Plan continued the focus on creation of transport capacity on the trunk routes of the railways which were carrying bulk freight traffic. Other line capacity enhancement works included projects such as converting 1600 miles of single lines to double lines, remodelling of major yards, opening of new stations on single line sections, improvements in signalling and construction of 120 miles of new lines. The new lines were mainly targeted at facilitating movement of minerals to industries. Some of the lines were Garwa Road-Robertsganj, Sambalpur-Titlagarh and Bimalgarh-Kiriburu, Ranchi-Bondamunda, Bailadilla-Kotavalasa and the new line to Haldia Port. Construction of an additional 200 miles of new lines was also planned for development of coal mines.

Upgrading Track

The need to carry heavier wagons necessitated improvement in the carrying capacity of the track. The standard type of rail used on the main routes of Indian railway used to be the so called 90R rail. The weight of this rail was 90 pounds (41 kg) per yard. The amount of traffic that could be carried over this track and the weight of the wagon that it could support were both limited. A new type of rail weighing 52 kg per metre was introduced to support the bigger wagons. Later even heavier rails weighing 60 kg per metre and having other special characteristics, which permitted carrying of more traffic, were introduced. The length of each rail used to be 13 metres. At the end of every rail was a joint connecting it to the next rail with plates and nuts. This was replaced by the use of longer rail panels, thereby reducing the number of joints, which had always been a potential safety hazard.

The push for rapid electrification of railway routes continued and 1100 miles of electrification was planned. The areas of focus were the lines serving coal mines and steel plants. The Mughalsarai (now Deen Dayal Upadhyay)-Kanpur route was also planned to be electrified. It was the heaviest density traffic corridor of that time, carrying coal to north India.

Wagon Design

The running of longer and heavier trains was aimed at maximising the utilisation of available line capacity. The design of new and larger wagons became a major area of attention.[36] The Research Design and Standards Organisation, (RDSO), set up in 1957, conducted research and developed designs and specifications for railway equipment. Over the years, RDSO developed a number of wagon designs to facilitate movement of specific commodities such as metallic ores, steel and loose minerals. In 1957–58 the RDSO developed a bogie type top open 'BOX' wagon for carrying coal and other loose materials. This wagon had an axle load[37] of 20.3 tons against the earlier 16.3 tons for a high sided four-wheeler wagon known as 'KC'. The cargo carrying capacity of the new BOX wagon was 55.6 tonnes compared to 23.67 tonnes for a KC wagons. The new wagon had roller bearing in the wheels, centre buffer couplers[38] and was capable of speeds up to 100 kilometres per hour. This represented a quantum jump in the ability to carry heavier freight. Coal was now carried in greater volume per train and the trains ran from origin to destination as a 'block rake', bypassing all marshalling yards and without the train's formation being disturbed.

Introduction of the new wagon brought multiple advantages in terms of higher cargo movement per train, elimination of delays at marshalling yards and higher speeds of freight trains. It may be recalled that the report of Robertson of 1903 had suggested similar actions to improve operations. All these factors helped to progressively enhance operational efficiency and reduce the unit operating costs of the Indian Railways. However, the change to running of full train loads of one commodity from origin to destination had other long-term implications for

---

[36] In the pre-Independence period, the task of designing equipment was generally sourced to foreign firms. To achieve integration and coordination amongst railway companies the Indian Railway Conference Association had been set up in 1902. An office for standardising designs and specifications of equipment named the Central Standards Office (CSO) had been set up in Shimla in 1930. After Independence the focus on the railways prompted the Government to set up the Railway Testing and Research Centre (RCTC) at Lucknow in 1952. The RCTC was mandated to conduct research and testing on rolling stock, railway track and other areas. In 1957 the CSO and RCTC were merged to form the Research Design and Standards Organisation (RDSO), with headquarters at Lucknow.

[37] Axle Load: The load exerted on each axle of a wagon. Old wagons had four wheels and 2 axles. The new BOX wagon had eight wheels and 4 axles. A load of 20.3 tonnes per axle implied that the total load that could be carried by the wagon would be $20.3 \times 4 = 81.2$ tonnes. This would include the weight of the empty wagon known as 'Tare'. For the KC wagon it would be $16.3 \times 2 = 32.6$ tonnes.

[38] Centre Buffer Coupler was a new system of joining one wagon to another. It was an improvement over the 'Screw Coupler' which was used earlier. The new coupling system was more robust, capable of withstanding higher strain due to enhanced cargo in the wagons, and the wagons could be coupled automatically by knocking against each other at a slow speed. The Screw Coupler had to be joined manually.

the Indian Railways, as we shall see later. It also required a radical change in the way coal was loaded from the major coalfields.

Systems of Coal Loading: Issues in Loading New Wagons

With the induction of new and larger wagons, the system of loading coal for transportation by rail had to go through a gradual transformation. In the Raniganj and Jharia fields, loading arrangements were mainly manual. The mined coal was kept as a heap near the railway loading platform. For loading of top open wagons, a wooden ramp was placed at the edge of the loading platform with the other edge of the ramp resting on the side of the wagon. The labourers used baskets to carry the coal from the heap to the wagon, the coal being dropped into the wagons after climbing the ramp. The size of the basket was not very large and several trips were made by each person. This was a slow process and filling up a KC wagon with a capacity of 23.67 tons took several hours. Loading a wagon which could carry two and a half times the cargo naturally took a much longer time. The labourers who would load the wagon were available from early morning till evening and thereafter the loading stopped. In the case of loading of top covered wagons, the process slowed down even further as the loader had to enter the wagons to access the interior of the wagon. Supply of wagons for loading the coal would have to be done overnight so that loading could commence early morning. This was an additional constraint imposed on the railway system.

There were very few colliery sidings which could accommodate a full train (called 'rake', in railway parlance). Consequently, wagons were supplied at several sidings and then taken to the nearest railway marshalling yard[39] for formation of a train. This was another time consuming process which resulted in wastage of transport capacity.

The eastern part of India, where the major coalfields are located, is a high rainfall area. There is a considerable drop in production of coal during the monsoon season from June to September. The seasonal fluctuation in loading is also responsible for creating additional burden on the transport capacity during the October to March period (March being the end of the financial year in India). This issue had been commented on by the Mahindra Committee Report too.

---

[39] Marshalling Yard: in railways marshalling yards are locations with multiple lines where wagons for various destinations would be collected, then sorted individually for each direction or destination after which a train would be formed for despatch to a particular destination. Incoming trains with wagons for various destinations would be sorted in a similar manner.

For higher volume of coal transportation, these systems needed to be replaced by round the clock mechanical loading arrangements, which loaded the wagons quickly and round the clock in all seasons.

Coordination with Railways for Distribution of Coal

In July 1964, the Government announced that the lower grades of coal (i.e. Grade II and below) were being taken out of the purview of the Coal Controller. This freedom resulted in a surge in the demand for rail transport of coal. In some cases, the demands were speculative in nature. To keep a control on the movement of the coal, and discourage speculative indents for wagons, the Indian Railways decided to continue with the system allotment of wagons after sponsorship of a consumer by a government authority, as in the past. In 1967, the Government decided to decontrol all grades of non-coking coal. At this time also, to protect the interests of the essential industries and preclude speculative demand, the Ministry of Railways decided to continue with the system of sponsorship of consumers (Ghosh Vol II, 1977, p. 279).

With the decontrol of non-coking coal by the Government in 1967, a railway officer, who had been attached to the office of the Coal Controller, shifted to the headquarters office of the Eastern Railway at Calcutta, and was designated as Joint Director, Coal. The work of receiving the sponsorship of various industries, accepting, issuing loading programmes and allotting the wagons for rail movement on a day-to-day basis was taken over by the railways. This office was later upgraded to Director, Rail Movement (DMR) in 1973 and later to Executive Director, Rail Movement (EDRM) in 1986.

Allotment of Railway Wagons for Coal Movement

The railways adhered to the earlier procedure for deciding allocation of coal. A consumer would have to be recognised by a government authority and consumers were segregated between core and non-core sectors. The allotment of railway wagons for consumers was finalised after going through a detailed exercise. As mentioned earlier, the Preferential Traffic Schedule (PTS) issued by the Ministry of Railways put coal under priority C. The PTS laid down a number of conditions for allocation of railway wagons for coal loading. Some of the important conditions were:

- Coal would include anthracite coal, bituminous coal, lignite coal, peat and other form of carbonaceous matter, sold or marketed as coal and also coke from colliery sidings, steel plants, washeries, coke oven plants, imported coal.

- Coal would be loaded only from a siding notified for outward booking of coal by the Railway Board.
- The programmes would have to be approved/ accepted by Railway Board/ Railways Director (Movement), Railways, Calcutta.
- Loading of coal would be in accordance with the programmes sanctioned or recommended by any authority and approved by the Railway Board.
- The programmes would have to be in accordance with the rationalised pattern of movement applicable to each coalfield. This could change from time to time depending on the policies of the railways.

The PTS also had a number of clauses which mentioned, inter alia, that (a) the list of sponsoring authorities would be as given in an annexure to the PTS, (b) the acceptance of a programme or the issue of a sanction would not guarantee either allotment or the supply of wagons, (c) the period of validity of a sanctioned programme would be laid down by the DMR from time to time (d) allotment and supply of wagons would be regulated in accordance with the availability of coal and operational exigencies, (e) allotment of wagons could be cancelled by the DMR, (f) allotment of wagons would not guarantee their supply (g) DMR had the power to allot wagons on 'out of turn' basis if a consumer was in distress.

At the beginning of each calendar year, the Director Rail Movement (DMR) called a meeting of all the sponsoring authorities from the states. The states were usually represented at these meetings by the Director of Industries (DIs). The representatives of the coal companies, steel plants and power companies also attended the meetings. Later, the demand of the industries in the core sector, i.e. defence, power, steel, cement and fertiliser were communicated separately to DMR's office. Demand for loco coal was communicated by the Railway Ministry to DMR.

The states provided a list of the industries requiring coal and mentioned, for each industry, the product manufactured, the quantity of coal required per year, the field from which they would like to draw the coal, and the grade of coal required by each industry. The coal was also divided in to two categories, 'steam' and 'slack'. Steam coal was lumpy in size and was used mainly for old boilers and for use in the locomotives of the railways.

The representatives of the coal companies responded to the demands of the states. If the demand was too high, the states were asked to prune it down. The same procedure was followed for the central sponsoring authorities, though they were given higher preference in allocation. After this, a matrix of the demand from each of the coalfields was prepared by the railways to examine whether it would be feasible to move the demanded quantities from the fields of choice. If not, then some adjustments were done in consultation with the coal companies and the states. A month wise breakup for each industry and each state would be prepared and shared with the coal companies and the DIs of the states.

The next stage was that the various sponsoring authorities sent their programmes for movement for a particular month or quarter to the coal companies from which movement was desired. The signatures of three persons authorised to submit the demand of the industry to the coal company and the railway had to be attested by the sponsoring authority.

After examination, the coal company would endorse the quantity of coal they were willing to provide. This endorsement on the programme was called 'consent'. After the consent, the programme would be sent to the office of the DMR for allotment of wagons. In the case of programmes for industries, the requirement was that the programmes for a particular month, along with consent, should be deposited with the DMR's office by the end of the preceding month and certainly not later than the first week of the current month. This discipline was required to ensure that the coal companies and railways got adequate time to satisfy the demands placed by the industries. The submitted programmes were scrutinised for their congruence with the programming pattern agreed at the beginning of the year. Thereafter, the programme was 'sanctioned' by the railways and became eligible for allotment of wagons.

The allotment of wagons was done on a cycle of 48 hours, (for example, the allotment of wagons for Monday of a particular week would be done on Saturday), the coal company would make an 'offer' for loading of coal on a particular day from various railway sidings in a coalfield. The offer would indicate the number of wagons to be loaded, whether the coal was steam or slack coal, its grade, and the industry for which was being offered. The list of industries was very large. The 'offer' from the coal company mentioned industries such as defence, railways, power, steel, cement, fertiliser, (in the core sector) and other industries such as pottery, glass, silk, rayon, heavy chemicals, light chemicals, paper, newsprint, brick kilns and several others for the non-core category.

A typical 'offer' from a coal company operating in the Raniganj coalfield for allotment of wagons, would state, for example, Siding XX, slack coal, grade Y, for pottery/ glass industry of a particular state, say Uttar Pradesh. The office of the DMR would examine the offer and depending on the feasibility of movement and the overall demand matrix, could possibly allot wagons for the pottery or glass industry in Uttar Pradesh. After the allotment was conveyed to the relevant railway division, the supply of wagons for loading on the date of allotment would be arranged. There was a detailed procedure for the validity of allotted rakes, defining the time within which the rake demanded by the consumer would have to be allotted, or else, the demand would lapse.

The overall scheme of rationalisation of railway movement determined broadly the direction of movement of coal from a particular coalfield. For example, the coal from Raniganj, Jharia or Karanpura coalfields would generally move to destinations in the east, northeast, north and northwest India, while coal from Korba and Kore-Rewa would generally move to the west and coal from Talcher to the south.

The office of the DMR was in charge of 'sanctioning' the programmes for all coalfields and imported coal, but allotment of coal was done only for the Bengal-Bihar coalfields (Raniganj, Jharia, Karanpura and Singrauli) and the privately owned mines of TISCO and IISCO. The allotment for Korba, Talcher and the outlying fields was done by the respective zonal railways. The office of the DMR also issued sanctions for movement of imported coal. Sanctions were, however, not issued for coal movement from the coalfields in Assam which came under the jurisdiction of the North East Frontier Railway. This was due to a judicial pronouncement following a court case.

At the beginning of each year, the office of the DMR would issue a policy circular laying down the guidelines for acceptance of programmes, issue of sanctions, allotment and other issues such as rules change of destination, if requested by a consumer, change of the coalfield from which the sanction had been obtained and a host of other issues. During the year subsidiary circulars would continue to be issued as problems were brought to the notice of the coal companies and the railways by the consumers.

The DMR was assisted by two officers, one in charge of programming, and the other for allotment. Scheduled meetings with the consumers were held once a quarter.

The entire job was quite complex, especially at the time of shortages of coal and /or railway capacity, as allocation would have to be pruned while keeping parity amongst a large number of consumers. This complex work was done manually with a dedicated team of staff and officers, generally to the satisfaction of all.

Later, in the 1990s, the power of allotment of railway wagons on a day-to-day basis was shifted to the divisions.

Given the provisions of the PTS, the Indian Railways virtually became the distributor of the coal. Allotment of coal would be governed not only by the 'offers' for loading from the coal companies, but also by the requirements and constraints of freight operations. A general guideline for allotment on a daily basis would be received prior to the allotment from the office of the Chief Operating Superintendent (COPS) of Eastern Railway, whose jurisdiction covered the Raniganj, Jharia, Bokaro, Karanpura and Singrauli coalfields. As the allotment process generated traffic for various directions and feasibility of movement of the loaded coal wagons had to be factored in at the time of allotment, the recommendations would form the general guideline for the purposes of allotment. For example, if the clearance for the north was inadequate and traffic had piled up, allotment for consumers in that direction would be regulated. This was an extremely important aspect of the functioning of the office of the DMR.

The allotment process being fairly complex, consumers operating factories far away from the coalfields were unable to remain up to date with the developments at Calcutta and remained unaware of the likely time of their demands coming to fruition. They, therefore, depended on middlemen or 'coal agents' who ran a thriving business in Calcutta. These agents undertook the work of submission of programmes on behalf of the consumers, of ensuring that the sanction of the programme was not delayed and keeping a watch on the process of allotment. They would regularly brief the consumers about the updated status.

There was also an issue of the quality of coal delivered to the consumer. Complaints about slippage in the grade of coal supplied were not uncommon. The agents, therefore, also undertook the task of supervising the loading of the coal consignments and ensuring that the proper quality of coal was loaded and transported after due weighment. With all these services being provided, the business of the agents was fairly lucrative. They formed various associations such as the Indian Coal Consumers' Association, Indian Coal Merchants Association, which represented the requirements of the consumers at various fora, including the headquarters offices of the railway zones, the coal companies and even the ministries in Delhi.

Decades later, in the era of liberalisation, the role of the office of EDRM would get pruned considerably. After the success of a system of computer-based allocation of iron ore loading, the programming and allocation of coal was also sought to be based on a software developed in house by the Railways around 2010.

Performance during the Third Five Year Plan

As mentioned earlier, the Third Five Year Plan ran into rough weather virtually from its beginning. Other than the two wars, there were severe droughts in 1965–66 and 1966–67 which affected the agricultural sector very badly and forced India to import huge shipments of food grain and other agricultural products. Industrial growth was poor and so was the overall growth of the economy. There was virtually no increase in the per capita income during the five-year period (1961–66). Major industries suffered from lack of demand and reported idle capacities. The production of coal reached a level of only 67.7 mt in 1965–66 against a target of 97 mt. Due to a fall in demand emanating from the slowing down of the industrial sector, the freight loading of Indian Railways which had been projected at 245 mt, reached a level of 203 mt and 117 billion tonne kilometres in 1965–66. The average lead of traffic on IR increased, though, from 564 kms to 576 kms.

After the Third Five Year Pan there were three Annual Plans during the years 1966–1969. These three years are usually referred to as the years of Plan Holiday. This term is a misnomer, as the Annual Plans were adopted as the country had gone through a period of turmoil due to external aggression and failure of monsoon. In order to bridge the trade deficit and encourage exports, the Government took the bold decision of devaluing the Indian Rupee in June 1966.

The economic condition improved slowly and by 1969, the total freight movement of Indian Railways had improved to 207.9 mt against an anticipated loading of 211 mt. The capacity of the Indian Railways for freight movement, at that time, seemed to be ahead of the demand.

Railway Finance: Higher Dividend Payment

For the Indian Railways, the economic hardship faced by the country not only affected the freight loading adversely, but also resulted in the Parliament increasing the dividend payout rate to the government from 4.25 per cent to 4.5 per cent from February 1963. The rate was further increased to 5.75 per cent in February 1964 for all capital invested in the railways after 31 March 1964. The Railway Convention Committee (RCC) of 1965 recommended that the rate should be further increased from 5.75 to 6 per cent. The payout of the dividend by the railways to the government on capital invested is in perpetuity. That is, the dividend had to be paid till the asset had depreciated and had been taken off the books. Hence, the increase in the rate from 4.25 to 6 per cent in a short period impacted the finances of the railways adversely, and for a long time to come. Some experts have pointed out that the railways did not have to pay dividend on investment in strategic lines and investment in the north east. Hence, the actual percentage of dividend paid by the railways is less than that mandated by the RCC. The assertion is true. However, the investment for strategic lines and the north east vary from year to year, and so does the financial load on the railways.

Power Sector

The development of energy sources within the country was one of the major focus areas of the Third Plan. Owing to the abundant coal reserves in the country, setting up of coal fired thermal power generation was an obvious choice. The Plan document observed that:

> Installation of large thermal units employing higher steam temperatures and pressures would result not only in increased thermal efficiencies but also in reduction of capital costs per kW of installed capacity. The thermal efficiencies attainable with modern plants of 30, 60, 100 and 120 MW units are of the order of 26, 29, 32 and 34 percent respectively. The capital cost per kW of installed capacity of 120 MW units is about 20 percent cheaper than for 30 MW units. In India the overall efficiency of thermal power stations in 1959–60 was 19.5 percent because many of the units were small and old. With the general adoption and operation of larger units, the overall thermal efficiency is expected to improve considerably, thus enabling more kilowatt-hours to be produced from each ton of coal utilised. (Planning Commission, 1961, Chapter 24, Para 39)

This marked the beginning of the coal based thermal power programme in real earnest, a path that has led India to be one of the largest generators of coal-based power in the world. As the programme developed and gathered momentum, demand for coal movement by railways increased rapidly.

Major Changes in Government Policy

The Fourth Five Year Plan covered the years 1969–74. The Government of India under the leadership of Prime Minister Indira Gandhi, was steering the country towards the path of creating an egalitarian society. Fourteen private banks had been nationalised in 1969. The general elections for the Parliament, held in March 1971, saw the Congress Party led by Mrs. Indira Gandhi win a very large majority. Having been reassured of the faith of the people in her leadership, the Prime Minister introduced further changes.

In the introduction to the Fourth Plan, the Prime Minister had observed that the '*… nationalisation of the fourteen banks is evidence of our determination to bring greater volume of resources within the area of social decision.*' She further added that

> there can be no doubt that the responsibilities devolving upon the public sector – without diminishing those of the private sector, in our mixed economy – will grow in range in range and volume. Socialism involves a reordering of society on a rational and equitable basis and this can only be achieved by assigning an expanding role to the public sector. Following the reorganisation of credit policies resulting from the nationalization of major banks, the public sector can be expected more and more to occupy the commanding heights of the economy. It alone would be in a position to undertake investments of the requisite magnitude in such industries of vital importance to us as steel, machinery, machine tools, power generation, ship building, petrochemicals, fuels and drugs. (Planning Commission, 1969, Introduction)

This policy pronouncement, made in 1970, was followed by a series of administrative actions of far-reaching consequences for the economy and gave the economy a direction which would affect the future operational strategy of the Indian Railways. The estimate of demand for freight movement by the end of the Plan for Indian Railways was planned at 280 mt. However, in December 1971, there was another war with Pakistan, which resulted in the creation of Bangladesh as a new nation. Prior to the war India received a massive influx of refugees from East Pakistan, who were fleeing from the atrocities against them. During the war, the eastern theatre of the country was taken up by military movements of the highest priority. This resulted in the slowdown of coal evacuation from the eastern states which were the largest coal producers. The freight target for railways for the Fourth Plan was reduced from 280 mt to 240 mt.

Owing to the shortfall in traffic, an impression was created that the investment in the Railways had been rather high. The Railway Convention Committee 1971 (Fifth Report submitted in April 1973) regarding requirement and availability of wagons was quite critical of the progress of wagon supply for coal loading on the railways. The Public Accounts Committee (1967) and the Railway Convention Committee (1971) urged the Ministry of Railways to plan the freight loading targets realistically, as resources were scarce and over investment in Railways was not desirable. The RCC observed while the originating freight traffic dropped from the original estimate of 265 mt to 215 mt, but the financial allocation was reduced from Rs. 1525 crores to Rs. 1400 crores only. It was regrettable that the capital expenditure in creating traffic capacity for railways was in excess of requirements. Scarce resources could have been gainfully utilised elsewhere (Railway Convention Committee, 1971, para 1.22).

The Ministry of Railways responded by pointing out that the true index of traffic output was net tonne kilometres and not originating tonnage. The railways achieved 150 billion tonnes kilometres against a target of 152 billion tonnes kilometres, which was very close to the target (Railway Convention Committee, 1973, Fifth Report, Para 1.29).

There was a severe drought in the country in 1972–73, which affected the agricultural output adversely. The sharp increase in global oil prices in 1973, together with other economic forces unleashed a severe inflation which resulted in diversion of resources from investment in infrastructure to public welfare.

The finances of the railway had come under considerable strain due to the factors mentioned in the foregoing paragraphs. The RCC of 1971 (Sixth Report submitted in April, 1973) recognised this, but kept the dividend payment to the government at 4.5 per cent on Capital borrowed up to 1964 plus a 1 per cent in lieu of passenger tax. For funds borrowed after 31 March 1964, the rate of dividend would be 6 per cent. Other features of providing relief on investment in strategic lines and in the northeast would continue.

Nationalisation of Coking and Non-Coking Coal

Coking Coal

In keeping with the stated objective of the Government controlling the commanding heights of the economy, the production of coking coal was brought under the ambit of the government in two phases. The first action of the Government was the promulgation of the Coking Coal Mines (Emergency Provisions) Act in October 1972. This Act provided for the taking over of private coal mines, in public interest, by the Government. The Coking Coal Mines (Nationalisation) Act of 1972 brought the coking coal mines under Government control and management with effect from 1 May 1972. The only exceptions were the coking coal mines owned by the Tata Iron and Steel Company (TISCO) and the Indian Iron and Steel Company (IISCO), as they were captive mines for the manufacture of steel at the TISCO plant at Jamshedpur in Bihar (now Jharkhand) and IISCO plant at Burnpur in West Bengal. The nationalised coking coal companies were put under one umbrella and the company was named the Bharat Coking Coal Company Ltd. or BCCL. More drastic action was to follow.

Non-coking Coal

In his book named Coal Industry in India, published posthumously after his tragic death in an air accident on 31 May 1973, S. Kumaramangalam, Minister for Steel and Mines, wrote in detail about the problems facing the coal industry in India and why bringing the industry under the control of the government was the only hope of increasing coal production to meet the challenges of a rapidly growing economy. Some of the issues mentioned in the book (Kumaramangalam, 1973) are:

1. The private mine operators did not follow rigorous safety procedures and compelled the worker to work in dangerous and unhygienic conditions.
2. As coal production expanded and mines became deep, the dangers workers were exposed to became greater. There was no permanent employment and payment was extremely poor.
3. Owing to leasing out of land in small parcels, many of the mines were extremely small and used dangerous methods of extracting coal.
4. The Coalfields Committee of 1920 had recommended the setting up of a Controlling Authority to regulate the issue of new leases. The Committee further had recommended that coal, being a non-renewable resource,

needed to be conserved and mined scientifically and this could be done only by the government.

5. The Coal Mining Committee, which submitted its report in 1937, had noted that the private mine owners placed their commercial and profit interests above those of safe mining. The Committee had observed that the state of affairs in the coal mining industry was indeed serious and urged immediate action for rationalisation and control of production, which could be an alternative to nationalisation. Two members of the Committee, Dr. Nag and Dr. M. S. Krishnan, had stated clearly that state ownership was the only long-term solution.
6. The consensus of the Committee had been that the coal industry did not have any tradition of investment for development. Nor did it have any tradition of scientific mining. Demand fluctuations were addressed through ad hoc measures of slaughter mining during rising demand and exploitation of workers during low demand. The book of the late Minister for Coal quoted a damning paragraph from the Report of the Coal Mining Committee. The Committee had recorded:

   > the coal trade in India has been rather like a race in which profit has always come in first, with safety, a poor second, sound methods an 'also ran' and national welfare a 'dead horse' entered perhaps, but never likely to start. Neither the Government nor landlords can escape responsibility for allowing this state of affairs to prevail for so long, but this does not alter the facts nor, still less, will it justify further inaction on the part of all concerned. (Quoted in Kumaramangalam, 1973, p. 28)

7. The findings of the Mahindra Committee (1945) were not much different from those of earlier committees. However, the terms of reference were wider and the Committee touched upon a large range of issues. The workings of uneconomic mines in Raniganj and Jharia areas were noted and the need for a sound and methodical mineral policy was recommended. The Mahindra Committee had also emphasised the need for conservation of coking coal and that its use should be restricted to the industries which needed it exclusively. They had further recommended that scientific mining of both coking and non-coking coal was inescapable. Although the Committee did not recommend nationalisation of the industry, it did advocate state control. The findings of the earlier committees regarding uneconomic mines, unsafe practices and exploitation of workers were endorsed.
8. The government had failed to act on the recommendations of the Mahindra Committee as those were turbulent times leading to the Independence of India in 1947.

9. The government of independent India set up, in 1951, an organisation named the Working Party for the Coal Industry. This organisation consisted of representatives from the coal industry, the workers and the government. The objective was to report on the status of small collieries. The report of the Working Party mentioned that, while the Indian Mining Federation and the Indian Colliery Owners' Association agreed that amalgamation of the small mines would be beneficial, they preferred this amalgamation to be voluntary. The Working Party's report recommended that government should enact legislation to merge uneconomic coal mines. No action had been taken by the government on this report.
10. In 1954–55 the Estimates Committee of the Lok Sabha, after examining detailed evidence concluded that in the long run the coal industry would have to be nationalised. However, at that time the government did not have sufficient technically trained manpower at its disposal to take over this gigantic task. Hence, the decision was that the process would move in measured steps. The Estimates Committee provided very cogent suggestions such as: (a) a coal commission should be set up immediately. (b) all new mines should be state owned and under the control of the Coal Commission. (c) as far as possible, all private mines producing metallurgical or high-grade coal should be brought under state control. (d) It recommended that the Government should lay down strict conditions regarding capital investment for increasing production to limits set by the state, use scientific methods of mining, introduce mechanisation and safe mining methods and follow government guidelines regarding the working conditions of mining labour. All collieries which did not conform to these standards should be taken over by the state.
11. The Government did not act on the recommendations of the Estimates Committee. Instead, it appointed in November 1955, another committee under the chairmanship of B. Mehta to examine the issue of amalgamation of collieries in depth. The report of the Mehta Committee, submitted in September 1956, painted a rather grim picture of the state of the mining industry in Bengal and Bihar. It stated that in there were 734 small mines in Bengal and Bihar of which 259 produced less than 600 tonnes of coal per month and there were 475 collieries which produced less than 2500 tonnes of coal per month.
12. The Government had accepted the recommendations of the Mehta Committee but decided to defer action on it till the middle of the Third Five Year Plan as production of coal at the beginning of the Second Five Year Plan could not be disturbed. Amalgamation of collieries was to proceed

voluntarily. The progress of this voluntary amalgamation was rather tardy and in the next 14 years, only 130 small mines were amalgamated into 59 units.

13. Estimates by experts had shown that the reserves of coking and blendable coal at current estimates would last only 50 years. The Mehta committee's recommendation of amalgamation of small mines would unlock the coal between the barriers of the collieries. The private mine operators were quite unmindful of the damage that they were causing and paid scant attention to the appeals for scientific mining.
14. The Government therefore decided to take over the coking coal mines in 1971.
15. The Fuel Policy Committee appointed by the Government submitted a report in 1972, which pointed to the small reserves of petroleum and emphasised that coal should be the primary fuel to power the economy towards long term growth. Based on a perspective plan drawn up by the Planning commission, the requirement of coal in 1978–79 would be 165 million tonnes, of which 43 mt would be coking coal and 122 Mt non-coking coal. The implication was the demand would double in about 7 years. An increase in production of this magnitude would call for massive investments and organisational improvements. After the takeover of the coking coal mines the owners of the non-coking coal mines had continued to resort to unsafe mining practices and exploitation of labour. Their financial position did not appear to be strong enough to undertake the magnitude of investments required.

> Further, private sector collieries defaulted in the payment of royalty and other dues to the State Governments and the deposits of provident fund; the amounts withheld by the private collieries were around the staggering figure of Rs. 30 crores. (Kumaramangalam, 1973, p. 44)

16. The overall situation made it clear to the Government that a takeover of the non-coking coal mines on the same lines as coking coal was warranted.

An Act named the Coal Mines (Taking over of Management) Act was promulgated in 1973. This Act gave the central government the power to take over the management of coking and non-coking coal mines in seven states in India. These included the coking coal mines which had already been nationalised. The Coal Mines (Nationalisation) of 1 May 1973 formally nationalised all the coal mines in the seven states. The nationalised mines were initially brought under the Coal Mines Authority Limited (CMAL), with headquarters at Kolkata. CMAL had four divisions, Eastern, Western,

> Central and CMPDIL (Central Mine Planning and Design Institute Limited) which was the research and designs organisation. The coal mines under the NCDC were brought under the Central Division (CCL). Later the BCCL, NCDC and CMAL were merged into one holding company named Coal India Ltd, with effect from 1 November 1975. The subsidiary companies under Coal India Ltd. were Eastern Coalfields (ECL), BCCL, CCL, Western Coalfields (WCL). The geographical spread of WCL and CCL was rather large and the government had ambitious plans of increasing coal production rapidly. Hence, to provide better managerial control, two new companies the South Eastern Coalfields (SECL) and the Northern Coalfields (NCL) were formed in 1985 by taking out areas from WCL and CCL respectively. The South Eastern Coalfields had jurisdiction over the Kore-Rewa, Korba and the Mand Raigarh coalfields, while the Northern Coalfields had jurisdiction over the Singrauli coalfields. Again in 1992, the Mahanadi Coalfields (MCL) was formed with jurisdiction over the Talcher and Ib Valley coalfields, by taking out the coal bearing areas from the ambit of CCL. Hence CIL now had 8 subsidiary companies, namely, ECL, BCCL, CCL, NCL, SECL, WCL, MCL and CMPDIL. The ninth entity is the coalfields in the northeast, controlled directly by CIL under the unit North Eastern Coalfields.

It is perhaps significant that both the dates of nationalisation of the coking and non-coking coal mines were the 1st of May, which is celebrated as the International Workers' Day. The then Minister in charge for the Ministry of Coal, late S. Mohan Kumaramangalam, was a great champion of labour rights.

The Singareni Collieries did not come under the ambit of nationalisation at it was a public sector undertaking with 59 per cent share of the Government of Andhra Pradesh and 40 per cent with the Government of India. At the time of the nationalisation of the non-coking coal mines, the production of Singareni was about 5 mt of coal.

The share of the production of CIL in the total coal production of the country from the time of nationalisation remained in the region of 84 to 85 per cent. This was because, other than the coalfields brought under the umbrella of CIL, there was only another coal producer of significance, namely, the Singareni coalfields in Andhra Pradesh.

The production achieved by the new organisation Coal India Limited as the holding company for all coking and non-coking coal mines in seven states in 1973–74 was 69.9 mt and it increased by 9 mt to reach 78.99 mt in 1974–75.

The share of the states which were major coal producers in the 1970s is presented below in Table 3.5.

Table 3.5: Coal Production in India – State wise Data 1971–76 (in million tonnes)

	Andhra Pradesh	Bihar	Madhya Pradesh	Maharashtra	Orissa	Tamil Nadu	West Bengal	Total (including other minor states)	Bengal and Bihar as Per cent of Total
1971	4.6	32.8	13.4	2.1	1.5	3.7	17.3	75.6	66.2
1976	7.9	42.4	20.1	3.6	2.1	3.9	24	104.6	63.5

Source: Statistics of Mines in India, Vol 1 (Coal), 2011, 2014. (Last column added by author)

It is clear that Bihar and West Bengal continued to be the main coal producers, and hence the strain on the railway transportation system continued.

The decision of nationalisation was welcomed by the managers and workers of the coal industry, though not by its erstwhile owners. The management challenge that was faced by Coal India Ltd. can only be referred to as gargantuan. The corporate headquarters at Calcutta and the subsidiary companies would have to put in place new administrative systems, management structures, improve technology, train manpower and deliver a level of production to match the aspirations of the country. A very large level of investment would be required, which was expected to be provided by the government.

Grading of Coal

Another area where a significant change came about post nationalisation, was in the grading of coal. Prior to the First World War, coal was not graded. After the setting up of the Coal Grading Board in 1925, a broad categorisation was introduced. However, coal continued to be sold generally on the basis of the experience of the users about quality of coal from various collieries. After the imposition of controlled distribution of coal through the Coal Controller during the Second World War, the grades of coal were as follows:

Selected A, Selected B, Grade I, Grade II and Grade III. The Coal Grading Board (1925) Act was abolished in 1959 through the Coal Grading Board (Repeal) Act. However, these classifications continued to be used in the Five-Year Plan documents of the government to set coal production targets.

After the nationalisation of coal mines in 1973, the grading and pricing came under the control of the Ministry of Coal, Government of India and/ or Coal India Ltd.

The grades were converted to the system of using the Useful Heat Value (UHV) of the coal. In an article in the journal Vikalpa, of the Indian Institute of Management, Ahmedabad, India, the authors Tiwari, Bhattacharya and Raghav note that:

> UHV took into account the heat trapped in ash (A) produced by burning the coal and the heat lost in removing the moisture (M) while burning the coal. Equal importance was assigned to the heat loss arising out of ash and moisture contents.
>
> For coal with high moisture content: UHV = 8900 – 138 (A + M) (1). For coal with low moisture and low volatile matter (VM) content: UHV = 8900 – 138 (A + M) – 150 (19 – VM) (2)
>
> The value of 8,900 kcal/kg adopted as the upper limit in Equations 1 and 2, represented the maximum heat value of Indian coal determined on pure coal basis. (Tiwari, Bhattacharya, Raghav, March 2015)

This marked the beginning of a more scientific system of grading coal. The move from UHV to Gross Calorific Value (GCV) would take place much later in 2011.

Coal was categorised under the UHV system into grades from A to G and the prices for each grade were announced by the Ministry of Coal at the beginning of each financial year. The prices for each grade were further divided into prices for steam coal and rubble, slack coal and washery middlings and run of mine coal (ROM). The UHV for different grades as laid down by the Ministry of Coal were:

Grade A: Exceeding 6200
Grade B: Exceeding 5600 but not exceeding 6200
Grade C: Exceeding 4940 but not exceeding 5600
Grade D: Exceeding 4200 but not exceeding 4940
Grade E: Exceeding 3360 but not exceeding 4200
Grade F: Exceeding 2400 but not exceeding 3360
Grade G: Exceeding 1300 but not exceeding 2400

There were separate prices for grades from A to D 'long flame coal', the prices being much higher.

Planning for Movement of Coal for Industries

One major development which had taken place with respect to coal movement was the formation in 1973 of the Short-Term and Long-Term Coal Linkage committees under the aegis of the Ministry of Coal. This step was taken to provide predictability of movement of coal to major customers, and would also benefit the coal mining industry and the railways. With this step, the efficiency of coal movement was expected to improve. The Committees consisted of representatives from the coal mining companies, Departments of Coal and Industrial Development, Ministry of Railways, Central Electricity Authority and Planning Commission. The Short-term Standing Coal Linkage Committee (SLC) met once in a quarter and finalised the movement of coal to the Railways, Power stations, Cement plants and Fertiliser plants. The quantum of coal to be consumed by each power station and the sources from which the coal would be moved was finalised with concurrence from the coal companies and the railways. This then became a stable matrix for movement over a quarter, which would not be disturbed except in the case of emergencies.

The Long-Term Linkage Committee met once in six months to discuss the coal movement matrix for new plants expected to come up in the near future.

In the month of May 1974, there was a general strike in the Railways, which lasted for 20 days. Services were severely affected during this period. Though the strike was ended through government initiative, several issues raised by the workers remained unresolved. The overall industrial relations situation in the country was not very peaceful, particularly in the eastern part of the country.

The V Plan (1974–78) was prepared at a time when the Indian economy was being buffeted by external forces, notably the sharp increase in oil prices which sent shock waves round the world. In her address to the National Development Council in September 1976, the Prime Minister stated:

> The presentation of the draft Fifth Plan unfortunately coincided with a major upheaval on the international economic scene which profoundly affected developed and developing countries. Economists and political leaders all over the world were reminded of the collapse of the international economic order in the thirties. The sharp increase in the prices of food, fertilisers and oil seriously upset the assumptions on which the draft Fifth Plan had been framed. These new developments also lent urgency to a time-bound programme of action in order to achieve a measure of self-reliance in food and energy. All other objectives had to be subordinated to the control of inflationary pressures caused by domestic as well as international factors. In the middle of 1974–75 we formulated an anti-inflationary programme which called for several hard decisions on the part of Central and State Governments. Our success in curbing inflation attracted world-wide notice. (Planning Commission, 1974, Foreword)

Imposition of Emergency and thereafter

Very soon, the political conditions in the country would be in the throes of unprecedented events. In 1975, the Prime Minister alleged that there was a serious threat to the internal security of the nation, and used an extraordinary provision contained in the Constitution of India to declare a state of Emergency in the nation from 25th June 1975. Under the Emergency rule, many civic liberties were curtailed and many political leaders were imprisoned. The state of Emergency was lifted on 21 March 1977. Though some authors claim that the organs of the government functioned very efficiently during the Emergency, the fact is that an atmosphere of trepidation was palpable.

Following the withdrawal of the state of emergency rule in the country, general elections were held in 1977 and the Congress party led by Indira Gandhi was defeated. A new coalition party named the Janata Party came to power. It called for a slew of reforms to veer away from the path of economic development adopted by the earlier government. The Fifth Five Year Plan was repudiated and replaced by a 'Rolling Plan', which aimed at flexible planning with short term, medium, term and long term horizons. The slogan was to move away from the Nehruvian model of investing in major industries and focus instead on small scale industries for the generation of employment. Another area of major emphasis was the agricultural sector, which in the view of the then elected Government, had been neglected.

Such unsettled political conditions could not fail to affect the industrial atmosphere. The performance of the coal industry and the railways during the second half of the decade of 1970s was quite dismal as would be seen from the following data in Table 3.6.

Table 3.6: Production of Coal and Transportation by Railways 1976–80

	Production of Coal and Lignite in Million tonnes						Revenue Freight Loading By Railways in mt	Coal Loading in mt by Railways
Year	Coal				Lignite	Total		
1	2	3	4	5	6	7	8	
	Coking Coal							
	Metallurgical	Non-Metallurgical	Non-Coking	Total	Lignite	Coal+ Lignite		
1975–76	22.19	7.93	69.51	99.63	3.03	102.66	196.8	64.3
1976–77	23.65	8.18	69.16	100.99	4.02	105.01	212.6	67.4
1977–78	23.33	8.10	69.65	100.98	3.58	104.56	210.8	69.1
1978–79	22.54	8.67	70.74	101.95	3.30	105.25	199.6	64.1
1979–80	24.19	6.68	73.07	103.94	2.90	106.84	193.1	62.0

Source: Economic Survey, 2002 and Indian Railway Key Statistics 1970–71 to 2012–13.

The production of coal increased from 102 to 106 mt and the freight loading of the railways actually registered some increase and then dropped to a level of 193 mt in 1978–79, which was below the level achieved in 1975–76. Clearly, the performance was a far cry from the Fifth Plan target for freight loading of 260 mt (with 98 mt coal) for 1978–79, the terminal year.

The decade ended on another dismal note as a severe drought in 1979–80 reduced agricultural production by about 16 per cent. Industrial production also declined marginally.

The decade from 1970 to 1980 had not been very productive in terms of output of either the coal industry or the railways. The coal industry had gone through a momentous change in its administrative structure and was grappling with the change. The Indian Railways was also going through a transition in its management practices and technology to keep abreast of the demands of the growing economy. Both the industries would have to face greater challenges in terms of output and availability of finances in the future.

The Economic Survey for 1980–81 identified the issues in the coal industry as shortage of power, disturbed law and order situation in the eastern region and low productivity of manpower due to use of obsolete technology. The Survey reported that CIL had attributed a loss in production of 13 mt of coal in 1979–80 due to power shortages, labour related issues and absenteeism. Improving the power supply position, introduction of modern machinery, skilling of labour and better administrative control were required. Help of the State governments would have to be sought for ensuring peaceful working conditions for the industry.

Though the installed capacity of power generation had increased from 1,360 megawatts (mw) in 1947 to 26680 mw at the end of the Fifth Plan, yet shortage of power had emerged as a critical component affecting the development of the country. Actions would be initiated soon to accelerate power generation, wherein coal would be a main component and railways would be the principal carrier. This initiative would have major repercussions for both railways and the coal industry, as would be seen later.

In the case of the railways, the Survey noted the transport capacity of the railways had not increased commensurately to keep pace with demand. This was mainly due to inadequate investments during the previous decade. Much of the assets of the Railway were old and required replacement. The old assets were creating maintenance and operational problems. On the demand side, the average lead of foodgrain and fertiliser movement had increased, and there was greater requirement for loading of coal. The Survey mentioned the inadequacy of investment in the railways. It stated:

> Para 3.41 At a time when the demand for transport has been expanding, with changing traffic configurations, the railways have suffered from a prolonged period of under-investment during the last decade. This among other things resulted in postponement of replacement of wagons, track etc. and progressive build-up of heavy arrears of replacement ... In this respect the problems of railways are substantially different from those of the other sectors where fairly large investments have been made in the past to permit expansion of capacity. By contrast, the existing capital stock of the railways is worn out and in need of replacement. Track renewals have not been carried out to the extent necessary, and there is inadequacy of line capacity in many areas.
>
> 3.42 There is a similar problem as far as the rolling stock is concerned. The stock of wagons has not increased at a rapid rate for the past several years ... If the perspective plan targets are to be attained it will be necessary to achieve a much higher rate of growth.
>
> 3.43 Improved Railway performance in the coming years is, therefore, critically dependent upon achieving a very substantial step up in investment and modernisation in this sector. The rate at which this can be done will be inevitably constrained by the overall availability of resources. It is essential, therefore, to maximise the effectiveness with which resources earmarked for expansion and modernisation for the Railways are utilised. (Economic Survey, 1981, para: 3.41–3.43)

Pointing to other reasons for the shortfall in movement, the Survey also stated that the use of overaged assets was not the only reason for loss of freight loading. The industrial relations within the railways also needed to be improved. The survey continued to state that in the past, passenger traffic had been accorded higher priority than freight. This was apparent as passenger traffic continued to increase when freight loading was declining. As passenger and freight trains run on the same track, there is tradeoff between the two streams of capacity on congested routes. '*In fact, the increasing use of high speed passenger trains necessarily ties up a large volume of slow moving freight traffic. Consideration should be given in future to contain the growth of passenger traffic where it can help to meet the requirements of freight transport. Among others, pricing policies should also help to achieve this objective.*' (Economic Survey, 1981, para: 3.45)

Efficiency of Railways

The Economic Survey had noted that the growing demand on the railway system had already begun stretching its capacity. The level of financial support from the government was as high as 72 per cent in the Fourth Plan and 75 per cent each in the Fifth Plan and the three Annual Plans. Railways had provided only 25 to 28 per cent of the capital from internal resources. A detailed examination of the adequacy of capital investment and the efficiency of its use is beyond the scope of this narrative. However, it is clear that the Indian Railways needed to do some introspection about the productivity of its assets and the investment planning process for ramping up transport capacity rapidly within the available resources.

As events in the decade of the 1980s would show, part of the existing problem in the railways was proper management of available resources and streamlining freight operations. The change over to new wagons and new pattern of operations created their own issues and these were also a part of the problem. Once systems stabilised, the productivity of assets increased. The other point noted by the Survey regarding the tradeoff between passenger and freight traffic on congested corridors did not get addressed as populist policies triumphed over economic logic.

Faced with the task of increasing freight loading rapidly, the management of Indian Railways decided to depend on longer, heavier and faster freight trains to absorb the growth in traffic. Track capacity expansion through adding of additional lines on existing congested routes progressed very slowly. This decision would create problems in the future.

As noted earlier, new BOX wagons were introduced as replacement of the existing fleet of wagons. The need for introducing larger wagons for transporting coal had been pointed out by Kelway Bamber in 1919. The idea was implemented half a century later. However, the new wagons of a different design created their own technical, management and marketing issues, which took some time to resolve.

New Wagons: Problems of Transition

As mentioned earlier, Indian Railways moved from a system of freight trains carrying consignments for multiple consumers to multiple destinations (called 'piecemeal' or 'break bulk' movement) to a system where the train moved from one origin to one destination carrying the cargo of one consignee (or multiple consignees if they all agreed to take delivery at the same destination). The new pattern of movement was called movement in 'block rakes'. The new BOX wagons were used for this movement pattern. The change was long term in nature as small consumers who loaded their consignments in a few wagons from small goods sheds could not participate in this exercise. The pursuit of this policy over the years had repercussions on the share of Indian Railways in the freight market. Transition from the existing system to a new system using new assets created certain problems which were addressed gradually.

The Problem of Wagon Couplings

Not all of the new BOX wagons could be converted into block rakes at the initial stages, as neither the consumers nor the loading entities were ready with the necessary infrastructure for handling large quantities of coal or other commodities. Hence, some number of BOX wagons were also loaded in 'piecemeal' and attached with 'mixed trains' which contained other types of rolling stock such as the KC (old type open-top wagon). As mentioned earlier, the BOX wagon and other new types of wagons such as the covered wagons BCX and CRT, had 'centre buffer couplers' which were a new item on Indian Railways. The old type wagons had 'screw couplers' which could not be coupled (joined) with the new wagons except through the use of a special 'transition coupling'. These special couplings were much in demand, but their supply was not adequate. During the period, when the author was a trainee officer in 1978–79, a huge railway marshalling yard like Mughalsarai (the largest marshalling yard in India) was choc a bloc with wagons which could not be coupled together due to the shortage of 'transitional couplings'. Senior officers from the Eastern and Northern railways were found camping at the yard to solve the problem. Incompatibility of couplings created a serious problem of shortage of wagons and mobility on the railway system.

The problem was solved by the Railway Board through an operational order stating that all wagons of a particular type with centre buffer couplers were to be segregated and run only as 'block rakes'. There was much consternation that this would lead to a loss of freight loading and revenue as some wagons would get temporarily sucked out of the system while the sorting operation was in progress. However, the Railway Board persisted with its policy and after some time the new wagons began running as pure formations. The positive results of the policy were reflected in the improvement of wagon productivity.

The financial position of the Indian Railways had deteriorated by this time and the assessment was that this was due to slow growth of traffic, rise in wage bills, increase in input costs and higher dividend payments. However, the expectation was that by increasing its efficiency, the Indian Railways would be able to make a positive contribution to financing its investments. The emphasis was on the increase of operational efficiency through the running of 'block rakes' and reduction in the 'cycle time' or 'turn round time' of wagons. During this period, bulk of the financial investment in the railways was earmarked for rolling stock.

The Janata Government did not rule for very long, and in the elections held in 1980, the Congress party under Indira Gandhi returned to power. We now turn to the next phase between 1980 and 2002 covering the periods of the Sixth to Ninth Five Year Plans and two Annual Plans.

CHAPTER 4

1981–2002: The Era of Liberalisation

The two decades between 1981 and 2002 witnessed dramatic political events and radical changes in economic policies of the government. It covers the periods of the Sixth to the Ninth Five Year Plans and two Annual Plans. In the earlier decade, the performance of the Indian economy had been adversely affected by internal and external factors. A second round of increase in oil prices in 1979–80 jolted most economies into recession. Reduction in savings and investments had a deleterious effect on demand for transport services. Amidst this difficult period, the government had taken proactive steps to increase coal production and improve rail transportation facilities. The coal industry had witnessed major changes in administrative structures, management practices and introduction of new technology. The learning curve was steep and the industry was doing its best to live up to the expectations of the nation. The railway had introduced new wagons, locomotives and changed its operational practices. The changes were beginning to stabilise. Thus, for both industries, it was work in progress.

The period 1982–91 witnessed bold attempts by the government to tide over the problems of the past decade and launch the economy on a high growth path. After 1992, there were major shifts in policies aimed at transitioning the economy from a government dominated to a market oriented one. The level of financing of the railways and the coal industry by the government was reviewed. This was also the period when the output of thermal power generation progressed rapidly, creating huge demand for coal. Indian Railways and the coal sector, particularly Coal India Ltd, negotiated these changes with varying degrees of success. The close coordination between these two industries remained strong and continued to fuel the industrial development of India.

The Sixth Plan (1980–85) attempted to erase the memories of the lean performance during the previous decade by launching an ambitious strategy to accelerate the pace of economic growth. A major component of the policy was an increase in investment in all the infrastructure sectors.

Performance during the Sixth Plan

During the first two years of the Sixth Plan, the economy grew at 6.5 per cent in real terms, exceeding the Plan target of 5.2 per cent per annum. Industrial growth also registered an increase of 5.6 per cent and 8.6 per cent in the first two years of the Plan. Unfortunately, the year 1982–83 saw drought, floods and cyclones in various parts of the country. The agricultural sector was badly affected and industrial growth also slowed down. However, the overall sense of the planners was that resource allocation for the major infrastructure sectors would have to be maintained (Planning Commission, 1983, para 1.9).

Prime Minister Indira Gandhi was assassinated in October 1984. The unfortunate event sent shockwaves throughout the country. However, her son, Rajiv Gandhi became the Prime Minister after winning a huge electoral mandate. The smooth transition of power steadied the economy and the core sector industries performed well. The Economic Survey of the Government of India for the year 1984–85 noted that the performance of the key infrastructure sectors had been satisfactory. The data provided in the Survey shows a commendable performance of the coal and power industries and the railways.

Table 4.1: Growth of Coal Production, Installed Power Capacity and Railway Freight Movement 1980–85

Item	Unit	1979–80	1980–81	1981–82	1982–83	1983–84	1984–85
Coal Production (excl. Lignite)	Million tonnes	103.94	113.91	124.23	130.50	138.22	147.41
Coal Pit head stocks	Million tonnes(mt)	14	18.3	21.1	23.3	33	29.2
Power Installed Capacity	'000 Megawatts	28.4	30.2	32.3	35.4	39.4	42.58
Goods Loading of Rlys	Million tonnes (mt)	193.1	195.9	221.2	228.8	230.1	236.4
Of which Coal	Million tonnes (mt)	62 (32.1)*	64.1 (32.7)	75.8 (34.2)	82.4 (36.1)	89 (38.7)	91.58 (38.7)
Coal for Power stations	Million tonnes (mt)	18.4 (29.7)**	21.9 (34.2)	27.5 (36.3)	37.1 (45)	40.7 (45.7)	

*Coal as percentage of total loaded by railways. ** coal for power stations as percentage of total coal loaded by railways

Source: Economic Surveys, various years, last two rows added by Author.

The data shows that coal output increased by 33 per cent between 1979–80 and 1983–84, while installed capacity of power generation increased by 38.7 per cent, and the goods transported by railways by 19.1 per cent during the same period. The focus on generation of power through coal based power stations is evident from the rapid increase in the coal for power sector transported by the railways.

During the Sixth Plan, the Indian Railways achieved a reduction in the turn round time for wagons and an improvement in the index of net tonne kilometres per wagon per day (which is an index of how much distance is covered per day by the cargo in a wagon). The improved performance was a dividend from the technological upgradation and changes in operational patterns following the introduction of the new BOX wagons and the running of block rakes.

Targets for the Seventh Plan

As the Sixth Plan had been successful, the economy entered the next Plan period in a buoyant mood. In the foreword to the Seventh Plan (1985–90), the Prime Minister emphasised the need for moving ahead in the direction of self-reliance and people oriented development. The outlay for expenditure for the public sector was expanded. At the same time the Plan document stressed the need to raise resources through improvements in efficiency. The document laid down a road map for development up to the year 2000. For coal and railways, the targets were:

Table 4.2: Coal Production and Railway Freight Targets for Seventh Plan

	1984–85	1989–90	1999–2000
Coal (in mt*) (without lignite)	147.44	226	417
Lignite	7.8	15.2	30
Originating Freight of IR in mt*	236	340	520

*million tonnes

Source: Planning Commission, VII Plan, 1985, Vol 1 para 2.41, para 2.74 and Vol 2 para 8.38.

The projected rate of growth of coal production up to the year 2000 was 9.5 per cent and for IR the projected rate was 7 per cent. These were very daunting targets indeed, given that the coal industry had grown at a compound rate of 6.63 per cent during the period 1980–81 to 1984–85, and the originating freight of IR had grown at a compound rate of hardly 4.81 per cent during the period 1980–81 to 1984–85. For Indian Railways, the target of 340 mt for the terminal year of the Seventh Plan comprised 152 mt of coal (44.7 per cent). The major increase in demand for coal would be from the power sector.

The demand projections for the Seventh Plan included a massive jump in the requirement of coking coal from 23.7 mt in 1984–85 to 41.1 mt in 1989–90. Requirement for the power sector was projected to nearly double from 62.21 in 1984–85 to 120 mt in 1989–90. It is noteworthy that the estimates of use of non-coking coal included an export component of 0.5 mt in 1989–90, thereby signifying adequacy in the availability of non-coking coal in the country. However, a small quantity of coking coal was to be imported.

Funds for Investment

Due to the long period of low growth in freight traffic during the previous decade, the financial position of the railways in 1980 was not very healthy. Though the performance had improved substantially in the next five years, still finding large resources for stepping up the freight movement as envisaged in the Seventh Plan was a tall order. The review of the Sixth Plan had again flagged the need for increasing the investments in the railways. In para 13.5 of the Mid Term Appraisal of the Sixth Plan had noted the following data regarding investment in the railways:

Table 4.3: Investment in Indian Railways 1981–84

	1980–81	1981–82	1982–83	1983–84 (BE)
At 1979–80 Prices (in Rs. Crores)	887	875	823	745

Source: Planning Commission, Mid Term Review,1983, para 13.5.

The appraisal observed that:

> It will be seen that the investments in the Railways in real terms have remained static or even decreased. Keeping this in view and the need for increasing the capacity of the Railways as mentioned earlier the investments in Railways would need to be stepped up. (Planning Commission, 1983)

In a radical departure from this view, the Seventh Plan document emphasised the need for public sector units to generate more resources internally. The railways were expected to contribute Rs. 4225 crores to the Plan finance, though most of this amount would go towards the depreciation reserve fund. In enunciating the framework of economic policy, the Plan document stated:

> 6.18 While public enterprises in several cases are expected to serve certain social purposes rather than to maximise profits, the major public enterprises which are in the core sector and in public utilities have been established in order that social ownership could ensure fast development of these vital sectors, and at the same time prevent concentration of wealth and monopolistic practices. In all the industrialised countries, major industries such as steel, aluminium, coal, power, and railways grow largely on the basis of surpluses generated by themselves, and to the extent equity finance was raised, an adequate rate of return had to be maintained. In India, too, these industries, though in the public sector, must generate surpluses through proper pricing and efficient operations. The needed resources are so large that they cannot be raised through market borrowings by the Government or through taxation. At present, the burden on the budgets for subsidising and funding public enterprises is too large for the health of the public economy. The reform of the public enterprises system with a view to making them efficient and capable of generating surpluses commensurate with the scale of capital invested in them must rank high in the agenda of fiscal reform. The aim should be to make the public enterprises financially viable and productive of surpluses. This financial autonomy must be matched by a corresponding managerial autonomy, with secretariat intervention being limited to policy guidelines and the direction of major investment programmes. An arms-length relationship between the commercial enterprises in the public sector and the government will also require major changes in the mode of organisation of departmentally-run activities. Several government committees have made recommendations oriented towards these ends. During the Seventh Plan period, the action that is needed to be taken on these recommendations must be completed. (Planning Commission, 1985, Vol 1, Chapter 6, para 6.18)

The spirit was well intentioned, but such reforms were not easy to implement in a multi-party democracy like India. The idea of financial autonomy and an arm's length relationship between the commercial enterprises in the public sector and the government remained on paper. Similarly, the issue of restricting the growth of passenger trains to provide room for expansion of freight traffic, which was mentioned in the Economic Survey of 1980–81, could not be implemented as there were continuous demands for new services from various quarters and new passenger trains were regularly introduced. Further, passenger travel, particularly the suburban and lower classes of travel, was highly subsidised. The Indian Railway was considered to be the vehicle for affordable transportation for the masses and any increase in tariff rates for passenger travel met with fierce opposition from the travelling public and political parties in the opposition benches in the legislatures. The losses incurred on passenger services were offset by regular doses of increase in freight tariff, which in turn adversely affected the ability of the Railways to generate surpluses by reducing its competitiveness vis-à-vis road.

For financing this ambitious Plan, the Central Public sector enterprises such as Railways and Post and Telegraphs were expected to net an additional revenue of Rs. 14, 240 crores. Deficit financing of the order of Rs. 14000 crores was planned. Clearly, the Government was over reaching itself.

The investment expenditure of the Seventh Plan was criticised later. The Preface to the Eighth Plan (1992–97) mentioned:

> While working out the financing pattern of the Eighth Plan, one of our major concerns was to avoid the trap that we had got into during the Seventh Plan. At the time of formulation of the Seventh Plan, it was envisaged that nearly 40 per cent of the total public sector outlay would be financed by the balance from the current revenues and by the contribution from public enterprises, both inclusive of additional resource mobilisation. Ultimately, the contribution from BCR (balance from current revenues) and public sector enterprises turned out to be only 20 per cent of the total outlay and the balance was met through borrowings. That created an internal debt-trap and acute BOP (balance of payments) crisis. We want to avoid that situation and confine the Public Sector outlay to an irreducible minimum level essential for ensuring the targeted growth. (Planning Commission, 1992, Preface Para 18)

Performance During Seventh Plan

In the coal sector, about 90 per cent of the output came from the subsidiaries of Coal India Ltd. The coal company, depending mainly on the government for capital investment, was opening up new areas, using modern technology and streamlining its management structure to live up to the great challenge facing it. There was commendable growth in coal production from states other than Bengal, which resulted in overall growth as would be seen from Table 4.4.

Table 4.4: Coal Production in India – State wise Data 1976–91 (in million tonnes)

	Andhra Pradesh	Bihar	Madhya Pradesh	Maharashtra	Orissa	Tamil Nadu	West Bengal	Total (including other minor states)
1976	7.9	42.4	20.1	3.6	2.1	3.9	24	104.6
1981	11.2	49.6	27.4	6.8	3.2	5.6	20.4	127.3
1986	16.2	56.7	44.2	11.9	6.9	7.8	19.7	170.2
1991	19.6	68.6	70.7	18.8	19.7	12.1	17.4	237.8

Source: Statistics of Mines in India, Vol 1 (Coal), 2014.

The production in Bihar increased in a North Karanpura area, where new mines were being opened. The Jharia area of Bihar did not register much growth. The shifting pattern of production to new areas, away from Bengal and Bihar (Jharia), indicated the success of the government's strategy. One worrisome feature was the slow growth in the production of high-grade coal from the underground mines in Raniganj and Jharia coalfields. The total production from underground mines of all states actually decreased from 76,199 tonnes in 1976 to 75,027 tonnes in 1986 (DGMS data). This distortion in the pattern of production led to a critical shortage of the high-grade coal produced by ECL, BCCL and CCL (South Karanpura). The supply of coking coal to the steel plants was adversely affected. Industries which required high quality coal for their boilers did not receive adequate supplies.

As has been mentioned earlier, the allotment of coal wagons from the coalfields of Bengal and Bihar (four companies under Coal India, viz, ECL, BCCL, CCL, NCL) was centralised at the office of the EDRM at Kolkata and that office used to be in a virtual state of siege by consumers of high grade coal demanding immediate allotment. The backlog was so large that the programmes submitted by consumers of high-grade coal had to be pruned down by 20 to 30 per cent to balance availability and demand.

The coal from the expanding coalfields like Korba and Singrauli (Madhya Pradesh) and North Karanpura (Bihar) was of low quality, which contained a large percentage of ash, sometimes as high as 40 to 45 per cent. The expansion of production of low-grade coal was welcome for the new thermal power stations which had been designed to use this coal. *However, the large percentage of ash being transported with the coal meant that the total calorific value delivered at the destination was low. This inflated the volume of coal required, and thereby increased the pressure on the transportation system. It also increased the level of pollution.*

The government invested heavily in coal production from the new coalfields as this was required for power generation. The midterm review of the Sixth Plan noted that at the end of December 1982, ninety-nine coal mining projects each of value more than Rupees five crores were under implementation. These projects, costing a total of 2339 crores Rupees would yield an output of 150 million tonnes of coal. Unfortunately, a large number of projects were running behind schedule by one to five years, due to various reasons like difficulties in land acquisition, late supply of machinery, insufficient geological data, and late development of evacuation facilities like railway sidings.

In his book 'Events in the Mining Industry', Anup Gupta, a senior officer of the coal industry observes:

> Since Nationalization of Coal mines in 1973 and up to March, 1990 Coal India Ltd. and its subsidiary companies invested above Rs. 9621 crores in coal projects.
>
> Plan Investment (in crore)
> 5th Five-year plan (1974–79) Rs. 832.00
> 6th Five-year plan (1980–85) Rs. 3258.54
> 7th Five-year plan (1985–90) Rs. 5530.65
> Total: Rs. 9621.19 (Gupta, 2004, p. 182).

A brief survey of the new machines that were introduced during various periods post the nationalisation of coal industry to boost productivity and output were:

For Open Cast Projects: (a) Draglines, in open cast projects (1970–80). These are heavy duty excavators which can mine a large amount of coal in a short time. (b) Small Shovel Dumpers (1980s) which are used to pick up the mined coal and load them onto trucks. Later, Large Shovel Dumpers (1999–2000) were also introduced. (c) Surface Miners were introduced much later to mine coal directly from the seams instead of retrieving coal after using the blasting method. This improved the quality of coal and provided assurance of standards. (d) Rapid Loading Systems which could load 4000 tonnes of coal onto a train in two hours.

For Underground Mines: (a) Load Haul and Dump (LHD) loaders (1980s) for rapid evacuation of coal and working in difficult conditions. (b) Side Discharge Loaders (1980s) which are used as loading machines for intermediate mechanisation. (c) Shearers in Long Wall Mining (1980s) (d) Continuous Miner (1990s) (e) Man Riding System (after 2000), which reduced the distance to be walked by the miners underground and the (f) High Wall Mining Machine (after 2010).[40]

These machines were expensive and their installation and use required the training and skilling of manpower. It is a tribute to the companies under CIL that they were procured and used intensively to increase output very rapidly.

Though the coal industry or the railways did not achieve the ambitious targets set for them, their performance was better than that in the earlier plan period. Coal reached a production level[41] of 213.69 mt (target 240 mt) and the Railways moved 309.97 mt (target 340 mt) of freight in 1989–90 of which 130.19 (42 per cent) was coal. The performance of both the sectors during the decade of the 1980s was a significant improvement over the poor outcomes of the previous decade. The Economic Survey for 1990–91 recorded that in the Seventh Plan, the overall performance of the Railways was satisfactory. However, the planned track renewals and electrification of routes fell short of the targets (Economic Survey, 1991).

Management of Change: Changes in Systems of Coal Loading and Rail Transportation

The improved performance of coal production and railway transportation during the Sixth and Seventh Plans were the result of sustained management efforts and coordination between the coal industry and railways. After nationalisation of

40 Only the names of the mining equipment have been mentioned here as a detailed account would be beyond the scope of this narrative.

41 There is a mismatch between the data of the DGMS data base and that provided by the economic Survey of the Government of India. Here the data of the Economic Survey has been used.

the coal industry in 1973, there had been a steady increase in production. The incremental production in three decades starting from 1961 to 1991 had been:

Decade	Additional Production
1961–71:	21.11 mt,
1971–81:	42.68 mt and
1981–91:	104.68 mt

From the Second Plan onwards, the macroeconomic planning process concentrated on setting up of large industries, for which transportation of large amounts of raw materials and facilities for despatch of finished products was required. To address the requirements of the times, the railway introduced BOX wagons and block rake running on a large scale from the 1970s. Later a new variety of wagon, the BOXN, was introduced. These new wagons were much larger than the old KC wagons which were used to transport coal. Further, the running of block rakes implied the loading and movement of a large volume of coal from one origin to one destination. This change in the pattern of transportation had an impact on several aspects of the functioning of the coal companies, particularly those such as Raniganj (ECL) and Jharia (BCCL), which had developed in the nineteenth century and had a large number of small mines. The areas from which coal mining had started in India were soon to be in the throes of very big changes in their systems of working.

The issues that arose related to (a) pooling of coal for loading a BOX rake, (b) the length of the coal loading sidings, (c) the time of supply of the wagons, (d) the time allowed for loading the new BOX wagons without charging penalty (demurrage charges), (e) weighment of the new BOX wagons, (f) taking care of the smaller consumers. All these issues were addressed over a period of time through exemplary cooperation between the railways, coal industry and the consumers and marked a major milestone in the management of change by the railways and coal industry.

(a) Pooling of Coal: BOX wagons were initially run in formations of 35 BOXs, carrying a total payload of 2000 tonnes. Later the number of BOX wagons in a train was increased to 44 and finally to 45, taking the payload of a rake to 2,600 tonnes. Small coal mines did not produce sufficient coal to load a full rake and had to pool coal from several mines. The consumers were no longer able to choose the mine from which to draw their coal. Consequently, a lot of quality related complaints surfaced. The industries lower down in the pecking order of the Preferential Traffic Schedule (PTS) of the Railways also mentioned that adequate supply was not available. The Ministry of Railways and the Government were, however, of the view that adequate rail transportation capacity was available.

(b) Length of the coal loading sidings: Issues arose regarding the placement of wagons for loading in the colliery sidings. Previously, the railway sidings which loaded coal had capacities for accommodating wagons on the basis of the output of the collieries. Most of the sidings could hold 15 to 20 of the old four-wheeler KC wagons, which were much shorter in length (5867 mm) than the BOX wagon (12800 mm). Many areas did not have sufficient coal to load a full train. Consequently, the new BOX wagons had to be distributed to various sidings and then collected together after completion of loading to form a full train (a full train composition is called a 'rake', in railway parlance). This was a cumbersome and time-consuming process, which defeated the very purpose of introducing block rake operations. It was not easy to amalgamate the colliery sidings as that would entail the reorganisation of road transport from several collieries to one rake loading point, but it was a task which had to be completed at the earliest.

(c) Time of supply of the wagons: Coal was traditionally loaded manually, using basket headloads, which was done only during daylight hours. The railways could not afford to keep the BOX wagons idling and insisted on loading of coal round the clock. Mechanisation of loading was slowly introduced by the coal companies. This had an impact on the employment of labour. The issue of employment is very significant sociologically, but beyond the scope of this work. Some collieries under NCDC introduced coal handling plants in the Karanpura area. The induction of mechanised loading enabled coal to be loaded from some sidings round the clock, which greatly benefited the mobility of railway wagons.

(d) Time allowed for loading the new BOX wagons without charging penalty (demurrage charges): With the advent of new wagons, the coal industry raised the issue of the time allowed by the railways for loading of trains as the volume of coal to be loaded had increased considerably, by about 1000 tonnes per train. The time allowed for loading was eight hours for manual loading and five hours for mechanised loading. If this time limit were crossed, demurrage charges would accrue, which had to be paid by the coal company. The coal industry felt that the time allowed for loading was inadequate and made several representations about it. This aspect was also highlighted by other industries which also were subject to stringent 'free time' regulations of railways for unloading of the trains. The issue was serious enough to feature prominently in the Final Report of the Rail Tariff enquiry Committee (1980).

Broadly, the issues flagged before the Committee were:

- The free time allowed should be on a case-to-case basis depending on the conditions obtaining at a particular siding.
- The schedule of locomotives sent for placing or withdrawing a rake needed to be specified and followed rigidly so the industries were not caught by surprise.
- If all the wagons of a rake were not loaded within the permissible free time, the wagons which were empty should be left behind and those loaded should be drawn out.
- For sidings where mechanical loading arrangements had been installed, the railways should provide a rebate on the freight charges to compensate the industry.
- The CIL also represented that the rebate of 10 paise per tonne being granted by the railways was insufficient as the cost of installing and running a 100 tonne weighbridge was about 36 paise per tonne.

The Report considered all these issues and suggested that:

1. The scheduling of locomotives for placement and withdrawal of rakes from colliery sidings should be based on time and motion studies, and once implemented should be adhered to.
2. In view of the large number of small sidings still in operation in the coal-fields, the railways should consider continuing supply of wagons to these sidings.
3. The free time for loading should not be uniform, but should vary from commodity to commodity depending on the results of actual field studies regarding time for loading.
4. The railways could consider increasing the rebate to CIL on weighbridges from 10 paise per tonne, with a ceiling of 10.5 per cent of the capital cost, to 18 paise per tonne and a ceiling of 13 per cent of the capital cost.
5. For industries which have invested in mechanical loading arrangement for loading of wagons, the railways could consider granting a suitable rebate on the freight. (Final Report of the Rail Tariff Enquiry Committee, 1980)

The railways did conduct time and motion studies for loading of coal from sidings using manual labour and those using mechanical methods. Obviously, it was not possible to have different rules for each siding, and hence the free time permitted remained at 8 hours for manual loading and 5 hours for mechanical loading. Further, every attempt was made to schedule placement and withdrawal times from the sidings and establish a robust system of communication at the field level between the railways and the collieries. Many coal companies deputed an officer to be present in the railway office every day to facilitate real time coordination. Supply of wagons in piecemeal to small colliery sidings continued for some time so long as the old four-wheeler stock was available.

(e) New Weighbridges for Weighment of New BOX Wagons:

Difficulties were faced with the weighbridges available with the railways for weighment of wagons. The old weighbridges had a capacity of 50 tonnes as they were designed to weigh four-wheeler wagons, which had a gross weight of 32.6 tonnes. The weighing table of these weighbridges were not large enough to accommodate an eight-wheeler wagon. The capacity of the weighbridges had to be increased to 100 tonnes as the gross weight of a loaded BOX wagon was 81.2 tonnes. Before the 100 tonnes weighbridges were installed, the weighment process of the BOX wagon was rather cumbersome. First one bogie of the wagon i.e. four wheels had to be placed on the weighbridge and the weight recorded. Thereafter, the second bogie was weighed. Thus, the whole process of loading of the wagons, their amalgamation to form a rake and their weighment were all rather slow and time consuming processes, which impinged on the transportation capacity of the railways and increased the turn round time of the new 'express' stock. The old weighbridges were of the analog type. Digital weighbridges had not been introduced as yet.[42]

Fortunately, the coal industry cooperated with the railways in introducing 100 tonnes weighbridges rapidly. The Rail Tariff Enquiry Committee Report of 1980 mentioned that CIL had installed 40 numbers of 100 tonne weighbridges which were weighing a total of 30 million tonnes of coal per year.

Digital weighbridges were introduced in the 1990s in the form of 'electronic in-motion' weighbridges. With this weighbridge, the wagons could be weighed while the train was in motion. This reduced the time taken for weighment

42 Analog weighbridges had dials which showed the weight. Digital weighbridges had an advantage of registering the weight in its memory. The cargo carrying capacity of a BOX wagon was 2.5 times that of the earlier four wheeler wagon. As some loading was done in BOX and some in the old wagons, the total loading was converted into a common denominator of a 4-wheeler wagon by multiplying the number of BOX wagons loaded by 2.5. So, if 10 BOX wagons and 10 four wheeler wagons were loaded, the result would be expressed as 20 = 35. This was the way to have a common basis for comparison, the total loading being expressed in 4-wheelers. The practice was discontinued much later after all 4-wheeler wagons had been phased out.

drastically. The stipulation of the new weighbridge was that the track had to be straight for one hundred and fifty metres and the gradient had to be no steeper than 1 in 400 at the location of the weighbridge. Further, the train had to move slowly and at a uniform speed over the weighbridge. It was not always possible to find this configuration of level and straight terrain near all colliery sidings. Hence in some cases, the weighbridge was installed at a distance from the loading site, often at some station on the main line of the railways. A weighbridge at a station away from the loading point could serve as an associated weighbridge for several loading points. Reduction in time taken for weighment was another major step towards improving the mobility of the rolling stock of the railways.

In case of overloading and underloading, there were penal charges and in case of gross overloading, part of the consignment had to be off loaded. When the weighment point was away from the loading point, the disposal of the off-loaded coal became an issue, which had to be addressed by the officers of the railway division.

The railways installed many such weigh bridges. Some were installed by major customers such as CIL too. The problem with private weighbridges, however, was that their accuracy needed to be monitored regularly. Over the years, a large number of in-motion weighbridges were installed at loading points. However, the goal of the Indian Railways to have 100 per cent weighment of all rakes could not be achieved.

(f) Taking Care of Small Consumers: Multi consumer Rakes and Coal Dumps

Small consumers who operated in a particular area often collaborated to form 'multi-consumer rakes', which would reach a specific destination and after unloading, the consignment would move by road to the respective consumers. The pressure on the small consumers also prompted some to opt for alternative forms of fuel such as oil.

The idea of coal dumps was a marketing exercise of CIL to help small consumers. Coal was moved by rail to certain locations and sold to consumers who could now buy small quantities. Starting from the early 1980s, Coal India Ltd. set up a number of coal dumps in various parts of the country and movement to these dumps started on a regular basis. By the early 1990s, the demand for coal from the core sector industries increased steadily and the movement to coal dumps dwindled. As the consumers were facing distress, the alternative of booking multi consumer rakes appeared to be better. The coal dump was slowly phased out by the mid-1990s.

The challenges involved in the management of all the issues delineated above was a formidable task. To the credit of the companies under Coal India Ltd., the reorganisation of loading points was started in phases in several areas, taking all stakeholders in confidence. When the author was officer in charge of railway operations on Dhanbad Division of Eastern Railway (now ECR), a lot of time was spent in touring the coal loading areas with senior officers of BCCL to identify the railway sidings that would be converted to full rake loading points and the coal mines that would serve a particular rake point. It was a great source of satisfaction that within a few years, large number of full rake points were in place in ECL/Raniganj and BCCL/Jharia.

At the unloading points too, the consumers had to develop sidings capable of handling full rakes. While this was done in the new power stations, cement plants etc. the smaller consumers faced considerable difficulty.

As the new operational patterns slowly stabilised, the running of block rakes by the railways provided a fillip to the transportation capacity. The turn round time of rakes carrying coal reduced substantially. The improved mobility enhanced the productivity of the new wagons and reduced the unit costs of operation of the railways.

The government was very keen to increase the production of coal rapidly and ensure its efficient transportation to the consumers, mainly to the major industries like power and steel. A three member committee under the chairmanship of Mr. J. G. Kumaramangalam (ex-chairman of Coal India) was appointed by the government in 1982 to examine the future of coal demand and the steps required for improving the efficiency of its transportation by rail. The committee submitted its report in 1983 and projected demand for coal in 2001–02 as 385 mt.

The committee also made some specific suggestions regarding reorganisation of coal loading. The important ones were:

- Loading of railway rakes should be done from sidings which can accommodate a full rake. Smaller sidings reduce the efficiency of movement.
- Coal companies should install rapid loading systems (coal handling plants or CHPs), with crushed coal being fed into loading silos. The CHPs should have in-built weighing systems so that separate weighment is not required. The crushing of coal would eliminate problems of supply of oversized coal.
- The capacity of the CHP would depend on the output of the coal mine. The committee recommended a rate of loading of 1200 tonnes per hour (tph) for mines producing up to two million tonnes per annum (mtpa), 2400 tph for mines producing four mtpa and 5000 to 6000 tph for mines producing more than 4 mtpa.

- The committee noted that even at that time some coal companies were planning to open mines of one mtpa capacity. This was particularly true of ECL, BCCL and CCL. (Kumaramangalam Committee Report, 1983)

These were very forward-looking suggestions at a time when most of the loading was done manually or through mechanical front loaders. If the suggestions were implemented, the transportation of coal by rail would have improved greatly. However, as we shall see presently, the installation of CHPs on a large scale did not take place.

It is noteworthy that the implementation of the recommendations of the Kumaramangalam committee report would have also solved the issue of free time for loading coal wagons.

Impact of Block Rake Operations: Closure of Small Goods Sheds

According to the traffic projections of the Seventh Plan, bulk commodities would comprise 85 per cent of the freight basket of Indian Railways. This was one of the results of centralised planning with great focus on large industries. The falling share of 'other commodities' in the freight basket of Indian Railways was compensated by a surge in movement by road. As the Railway Ministry had adopted a policy of gradual shift to loading of full rakes only, the small goods sheds at wayside railway stations were progressively closed. In many places, where roads were not well developed, the closure of the railway facilities was a blow to the business prospects of small traders. When the author was an officer on a field posting in the early and mid-nineteen eighties, traders would express their deep concern about their own future if the railway services to small goods sheds were withdrawn. The policy continued nevertheless as, in the macro perspective, the railways had a larger role to play in the economy.

Introduction of New and Heavier Wagons by Railways

A new wagon, named BOXN, was designed by RDSO in 1976. It was a significant improvement over the BOX and was introduced in the coal circuits in the mid-1980s. The BOXN had the same axle load of 20.32 tonnes as the BOX, but its side walls were a little higher than the BOX and its length was shorter. Consequently, 58 wagons of BOXN could be accommodated in a train (rake) as against 45 for BOX. The payload of a BOXN wagon, as designed, was 58.08 tonnes. Thus, 3369 tonnes could be loaded in a train of 58 wagons as against 2600 tonnes in a 45 wagon BOX rake, an increase of 29 per cent. The track loading density (load per metre of track) went up from 5.925 tonnes per metre for BOX to 7.59 tonnes per metre for BOXN. Track quality had to be monitored and upgraded. The payload to tare ratio was also higher, being 2.5 as against 2.25 for BOX. The BOXN also introduced a much superior braking system, using compressed air, which made braking fail safe.

The introduction of the BOXN was accompanied by the BCN, which was a covered wagon, with much greater carrying capacity than the earlier BCX wagon. These two wagons virtually eliminated all players who were not capable of booking and handling bulk consignments.

The introduction of the BOXN once again brought in its wake several issues which required exemplary cooperation between the railways, coal industry and coal consumers. It is a tribute to the management of all industries that the issues were resolved expeditiously.

Coal Loading Using Payloaders

The loading of coal round the clock using part manual and part mechanical appliances had stabilised in the era of the BOX wagon. Some mechanised coal handling plants had been installed. The BOXN carried much more coal and their sidewalls were higher than the BOX. Manual loading of BOXN became impossible. As the installation of CHPs had not progressed satisfactorily, the use of motorised 'pay loaders' on a large scale came into vogue. These machines, which had been in use for some time, were equipped with large buckets which lifted the coal from the wharf adjacent to the railway siding line (on which the coal was dumped after coming from the mines) and loaded the coal into the railway wagons. If sufficient numbers were used, a rake of fifty eight BOXN wagons, which carried approximately 3500 tonnes of coal, could be loaded within the stipulated time of five hours. In some cases, very efficient operators employed more payloaders and loaded rakes in three hours. In cases where the older BOX wagon was supplied, the loading would be completed in less than three hours. Encouraged by this development, IR introduced in the 1980s, the system of 'engine on load' (that is, for some sidings where loading was efficient, the engine would remain attached to the train during the loading process). The advantage of this scheme was that the rake would enter the siding, the engine would remain attached to the train, and it would depart for its destination after three hours, improving the mobility of the rolling stock substantially. This way, the coal companies also utilised their siding capacities more intensively. With the great success of rapid loading of rakes with pay loaders, the tempo for installation of coal handling plants for loading of non-coking coal went onto the back burner. The introduction of mechanised loading at several sidings stabilised the system of coal being loaded round the clock, which was imperative for delivering large quantities to the customers.

At the unloading end, the tipplers (mechanical devices for unloading wagons) had to be modified to accommodate the larger BOXN wagon. This was done expeditiously by all major consumers.

BOBR Wagons

Later, in 1994, persisting in its strategy of improving the efficiency of operations through reduction in the turn round time of wagons and improving customer experience, the Railways introduced a new wagon named BOBR. The new feature was that it had an arrangement for discharging coal from the bottom of the wagon. The facility enabled multiple wagons to be unloaded over 'track hoppers' (trenches with conveyor belts) while the train was in motion. A train could be unloaded in three hours as against about eight hours taken in the process of tippling of BOXN. Further, the discharge arrangement of the wagons did not allow large sized coal to be unloaded, which was a great relief for the consumers. The coal companies started using surface miners, which mined coal directly from seams (instead of using the blasting method) to ensure proper sizes. The BOBR was extremely useful for short lead closed circuit movement and had been in use by NTPC in their pit head power stations for some time.

Here again, the customers receiving the BOBR wagons had to install special unloading arrangements (track hoppers) in addition to the existing unloading systems. It must be said to the credit of the managers of the railways and the consumers, especially the power stations and steel plants, that they recognised the merit of the new system and undertook the necessary capital expenditure. Many of them now had wagon tipplers for unloading BOXN wagons and track hoppers for BOBR wagons. This was yet another example of excellent cooperation between the railways and its major customers.

Thus, from the 1980s to the middle of the 1990s, the coal industry and railways collaborated to bring about a sea change in the methods of coal loading, weighment and movement. The major consumers also played an important role by adapting their infrastructure to accommodate the new railway wagons and larger quantities received. Overall, it was a wonderful example of collaboration between three sectors to manage change of systems and helped to take the production and transportation of coal to new heights.

Railways: Systemic Issues Impinging on Optimum Utilisation of Assets

While the Indian Railways was adding to its transportation capacity by adding modern wagons and locomotives and upgrading tracks and signalling systems, its track network was growing rather slowly. This was particularly true of the important routes which carried coal to the major industrial consumers. The problem got exacerbated as the level of loading and movement increased.

Due to the mixed composition of traffic, which included large number of passenger and freight trains on the same track and the concentration of traffic on few arterial corridors, the inadequate expansion of the track network would become a limiting factor on the optimum utilisation of the new wagons and locomotives. The capital investment planning perhaps failed to consider all aspects of traffic operations. Here it is not intended to critique the capital investment planning policies of Indian Railways. It is only intended to highlight that a better balance between expansion of track network and induction of new wagons and locomotives could have led to superior results. The slow rate of growth of track network had an impact on the ability to satisfy burgeoning demand for coal movement during the late 1990s and first two decades of the twenty-first century. At that time too, adding to the cargo carrying capacity of each wagon came as a major solution. We shall come to that later.

The following three sections examine the impact of the slow growth of network on the fluidity of freight movement on Indian Railways.

Slow Growth of Track Network

Indian Railways had inherited a network consisting of multiple gauges, the 'broad gauge'[43] (BG) (1676 mm), 'metre gauge' (MG) (1000 mm) and 'narrow gauge' (NG) (762 mm and 610 mm). The construction of lines with different gauges in the country had been a historic blunder. It was difficult to run an integrated railway system with break of gauge transhipments[44] at several points. The long term objective of the government was to convert the entire network to broad gauge. However, funds were scarce and the focus had to be on creating freight transportation capacity in the areas of mineral deposits and industrial clusters to facilitate economic growth. The coal and mineral deposits as well as the major industries were all in areas which were already covered by the broad-gauge network. We have noted that during the first three Five Year Plans, the decision was to concentrate on creation of transport capacity in these areas by even sacrificing investment for passenger traffic.

---

[43] The 'gauge' of a railway track denotes the distance between two rails. Thus, Broad Gauge refers to a distance of 1676 millimetres between two rails and so on. Wagons of one gauge cannot run on another gauge.

[44] Transhipment refers to offloading consignments from wagons of one type of gauge (say MG) and loading it on to wagons of another gauge (BG). This takes place at the junction points of two types of gauges.

An examination of the growth of the track network reveals that the growth of the broad-gauge network, which was carrying the preponderant part of the traffic, was pitifully slow.

Table 4.5: Growth of Track Network 1971–91

	TOTAL Route kms	of which BG	of which MG	of which NG	Double Lines BG
1970–71	59,790	29,449	25,865	4,476	10,694
1975–76	60,216	30,497	25,427	4,292	11,991
1980–81	61,240	31,827	25,167	4,246	12,623
1985–86	61,836	33,669	23,921	4,246	13,222
1990–91	62,367	34,880	23,419	4,068	13,955
Growth since 1970–71	2,577	5,431	–2,446	–408	3,261

Source: Ministry of Railways, 2013.

The data clearly shows that, if conversion from MG and NG to BG are excluded, the overall growth of the total network in twenty years between 1970–71 and 1990–91 was only 2557 kilometres. That is, an average of only 128 kilometres per year. In the case of double and multiple lines, the addition was 188 kms per year during the decade of the 1970s, and reduced to 129 kms per year during the decade of the 1980s. The addition to route kilometres on BG reduced even further during the decade of the 1990s. We might recall that there had been great emphasis on progress in this area during the second and third plan periods.

Growth of Traffic and Line Capacity Issues

Unlike many major railroad systems in the world, Indian Railways carries passenger and freight traffic on the same track. That is, there is no separation of passenger and freight corridors. This system has its own limitations due to the difference in speeds between fast passenger trains and slower freight trains. The freight trains have to be stopped frequently to allow faster mail/ express trains to pass. It can be compared to the flow of cars on a city road being stopped frequently to allow VIP convoys to pass.

The problem gets exacerbated further if there is a skew in the pattern of traffic movement on the network. Six routes on IR which connect the four metropolises of Chennai, Delhi, Kolkata and Mumbai are referred to as the Golden Quadrilateral (GQ) and its two diagonals. In the early 1990s, these six routes, comprising 16 per cent of the route length of the network carried 56 per cent of the freight and 52 per cent of the passenger traffic. These arterial routes had started getting very congested by the 1980s. The issue of line capacity for freight traffic was sought to be addressed much later through the development of the Dedicated Freight Corridor (DFC), which we shall come to presently.

The growing demand for coal created serious issues of line capacity on certain specific coal corridors, which were also on the Golden Quadrilateral. Traffic from the following major coalfields moved on the routes of the Golden Quadrilateral:

- From Raniganj, Jharia and Karanpura coalfields: Moving towards the north on the Howrah-Delhi route via Asansol-Dhanbad-Gaya-Sone Nagar-Mughalsarai-Allahabad
- From Ib Valley and Korba coalfields: moving towards the west on the Howrah-Mumbai route via Jharsuguda-Champa-Bilaspur-Nagpur
- From Talcher coalfield: moving towards the south on the Howrah-Chennai route via Khurda Road-Waltair-Vijayawada
- From Singareni coalfield: moving on the route via Vijayawada to destinations in southern India and via Wadi to destinations in western India.

It would be seen that traffic from all the major coalfields came onto the GQ. Passenger traffic on these routes was extremely heavy. Unfortunately, addition of new lines/ multiple lines on these important corridors progressed very slowly. The mix of slow running freight trains and fast moving passenger trains created serious constraints of line capacity. Further, the growth of future coal traffic was also expected to be on these routes as was evident from the coal linkages of the SLC. The level of saturation on important freight corridors continued to increase steadily.

A map showing the routes of the GQ may be seen at Appendix 3.

Slow Freight Train Speeds: Hauling Capacity of Locomotives, New Wagons and Configuration of Traffic

Given the limitations of utilisation of track capacity due to the speed differential between passenger and freight trains, it would have been ideal if the Indian Railways could devise a method of running the freight trains at very fast speeds. This was not possible due to a mismatch between the hauling power of the locomotives and the steadily increasing gross weight (load) of the freight trains.

In the 1980s, the most powerful electric locomotive on IR was the WAG5, with a horse power of 3,900, and its diesel counterpart was the WDM2 having 2,600 horse power. To utilise available line capacity optimally, freight trains hauled by these locomotives would have to run at speeds similar to the passenger trains, i.e. about 90 to 100 kmph. With the advent of the new wagons and heavier trains, this became impossible as the locomotives were not powerful enough to achieve such speeds when hauling loaded wagons, especially in the coal loading areas, where the terrain is usually undulating and a gradient of 1 in 200[45] or steeper is normally encountered. The Indian Railways did not have sufficient locomotives to use two locomotives per coal train. So, the usual speed that a loaded train attained was a about 30 to 35 kmph in graded areas and about 40 kmph on level terrain. Double locomotives were used only in areas where the steep gradient did not permit a single locomotive to haul a train. Due to the reasons mentioned, the speed potential of the new wagons was not utilised.

During the author's tenure as the officer in charge of traffic operations at Dhanbad division of the Eastern Railway, a coal rake loaded from a colliery area like Patherdih, or Kusunda or Katrasgarh would leave the yard with two locomotives to negotiate the graded sections. This formation would travel about 180 kms to a station named Bandhua (near Gaya), where one locomotive would be detached and it would run back all the way, without hauling any train, to the colliery area to assist another train to move northwards. It was a difficult exercise to match locomotives and the train loading pattern of the collieries and freight trains often had to wait for hours for the second locomotive. The saturation of the network and inadequate hauling power did not allow the last component 'faster' of the triad 'Heavier, Longer and Faster' to operate. This stunted the efficiency of the rolling stock, which suffered substantial delays enroute due to the pressure of passenger traffic and saturated line capacity.

The BOXN had a new braking system and it required a new breed of locomotives suited for air brake wagons. The locomotives soon became available. However, till such time as both BOX and BOXN coexisted with their distinct braking systems, the variables to be dealt with in freight operation multiplied.

In an effort to rectify the situation, the Indian Railways introduced two new breeds of more powerful electric locomotives and a new diesel locomotive in the 1990s. The electric WAG7, with 5000 horse power was introduced in the early 1990s. This locomotive enabled the freight trains to run faster and the need for a second locomotive was not felt unless the gradient was steeper than 1 in 180. In the late 1990s the WAG9 electric locomotive with 6000 horse power and a new diesel locomotive WDG4 with 4000 horse power were inducted. The induction of these new locomotives increased the speed of traffic, which improved mobility of freight services and enabled the railways to keep

---

45 Gradient of Railway track: An upward gradient of 1 in 200 means that the level of the track rises by 1 metre every 200 metres or by 0.5 per cent.

the freight services abreast of the rapidly growing demand. However, even the new locomotives could not match the speeds of the fast-moving passenger trains. The issue of line capacity got addressed to some extent, but the rapid growth of traffic soon nullified the advantages gained.

It is important to note that the emphasis continued to be on using the available and slowly expanding network more intensively. The exercise reached a new level after 2004. We will come to that presently.

Recommendations of SLC: Stable Movement Matrix and Maintenance of Wagons

As mentioned earlier, recommendations of the Standing Linkage Committee (Short Term) used to generate a stable matrix of origin and destination flows with well-defined corridors linking the coalfields to the consumption centres. This pattern suited the coal industry, railways and the consumers. Taking advantage of this, the railways created wagon and locomotive maintenance depots at strategic points on each defined coal movement route.

The movement of coal is almost entirely in open-top BOX or BOXN wagons. These wagons are not suited for loading of bagged consignments like foodgrain or cement, which may be damaged when exposed to the elements. The BOX rakes moving from east and east-central India to the north, west, south and the northeast usually return empty as suitable cargo for open top wagons is not available. The introduction of block rake movement had resulted in the closure of several marshalling yards, which were the mainstay of freight operation in the era of piecemeal (break bulk) traffic. These yards were slowly converted by railways into block rake wagon maintenance depots and freight rake examination points. The BOX rakes plying on a particular axis were converted into 'Closed Circuit Rakes'[46] (CC Rakes), which would be examined at a particular depot. Thus, on the eastern-northern axis, Mughalsarai yard became the examination base for CC BOX rakes running on the eastern-northern route, carrying coal from Jharia and Karanpura to the north and north west. Similarly, Bhilai and Katni marshalling yards were nominated for the CC Rake streams moving from Korba and Kore-Rewa areas to destinations in the west and northwest, the Andal yard on Eastern Railway was the nodal yard for examination of CC rakes moving to

[46] CC Rakes: Closed Circuit Rakes which operate on a defined circuit in a particular geographical area and their fitness for operation is certified at a nominated depot.

the east and northeast and Waltair yard was the nodal yard for examination of CC rakes returning from south India.

An inherent weakness of this system was that it assumed that the movement matrix would remain static. A change in the pattern of movement would directly impact the wagon maintenance system of the railways, as wagons could move away from the nominated circuits and would have to be returned to their base depots for maintenance and repair in a planned way. This could entail some infructuous running. As events would show later, the movement patterns became quite fluid due to compulsions of demand and supply and liberalisation of economic policies.

Four coalfields namely, North Karanpura (in Bihar, under CCL), Korba (in Madhya Pradesh, under SECL from 1985), Talcher and Ib Valley (both in Orissa, earlier under CCL and then under MCL from 1992) emerged as the main coal production centres. With the changes in the production pattern of the coalfields, the movement matrix had to be modified periodically as coal companies such as ECL and BCCL were unable to meet the growing requirements of coal from new power projects and expansion of existing projects in north India. The production from Singrauli under NCL also increased, but it was mainly consumed by power stations in its vicinity.

A map showing the major coalfields of India and the adjoining railway routes in the 1990s is placed at Appendix 4. It is clear from the map that the concentration of coal production in a geographical sector would create pressure for railway movement on a few specific routes.

Rapid Growth in Coal Demand from Power Sector: Impact on Coal Industry and Railways

The government had set up the National Thermal Power Corporation (NTPC) in 1975 to develop coal-based power stations with large generating capacity all over the country. The first power station to be set up by NTPC was Singrauli in Uttar Pradesh in 1982. This was located very near the coal mines of the Singrauli coalfields under the Northern Coalfields Ltd. To undertake the short distance movement of coal to the power plant, NTPC developed its own railway system. Other power plants near the mines (known as 'pit head' plants in India) were also set up by NTPC with its own railway transportation systems. These plants were, Korba in 1983 (in Madhya Pradesh, now Chhattisgarh) linked to the Korba field of SECL, Farakka in 1986 (in West Bengal) linked to Rajmahal field of ECL, Rihand in 1988 (in Uttar Pradesh), Vindhyachal in 1987 (Madhya Pradesh) both linked to the Singrauli field of NCL, Talcher (Orissa, now Odisha) linked to Talcher of MCL and Ramagundam in 1983 (Andhra Pradesh, now Telangana) linked to the Singareni coalfield. The Singrauli coalfields area of NCL, with several large power plants became a large hub of power generation.

Location of Power Plants

The industrial development of the country was led by the states in the west, north and south, rates of industrial growth in the eastern and the northeastern states being comparatively less. The installation of power stations also followed the demand pattern from industries. Though it could be argued that it would be cheaper to generate power near the coal sources and transmit the electricity, the various state governments and the private sector opted for setting up power stations near the centres of demand. One reason was that the transmission of electricity over long distances was not very economical at that time. The desire of state governments to have administrative control over power generation was also, perhaps, an important consideration. Overall, during the period 1974 to 1990, many new coal-fired thermal power stations were installed in the country. Most of the power stations had capacities around 200 to 210 MW, which is low by today's standards.

This drive by the Government for adding to coal based power generating capacity resulted in a phenomenal increase in demand for coal as would be seen from the data in Table 4.6:

Table 4.6: Growth in Coal based Power Generation

Power Generating Capacity (all modes) at the end of each Five-Year Plan period in MW		Share of Coal based Power Plants in MW
End of Fourth Plan 1974	16664	8652 51.9%
End of Fifth plan 1979	26680	14875 55.7%
End of two Annual Plans 1980	28448	15991 56.2%
End of Sixth Plan 1985	42585	26311 61.8%
End of Seventh Plan 1990	63636	41237 64.8%

Source: Report of Central Electricity Authority, 2020.

Thus, in 16 years between 1974 and 1990, the coal based installed capacity for power generation grew nearly 4.8 times, a very commendable growth by any standards.

From the standpoint of logistics, the important criterion was the actual location of the power stations and the coalfield from which they received coal. The region wise addition to capacity is presented below in table 4.7:

Table 4.7: Number of *New* Coal based Power Units Installed in each Region 1971–90

	Number of *New* Coal based Power Units set up in each region	
Region	**1971–80**	**1981–90**
Northern: including states of Delhi, Haryana, Punjab, Rajasthan and UP and also power stations under Central Projects	5	28
Western Region: including the states of Chhattisgarh, Gujarat, Madhya Pradesh and Maharashtra and also power stations under Central Projects	7	36
Southern Region: including the states of Andhra Pradesh, Telangana, Kerala, Karnataka And Tamil Nadu and also power stations under Central Projects	4	19
Eastern Region: including the states of Bihar Jharkhand, Odisha and West Bengal and also power stations under Central Projects	0	19

Source: Derived from CEA, 2020, CEA, 2021.

Location of new power units distant from coalfields meant higher revenue earning for railways. However, railway infrastructure had to be put in place on a war footing at the major growth areas of coal production. In most of the cases the new and growing areas had been provided with rail connectivity. The capacity of the connecting lines would have to be increased as the production grew by adding additional lines, improving the system of signalling and the like.

In the case of the Korba coalfields, the Champa to Korba link, connecting the coalfield to the Howrah-Bombay trunk route had been established in 1956, and the Korba to Gevra link, within the coalfield area, had been completed in 1965. For evacuation of coal from the Talcher coalfield, the Cuttack to Paradip Port line was completed in 1973 as a single line and was to be used for carrying coal from Talcher by rail-cum-sea route to destinations in South India. On the Eastern Railway, the infrastructure in the North Karanpura area was rather rudimentary and needed augmentation. For the Singrauli coalfield under the Northern Coalfields Ltd., the line connecting Garwa Road-Chopan-Singrauli was completed in 1970 as also the line between Singrauli and Mahadiya. The line to Mahadiya would provide an outlet towards Katni and Bina on Central

Railway. The line connecting the Shaktinagar station, which was in the heart of the Singrauli coalfield to Karela Road, which was a station on the Chopan-Singrauli line, was completed in 1984. The line provided an outlet of coal from Singrauli for power stations in the vicinity like Anpara and Obra. The Karela Road-Shaktinagar line traversed a rather difficult terrain and was considered to be a great feat of civil engineering.

Finance: Internal Generation of Resources by Railways

It had been noted that from the Sixth Five Year Plan there was emphasis on the need to enhance internal generation of resources. Broadly, internal revenue generation refers to the surplus of revenue earned over revenue expenditure, the balance being available for capital investment and other necessary expenses. The revenue earning of Indian Railways was mainly from passenger and freight traffic and pricing of these services was (and still is) determined by the Government. The Railways also undertook some social obligations such as running of passenger services on uneconomic lines and carrying some essential materials such as foodgrain and fertiliser at low rates. There is considerable evidence to show that over the years, the passenger services had been underpriced, whereas freight services had been overpriced. At the same time, the cost of social service obligations had increased steadily. The pricing pattern and the new operational strategies adopted to serve the core sector industries had resulted in loss of share of the railways in the freight market. The profitability of the railways as a commercial enterprise got compromised due to loss of market share and unrealistic pricing policies.

Given the circumstances, it was not possible for the railways to generate resources required for servicing its requirements. Anticipating the continuing trend of reduction in financial support from the Government, the Ministry of Railways had created, in 1986, an organisation known as the Indian Railway Finance Corporation. The website of IRFC states:

> The primary objective of IRFC is to meet the predominant portion of 'Extra Budgetary Resources' (EBR) requirement of the Indian Railways through market borrowings at the most competitive rates and terms. The Company's principal business therefore is to borrow funds from the financial markets to finance the acquisition / creation of assets which are then leased out to the Indian Railways.

The change in the pattern of financing the railways from the First to the Seventh Plan is represented below:

Table 4.8: Pattern of Financing of Capital Expenditure of Railways

Plan	Internal Resources (In Per cent)	Borrowings (In Per cent)	Total Internal Plus External (In Per cent)	Capital from General Exchequer (In Per cent)
I	66		66	34
II	45		45	55
II	32		32	68
Annual	42		42	58
IV	28		28	72
V	25		25	75
Annual	25		25	75
VI	42		42	58
VII	43	15	58	42

Source: Sriram, 2000.

The era of dwindling Government support and borrowings from the market continued from Sixth Plan onwards and the situation would get exacerbated further, as we shall see presently.

Economic Liberalisation and Changes in Policies: 1991–2002

General Elections for the Lok Sabha were held in 1989 and a new multi-party coalition government headed by V. P. Singh as the Prime Minister (PM) came to power. However, V. P. Singh had to resign very soon and Mr. Chandra Sekhar became PM in 1990. He too resigned less than a year later as he did not enjoy majority support in the Lok Sabha (the lower house of Parliament). Fresh elections were held and the Congress came to power again in 1991 with Mr. Narasimha Rao as the PM. During this political turmoil, the Eighth Plan could not take off in 1990. The years 1990–91 and 1991–92 were treated as Annual Plans, and the Eighth Plan covered the period 1992–1997.

With the new government, came a new era of economic thinking in favour of a market-oriented economy. The financial policies followed during the Sixth and Seventh Five-year Plans had created a difficult financial situation. The Eighth Plan was launched in 1992 in the backdrop of a severe financial crisis facing the nation and was presented as a '*a Plan for managing the change, for managing the transition from centrally planned economy to market-led economy without tearing our socio-cultural fabric*'. (Planning Commission, 1992)

In the Preface to the Eighth Plan, it was noted that:

> For rapid economic development, the priority sectors identified for the growth of infrastructure are power, transport and communications. The basic assumption is that if we can provide these three essential ingredients in the urban and rural areas, it will lead to accelerated economic growth. The Plan attempts to correct the fiscal imbalances from which the Sixth and the Seventh Plan suffered. The funding of the Plan has to be done in a non-inflationary manner by avoiding the debt trap, both internally and externally. This calls for reduction in Government's dissavings, higher resource mobilisation both by the Centre and the States and improvement in the performance of public sector units (Planning Commission, 1992, Preface).

The intention of the Government was clear. Sectors like coal and railways would have to deliver results, but should not depend on substantial financial support from the Government. The approach of the government led to a sharp reduction in financial support for the coal sector and the railways.

Target and Plan for Coal Sector

In 1990–91 the production of coal was 211.73 mt and railways had moved 318.4 mt of traffic in the same year. The targets for 1996–97, the terminal year of the Eighth Plan were ambitious. Coal production target was set at 308 mt. Demand from the power sector was assessed as 185.3 mt due to an improvement in the plant load factor.[47] Some estimates put the demand from the power sector at 215 mt. In the case of steel, the demand for coking coal was expected to increase from 31.66 mt in 1991–92 to 42 mt by 1996–97. It was recognised that importation of about 3 mt of coking coal would be inevitable.

Looking at the rapidly increasing demand for coal, the Eighth Plan aimed at increasing the tempo of coal exploration, and maximisation of coal production and transportation. Improving the level of coal washing of both coking and non-coking coals was also an area of focus. New potential areas and new coal deposits were identified in areas such as East Bokaro coalfield in Bihar (now in Jharkhand), Birbhum in West Bengal and Mand Raigarh in Madhya Pradesh (now in Chhattisgarh). It was recognised that the output of good quality coal was unlikely to increase and the country would have to live with low quality high ash coal. The proportion of low grade coal and ungraded coal was as high as 72 per cent of the total. As we have observed earlier, the lower grades of coal contain a high percentage of ash, varying from 35 to 45 per cent. The usage of high ash coal inflates transportation demand and also contributes to atmospheric pollution.

---

[47] Plant Load Factor or PLF, is the average capacity utilisation of a thermal power station.

To assure customers of adequate supply of coal, tripartite fuel supply and transportation contracts between the coal supplier, transporter and the power stations, with financial penalties for failure, was proposed. A number of negotiations were held with interested parties. This strategy could not be implemented across the board as the mixed traffic corridors of the Indian Railways did not permit freight trains to be accorded priority over passenger trains.

Financial Support to Coal India Ltd.

Predictably, the macroeconomic policies of the government led to a reduction in the level of capital support to both the coal sector and the railways. After nationalisation of the coal industry, Coal India Ltd. (CIL) was virtually the monopoly coal producer in the country, with the Singareni Coalfields a very distant second. The logic which had been followed by Coal India was that increasing production was of paramount importance. The pattern of funding of Coal India is lucidly stated by P.S. Bhattacharya in his book, 'When Coal Turned Gold'.

> 'Coal mining was nationalised primarily to enable the government to provide funds for its operations and growth. Right from inception, CIL received funds from the government to meet its capex requirement. These funds were disbursed from the government's overall plan outlay, loosely referred to as budgetary support. Roughly fifty percent of the support was by way of equity infusion by the government in the company, while the remaining fifty percent was by way of an interest-bearing plan loan with a defined payment term.' (Bhattacharya, 2018, p. 9)

Given the environment of funding and the focus of higher production for overall economic gains, new projects were sanctioned on the basis of the overall contribution to the economy rather than only the financial return from the project. *'As a result, many coal projects that were set to be loss making were approved and implemented—the Rajmahal project being one of the largest and most prominent'* (Bhattacharya, 2018, p. 11).

Later, the Rajmahal project became profitable when NTPC agreed to pass on some of the benefits that accrued to its power stations from the Rajmahal project to Coal India.

Between 1975 and 1991, Coal India had achieved a cumulative average growth rate of 5 per cent in production. However, despite government support, the company was incurring losses. In spite of the losses, the new government reduced support for capital expenditure from 50 to 30 per cent. To avoid investing in loss making projects, the Ministry of Coal advised Coal India to focus on projects which yielded an Internal Rate of Return[48] of more than 16 per cent. This decision affected the production of coal as opening of new mines slowed down. The decade of the 1990s continued to be one of struggle for the coal industry as it grappled with changes in the financial schemes of the government. In 1996, the central government approved a financial restructuring of Coal India.

> It comprised an interest waiver of Rs. 892 crore, conversion of plan loan arrears of Rs. 904 crore to eight-year preference equity and a three-year moratorium on interest accrual and repayment of non-plan loan arrears of Rs. 433 crore, repayable in three annual instalments with interest. (Bhattacharya, 2018, p. 24)

After financial restructuring, Coal India was able to negotiate and secure one billion USD sectoral loan from the World Bank and Japanese Bank for International Cooperation (JBIC) to invest in twenty-four profitable open cast projects.

Coal Production

The actual production of coal in 1996–97, the terminal year of the Eighth Plan was 308.2 mt including 22.54 mt of lignite, in line with the projected demand of 308 mt. The production was, however, less than the demand from the core sector. This had been anticipated.

Addition to power generation during the Eighth Plan was 9488 mw against a target of 14430 mw. Though the addition to generation capacity was less than the target, higher PLF of existing plants and the added generation capacity increased the demand for coal to a level which the planned coal production was unable to meet. The steel and cement sectors also experienced shortage of coal. This was the first time that a significant shortage of non-coking coal was experienced. Import of coking coal was nine million tonnes against a plan of three million tonnes.

The Ninth plan document, in its review of the Eighth Plan mentions the reasons for the shortfall in coal production as:

> The main reasons for shortfalls in the availability of domestic coal are regional demand supply mismatches, quality problems and inadequate rail evacuation facilities. Besides, the constraints of domestic coal production have affected the demand materialisation in the later part of the Eighth Plan. (Planning Commission, 1997, Vol 2 Para 6.152)

---

48 The Internal Rate of Return of a project is the expected compound annual rate of return that will be earned from the project.

Regarding the coking coal scenario, the Plan document noted:

> Delays in completion of the modifications/retrofitting of existing washeries as per the Altekar Committee recommendations and delays in implementation of new washery projects have resulted in the shortfall of washed coking coal availability. Shortage of suitable raw coal feed to the washeries has also affected the washery performance The proposed utilisation of Low Volatile Medium Coking coals (LVMC), to increase the availability of raw coal feed for coking coal washeries supplying coal to the steel sector, has not come up to the required extent. (Planning Commission, 1997, Para 6.158)

Faced with the demand and supply mismatch for coal, the government had decided in 1993 to allow captive mining of coal for specific industries like power, steel and cement for their own use. A large number of such mines were allocated between 1993 and 2014. This story would, however, later unravel in an unfortunate way, as we shall presently see.

The rising imports of both coking and non-coking coal created a new challenge of evacuation of coal from the ports for the railways, as the railway connections to the ports and the coal handling facilities at the ports needed to be strengthened. Some projects for strengthening the connectivity to ports were sanctioned. Augmentation of capacity of Paradip port for handling higher coal cargo was one of them.

Performance of the Railways

For the railways, the target for 1996–97 had been pegged at 418.4 mt, which implied a growth of one hundred million tonnes over the level of 1990–91. Against this target, the actual movement was 409 mt and 277.57 billion tonne kilometres (btkms) in 1996–97.

Reduction in Financial Support to Railways

As mentioned earlier, the Indian Railways works as a department of the government, but is also treated as a commercial organisation. The costs incurred by IR consist largely of fixed expenditure on salaries and pensions, cost of fuel and cost of providing subsidies mandated by the government. The rate of inflation obviously has a great impact on the escalation of costs of inputs. The revenue is largely dependent on earnings from freight and passenger traffic, the tariff for which is also mandated by the government. Passenger transport as a whole incurs losses and is cross subsidised through income from freight. Thus, the room for manoeuvring revenue is limited to increasing the freight tariff and achieving economies in costs through reduction in unit costs of operation. Over the years, due to the induction of new technology in the form of new wagons, locomotives, signalling etc., and increase in quantum of freight moved, the unit costs of freight operation had reduced steadily.

In the book 'Bankruptcy to Billions', the authors mention that, at constant prices, the unit costs of freight operation had declined steadily from 10 paise in 1991 to about 4.3 paise in 2004. This is a very substantial reduction in costs. (*Sudhir Kumar & Shagun Mehrotra,2009*)

The financial support for the railways from the general exchequer was reduced significantly in the Eighth Plan, dropping to a level of 23 per cent from 42 per cent in the Seventh Plan. Internal generation accounted for 58 per cent and 11 per cent was generated through extra budgetary resources. This level of funding by the Government was not enough, and the dependence on extra budgetary resources, which required higher rates of interest payment, was not a path that could be pursued for long. High rates of inflation during the 1990s and a large payout to employees to implement the recommendations of the Fifth Pay Commission compounded the problem.

The Economic Survey of the Indian economy for the year 1997–98 noted:

> Over the years, the Railways have increased their reliance on extra-budgetary resources. The pressure on resources has, however, increased due to higher expenditure on account of implementation of the Fifth Pay Commission's recommendations, growing lease rentals, etc. Besides market borrowings, private sector participation through schemes like Build-Own Lease-Transfer (BOLT) and Own-Your-Wagon Scheme (OYWS) is also being encouraged. (Economic Survey, 1998, Chapter on Railways para 35 and 36)

As the demand for coal transportation increased, the need for a large dose of capital investment for adding to track capacity on the arterial coal routes became extremely important. The railways did not have the requisite funds and the situation continued to drift.

The critical shortage of funds for the railways was also recognised and commented upon in several documents. Commenting on the declining Budgetary support for the Railways, the Ninth Plan document recorded:

> The budgetary support for the transport sector has been declining consistently over the years. For example, in the railway sector, the budgetary assistance declined from as high as 75% in the Fifth Plan to a mere 23% in the Eighth Plan This combined with the policy of keeping the passenger fare low, forced the railways to resort to market borrowing, whose heavy servicing burden further eroded the internal surpluses of the system There is a strong case for a higher budgetary support on both theoretical and practical considerations. The transport infrastructure has important externalities in view of its catalytic role in economic growth. Many of our transport enterprises cannot take tariff and investment related decisions on purely commercial lines. When projects are taken up on strategic considerations or uneconomic routes have to be served on social

> policy grounds or essential commodities are to be carried at concessional freight, it is only proper that budgetary compensation is provided in order that the financial health of the transport entity is not affected. In view of these considerations, the budgetary support to the transport sub-sectors will have to be enhanced. For development projects, which are commercially not viable, financial support will also be tapped from the beneficiary States which should share in the operational costs of such suboptimal investments. (Planning Commission, 1997, Para 7.1.33)

The sentiments expressed in the Ninth Plan document were echoed by the report of the Railway Convention Committee on the Infrastructural Requirements for Indian Railways in the Ninth Plan period (1996, submitted in March 1997). Commenting on the predicament of the railways, the RCC highlighted the following issues:

- The Indian Railways needed a higher level of financial support from the government.
- The expansion of the rail network has not kept pace with the expansion of traffic.
- Lease charges paid by IRFC were mounting.
- No railway system in the world can survive on borrowed money. The government should provide funds from the general budget for Indian Railways.

Fundamentally, the RCC was suggesting that the Indian Railways should be financed from the Government revenues like roads and ports and a mechanism for recovering the money should be created as in the case of roads through a cess on the fuel used by road vehicles.

In the Final Budget speech for 1998–99, for the Railways, the hon'ble Minister for the Railways forcefully reiterated the demand for more funds from the Government.

Investment Choices: Gauge Conversion

With the government reducing the flow of capital to the railways, it was important to target scarce resources to the right areas. The achievements of the Eighth Plan in terms of acquisition of new wagons and locomotives were modest due to lack of resources. In the case of track, however, the Ministry of Railways decided to launch 'Project Unigauge' in the year 1992. The aim was conversion of metre gauge routes to board gauge at a rapid pace. The vision of a uniform gauge all over the network was a laudable objective. Perhaps the timing for this venture was not quite right as the scarce resources could have been used for adding capacity on congested broad gauge routes for meeting the rapidly growing demand for transport. Very few metre gauge routes were alternatives for congested broad gauge lines. The conversion of gauge added to capital requirement as after conversion, additional rolling stock suitable for broad gauge had to be procured for use on the converted lines. The metre gauge stock was rendered redundant. Table 4.9 presents the data of the progress of gauge conversion between 1991 and 2001:

Table 4.9: Expansion of Broad Gauge Network 1991–2001

Year	MG+NG In Kms	BG In Kms	Growth of BG in Kms. Excluding Gauge Conversion	Double Lines on BG
1991–92	27439	35109		14224
2001–02	18041	45099		16041
Net Growth in 10 years	(–) 9398	9990	592 Average 59.2 kms per year	1817 Av. 181.7 kms/year

Source: Indian Railway Year Books, various years.

It is clear that the growth in the BG network was almost entirely attributable to gauge conversion. The increase in the number of double and multiple lines was better, at the rate of 181 kms per year at the all India level. The progress on the coal routes was a fraction of the all-India average. Reviewing the performance of the Railways during the Eighth Plan, the Ninth Plan document stated:

> The Indian Railways have extended their route length from 53,596 kms. in 1950–51 to 62,725 kms as on 31.3 97 registering an increase of 17% only. On the other hand, freight in tonne kms carried has risen six-fold, while passenger kms, have grown by five times during the same period. On an average, only about 2000 kms have been added to the system in each decade, while the Eighth Plan contribution, was even lower at 267 kms. Further, the Indian railway system is a multigauge one and the Broad Gauge part is 41,971 kms, of which only about 15,000 kms. are double/multi-track, despite the heavy congestion in the high density corridors. (Planning Commission, 1997, Vol 2 para 7.1.4)

The strategy of using the existing resources more intensively through technology upgradation and better management appeared to be reaching a saturation point and this fact was duly recognised in the official documents. The impact of inadequate growth of the railway network on the market share of Indian Railways was also commented upon in the Ninth Plan document, which stated that the decline in the share of the railways in the freight market was due to the inability of the system to grow at the rate warranted by the growth of the economy.

The system, which is wholly government owned and funded, has suffered from underinvestment. In the face of severe capacity constraints, the railways chose to concentrate on transportation of bulk materials for the industries in the core sector, thereby losing the traffic from the high-value non-bulk segment. The tariff policy was skewed against the freight sector as passenger tariff was cross subsidised by continual increases in freight tariff. This was another reason for the migration of non-bulk traffic from rail to road. The policy of the government to have a liberal regulatory and permit system for road, low cost finance from banks and subsidies on price of diesel created a congenial environment for the largely privately owned road sector. The railways continue to pay very high tariffs for electricity consumed in transportation (Planning Commission, 1997, Vol 2 Para 7.1.13).

Despite the strong statements made in the Plan document and by the RCC, the government did not take any decisive action to address the twin issues of saturation of line capacity and the cross subsidisation of passenger services through high freight tariff. In the case of expansion of network, the growth of double lines/ multiple lines during the Ninth Plan period was actually less than that in the Eighth Plan period.

Investment Choices: New railway Zones

As noted earlier, the Indian Railways had started with six operating zones, which were expanded by 1965-66 to nine zones. Representations from public representatives and other quarters continued to be received regularly for the creation of new zones. In 1986 a high-level committee named the Railway Reforms Committee (RRC) had been set up to examine the workings of the railways. Among other recommendations, the RRC had advocated the creation of four new zones, which were to be carved out of existing zones. Subsequently, in 1994–95, the Railway Board set up an internal committee of senior officers to go into the question of requirement of new zones to improve the administrative and operational functioning of the railways. This committee too suggested the creation of four new administrative zones. However, in 1996, the Union Cabinet cleared the proposal for creation of six new zones. Another one was added in 1998. Thus, a decision to have a total of sixteen administrative zones headed by General Managers was arrived at. Investment for establishing the new zones started in the 1990s and the new zones got commissioned in 2002 and 2003. Later, in 2010, the Metro railway at Kolkata was also named as a separate zone, making it the 17th. The creation of new zones was accompanied by the creation of nine new divisions as well. It is a moot point whether this exercise of creating new administrative zones and divisions, which involved considerable expenditure and relocation of personnel, was beneficial for the railways as an organisation, particularly at a time when the railways was critically short of capital for investment. Commenting on this aspect, the Report of the Bibek Debroy Committee for Mobilisation of Resources for Major Railway Projects and Restructuring of the Railway Ministry and Railway Board, (submitted in June 2015) states very clearly that that the efficiency parameters of Indian Railways were definitely better with nine zones (Final Report of the Bibek Debroy Committee for Mobilisation of Resources for Major Railway Projects and Restructuring of the Railway Ministry and Railway Board, 2015, para 1.7 pp. 33).

Continuous Increase in Freight Tariff to Garner Resources

In an effort to bolster revenue and offset the losses due to low passenger tariff, there were regular doses of increase in freight tariff. This is reflected in the earning per tonnes of freight transported. The rate of increase in earning per tonne for coal was the highest, perhaps reflecting the attempt of Indian Railways to boost earnings from a commodity whose importance in the total freight basket was growing rapidly.

From the data of earning from freight for all commodities and specifically for coal presented in table 4.10 below, it may be observed that the average earning from all commodities other than coal was consistently more than that from coal. This was due to the presence of some high rated commodities like petroleum products and steel, which are charged at rates much higher than that for coal. However, the CAGR of earning per tonne from coal in the period from 1975–76 to 2000–01 was 10.6 per cent, whereas the growth rate for all commodities, excluding coal, was 8.6 per cent. That is, the rate of increase in earning per tonne from coal was higher than that for the basket of all other commodities. This indicates that the tariff for coal increased at a comparatively higher rate than that for other commodities taken together. The average lead for coal was always lesser than the average lead for basket of all other commodities. The consumer price index increased at a cagr of 7.96 per cent (World Bank data) between 1975 and 2001.[49] Thus, the cagr of both 'all other commodities' (8.6 per cent) and coal (10.6 per cent) was more than the cagr of the consumer price index. Hence, it does appear that the Indian Railways sought to improve its revenue earning through a steady increase in freight tariff.

[49] The data for Indian Railways is in terms of fiscal year (April to March), whereas the data for world Bank is for calendar year January to December. To compare with the World Bank data 1975–76 has been taken as 1975 and 2000–01 has been taken as 2000.

Table 4.10: Loading and Earning from all Commodities and Coal 1976–2001

Year	Total Loading in mt	Total Earnings in Rs. mill	All Commodities Earning/ Tonne in RS.	Coal Loading in mt	Coal Earning in Rs. millions	Earning per Tonne from Coal in Rs.	Total loading minus Coal	Earning per tonne from goods other than coal
1975–76	196.8	10,957.4	55.68	64.3	2,459.8	38.26	132.5	64.13
1980–81	195.9	15,509.3	79.17	64.1	3,170.5	49.46	131.8	93.62
1985–86	258.6	42,321.9	163.66	101.6	13,626.5	134.12	157.0	182.77
1990–91	318.4	82,470.4	259.02	135.2	31,141.1	230.33	183.2	280.18
1995–96	390.7	149,727.8	383.23	184.4	64,057	347.38	206.3	415.27
2000–01	473.5	230,454.1	486.70	223.7	105,521.6	471.71	249.8	500.13

Source: Indian Railway Year Books.

Liberalisation: Partial Deregulation of Price of Coal

In pursuance of the new economic policies, in March 1996, an important decision was taken to deregulate the prices of A, B and C grades of non-coking coal and coking coal. Their distribution was also deregulated. CIL was empowered to fix the prices of these grades of coal. A year later, in March 1997, the prices of hard coke and Grade D coal were also decontrolled. This was indeed a major departure in policy from the past. Coal India was able to determine the prices of all grades of coal.

Ninth Five Year Plan at the Turn of the Century

The Ninth Five Year Plan covered the period 1997–98 to 2001–02. Most of the Plan period was under the guidance of Atal Bihari Vajpayee who was Prime Minister from 19 March 1998.

The Planning Commission forecast a rate of growth of 7 per cent per annum for the economy during the Plan period. The Indian Railway too had ambitious plans of regaining its lost share in the freight transportation market, which had reduced from 89 per cent in 1951 to 40 per cent in 1994. To retain its dwindling market share, Indian Railways needed to increase loading of freight by at least 7 per cent per year and, to increase its market share, the challenge for IR was to grow at a rate greater than 7 per cent. The total freight loading in 1996–97 had been 409 mt. IR would have to reach 574 mt by 2001–02 to maintain its market share. The main component of IR's freight traffic was coal and its production would also have to increase dramatically. The growth of coal production between 1991 and 1997 had been from 225.5 to 308.2 mt, i.e. at the rate 5.3 per cent.

Strategy for Financing Railway Investment and Loading Target for Railways

The strategy for higher level of freight transportation proposed by the Ninth Plan was:

> The task of lifting additional freight traffic and meeting the requirements of different user sectors requires both short-term and long-term strategies. In the short-term, the capacity would be augmented through acquisition of additional rolling stock, improvement in terminal operations and speed of goods trains, encouraging private sector participation in the acquisition of rolling stock etc. In the long run, the capacity would be augmented through improvement in the handling systems at terminals in close coordination with the users, improvement in wagon designs, development of high horse power locomotives and introduction of heavier trains, construction, and operation of heavy haul freight routes etc. Sharing of cost between the Railways and the user sectors for introducing mechanical handling devices to reduce wagon detention time will also be considered. (Planning Commission, 1997, para 7.1.74)

To create capacity on existing routes, doubling of 2500 kms of track was targeted. Procurement of 1,36,000 wagons, 785 diesel and 851 electric locomotives was also planned. With the paucity of finances available with the railways, it was a moot point how these targets would be achieved.

The target for freight movement for the terminal year of the Ninth Plan 2002–03 was set at 525 mt, and 353 btkm. which implied a growth rate of just over 5 per cent per year. Thus, if the economy actually did grow at 7 per cent, the planned growth of Indian Railways would lead to a further erosion of its market share. The budgetary support for the Ninth Plan was proposed to be enhanced.

Funding of Railway Infrastructure by Coal Industry

Recognising the paucity of resources for railway projects, specific routes were identified in consultation with the Ministry of Coal and a funding mechanism developed. The specific suggestions mentioned in the Ninth Plan document are:

> Augmentation of rail movement capacity by implementing the already identified critical rail links in potential coalfields is essential in the Ninth Plan to avoid mismatches and help materialisation of coal demand The MOC has listed the following rail network constraints:
>
> (i) For movement of coal to the Northern India power stations an additional 14 rakes will have to be moved per day in 2001–02, through Mughal-Sarai Junction over the current average movement of 24 rakes a day. In addition, there will be movement to non-power consumers at about 5 rakes a day in 2001–02 Thus, movement through Mughal-Sarai needs to cater to about 43 rakes a day in 2001–02

(ii) A new rail link between Korba and Korea-Rewa coalfields, which will enable coal companies to take up rapid expansion with least investment in Korba, to cater to the demand from Western India
(iii) The identified important rail links in MCL covering Talcher and lb Valley as per the Master Plan need to be completed
(iv) In CCL, the Tori-Dhonia (Danea) link is critical for tapping the vast potential of NKP area
(v) In ECL, the Pirpainti to Madhupur link in the Rajmahal coalfield is vital for expanding the production potential of this field. (Planning Commission, 1997, Para 6.187)

The Plan went on to record:

> While the trunk routes are looked after by the Ministry of Railways (MOR), the movement facilities Irom the coalfields to the trunk routes is lagging due to resource crunch being faced by the MOR. It is, therefore, felt necessary by the MOC that it would have to fund these new infrastructural rail links through collections from excise duty leviable under Coal Mines Conservation & Development Act (CCDA) 1974, which is also meant for improvement of transport infrastructure in the coalfields. Presently, approximately Rs 335 crore is lying unspent in the consolidated fund of the Government of India which were collected in the form of excise duty since the inception of CCDA in 1974. As per the estimates of the MOC, rail line for a distance of 490 kms in different coalfields of CIL is required to be covered with an estimated cost of Rs. 1127 crore. (Planning Commission, 1997, Para 6.188)

These were very practical suggestions and the offer for funding development of capacity on coal routes was yet another example of the high level of coordination between the coal industry and the railways.

Coal Production Targets

For the terminal year of the Ninth Plan 2001–02, the coal production target was fixed at 370.6 mt, which implied an annual rate of growth of 5.3 per cent. The growth in the Eighth Plan had been 4.5 per cent. The production pattern planned is shown in table 4.11.

Table 4.11: Coal Production Plan for 2002 (in million tonnes)

CIL	SCCL	TISCO/IISCO/DVC	Captive Blocks	Total
314	36	7.60	13	370.6

Source: Planning Commission, 1997, Table 6.22.

The projected demand for coal by the end of the Plan was 412 mt. Thus, the production planned at 370 mt was well short of the demand. The total production included an addition of 73 mt of coal from new projects within the Ninth plan period. This was perhaps a very optimistic assumption. Import of 19 mt of coking coal by the steel sector and 2.3 mt of non-coking coal by the power sector still left an uncovered gap of 20.7 mt Close monitoring of the end use of coal and encouragement of private mining was contemplated by the Government to improve coal availability. Inadequate availability of non-coking coal was becoming a major issue and recognising this, the Plan document mentioned the need to import coal.

The document recorded:

> Coal will continue to be the major fuel for the power sector in India Based on the study conducted in the Planning Commission on cost of generation with different fuels, it has emerged that the domestic coal and the natural gas at current price level are the cheapest fuels for power generation. However, the domestic production of coal and gas is projected to fall short of the requirements during the Ninth Plan period. In order to meet this situation, increased imports of coal and gas may be necessary. (Planning Commission, 1997, Para 6.108)

The problem of importation of coal was that the ports in India, at that time, were equipped to handle only 8.5 mt. Thus, the option of large-scale importation of coal did not appear to be feasible till the capacity of ports and rail connectivity were improved. To address this issue, infrastructure upgradation of the Paradip, Haldia and Ennore ports was initiated

To augment the availability of coal a new initiative was introduced to make exploration and production competitive. Entry of private entities for captive coal mining for certain industries had already been started. A number of coal blocks continued to be allotted. However, the production from captive mines was very small compared to the overall requirement.

Coal Beneficiation

As the preponderant part of the additional coal production was to be of inferior grade coal, which contained a large percentage of ash, the beneficiation of non-coking coal was suggested by the Plan. This would immediately reduce the transportation requirement and also the pollution caused at the consumption point. Specifically, the Plan document recorded:

> The notification dated 19.9.1997 issued by the Ministry of Environment & Forests (MOEF) makes it mandatory for thermal power plants located 1000 kms from pithead and also those located in urban areas/sensitive areas/ critically polluted areas, irrespective of their distance from pithead, excepting any pithead thermal power plant, to use beneficiated coal with ash content not exceeding 34% from 1st June, 2001. As there is only one non-coking coal washery, namely Piparwar (in CCL), there is an urgent need to create the required capacities for beneficiating non coking coal to comply with the MOEF notification. Also, 37% of the total despatches to the power sector, currently, are

> over long distances This implies that about 120 mt of washing/beneficiation capacity would need to be created by 2001–02, which would require a capital investment of about Rs. 3000 crore at a specific investment of Rs. 25 to 30 crore per million tonne. (Planning Commission, 1997, Para 6.199)

The norms would be made more stringent later as we shall presently see.

Setting up of Non-coking Coal Washeries

Other than the Piparwar washery which was set up in 1997 in CCL, the Bina de-shaling plant was set up in 1999 in NCL and the Dipka washery in the Korba area in 1999–2000. The Dipka was a large washery with a capacity of 14.5 mt per annum. Some power stations in western and northern India started using beneficiated coal. Other non-coking coal washeries in the private sector were set up later.

Coking Coal Washeries

The Plan document also flagged the serious issue of inadequate beneficiation of coking coal by the washeries of CIL. It recorded:

> It was envisaged that the average ash content in the washed coking coal for steel plants at the desired level of 17% +/– 0 5% would be maintained by the coal industry by undertaking the necessary modifications and retrofitting etc. of existing washeries as per the recommendations of the Altekar Committee by 1994–95. However, the problem of higher ash content has not been overcome and the steel industry is increasingly depending on imports mainly due to inconsistencies in the quality of washed coking coal being supplied by CIL at about 21% ash The washed coking coal production from CIL washeries has almost remained stagnant at around 9 mt in the Eighth Plan The yield of the washeries has come down from 54% in 1992–93 to about 51% in 1996–97. The two new coking coal washeries namely Kedla and Madhuband which were scheduled to be commissioned during the Plan have not been commissioned. (Planning Commission, 1997, para 6.155)

Coal Demand and Output

The demand for coal during the Ninth Plan period did not fructify due to fall in global coal prices, reduction in import duties for coal and slow commissioning of thermal power projects. According to the data available from the CEA's National Electricity Plan Vol-1, of 2018, the main reason for the shortfall (all modes of generation) was the slow progress in the capacity additions from the private sector (30 per cent of target) and the central sector (38 per cent of target). The low demand for coal prompted Coal India to use only half of the amount of the loan available from the World Bank and JBIC. This decision to go slow on new projects would create problems a few years later.

The production of coal in 2001–02, the terminal year of the Ninth Plan was 352.6 mt including 24.8 mt of lignite, which was considerably less than the target of 370 mt. CIL produced 279.65 mt, about 85 per cent of the total. From the point of view of the coal industry, investments in new projects had been deferred as demand was low. However, demand from the power sector was expected to rise sharply in the near future. The midterm review had warned that the *'shortfall in coal production capacity addition, may lead to a large gap in the Tenth Plan and beyond unless the identified new projects (i.e., formulated and awaiting approval) are implemented.' [Mid Term Review of Ninth Plan]*

Performance of Railways

The freight movement of the Railways in 2001–02, the terminal year of the Ninth Plan, was 492.50 mt, considerably less than the target of 525 mt. The share of coal had risen to 229.82 mt or, 46.5 per cent. The financial condition of the Railways did not improve.

In the case of the Railways, the Mid Term Review raised certain important issues:

- The movement of freight was sluggish up to 2000 due to lack of demand. However, the passenger traffic was growing very rapidly.
- *The Railways continues to spread its available investible resources thinly on several projects. The investment strategy needed to focus on projects which would create capacity in the system to carry more traffic.* [Italics added by author]
- The financial health of the Railways had deteriorated during the first three years of the Plan due to slow rate of growth of freight offerings and the implementation of a wage hike following the report of the Pay Commission in 1997.

Progress of Railway Projects for Coal Movement mentioned in Ninth Plan

It is worthwhile recording here that among the coal evacuation lines mentioned in the Ninth Plan document, the Korba-Korea-Rewa connecting line was under construction in 2019–20, through a Special Purpose Vehicle named the Chhattisgarh East-West Railway Corporation. The Tori-Danea link was not constructed, nor was the Pirpainti-Madhupur link. Some portions of the master plan for the Talcher and Ib Valley coalfields were constructed and these line capacity works facilitated evacuation of coal from these two areas. The progress of line capacity enhancement works gives a fair idea of the level of capital investment and focus on this critical area.

The Coal Ministry had correctly identified Mughalsarai as an important area. The pressure of traffic was growing as demand from north India was on the rise and three coalfields ECL, BCCL and CCL were moving coal in that direction. Among them, CCL was the fastest growing field. The coal moved on a double line section from the colliery area to Sone Nagar which was on the Grand Chord (GC). The Sone Nagar-Mughalsarai section (120 kms) was the busiest traffic corridor in the country and its capacity was saturated. A third line between Sone Nagar and Mughalsarai had been planned and the work was completed only around the year 2000. After Mughalsarai, there were two routes to the north, one via Allahabad (now renamed Prayagraj) called the 'A' route and one via Lucknow, named the 'B' route. The Lucknow route was not electrified till much later and this necessitated a change of traction from electric to diesel at Mughalsarai, with the inevitable delays. Beyond Mughalsarai, the line capacity on the A route was also saturated. A third line had been planned. This project progressed slowly and its importance dwindled after the announcement of the Dedicated freight Corridor in 2006.

There were other areas too where the rapid increase in coal loading from specific areas such as Ib Valley, and Korba, led to pressure on available line capacity on the trunk routes. The Jharsuguda-Champa-Bilaspur section was a double line track. Coal moving from Ib valley and Korba towards Katni needed to cross the Bilaspur-Anuppur section (appx. 150kms) which was single line with steep gradients. This line was slated for doubling. The work was sanctioned in three phases between 2004–05 and 2006–07 and finally completed in 2019. Similarly, there was the need for a third line between Bilaspur and Raipur as this was the route for movement of coal from Korba and Ib Valley to the west via Nagpur and there were a number of cement plants, limestone quarries and the Bhilai Steel Plant in that area. This work was completed in 2016. A third line between Jharsuguda and Bilaspur was proposed in 2008–09 keeping in view the huge coal traffic anticipated from Ib Valley and Korba coalfields. This project was completed in 2020.

On the east coast, the rapidly growing coal loading from Talcher coalfields created line capacity issues in two areas. First, the movement from Talcher to Paradip Port, was via the Kendrapara Road-Cuttack section, which had two major bridges over the rivers Birupa and Mahanadi. These two bridges had been retained as a single line on an otherwise fully double line section. Beyond Cuttack, there were two more bridges over the rivers Katjuri and Kuakhai which were also single line. The two bridges on Birupa and Mahanadi were crucial for moving coal from Talcher to Paradip port. These two bridges were converted to double line in 2004 and 2008 respectively. The second constraint was a single line section between Cuttack and Paradip Port, which had been identified as the loading point for movement by rail-cum-sea route for coal from Talcher to Tamil Nadu and

Karnataka. Paradip port was handling coal, iron ore and fertiliser traffic and as the loading from Talcher increased, the section became very congested indeed. The section was proposed for doubling and the work was finally completed in 2005.

Other Issues Mentioned in Ninth Plan

For the first time, the Plan mentioned the need to restructure the Indian Railways and also the need to set up an independent Tariff Regulatory Authority for railway tariff so that the decisions on setting of tariffs could be taken independently. Some restructuring of the management cadre of the Railways began after the second decade of the twenty-first century. The efficacy of the restructuring will not be known immediately. The Tariff Regulatory Authority has not been set up till 2023.

Many of the projects planned for the Ninth Plan did not materialise as the Indian Railway ran into severe financial turbulence by the end of the century.

Expert Committee

A committee of experts headed by Rakesh Mohan of the National Council of Applied Economic Research had been formed and submitted its report in 2001. It was called the 'Indian Railways Report 2001: Policy Imperatives for Reinvention and Growth'. Commenting on the status of the Indian Railways, the report highlighted the precarious financial position of the Indian Railways. The Operating ratio had reached 98.8 in March 2000. The report further highlighted that the fund balances of the railways had dropped from Rs. 3564 crores in 1997–98 to Rs. 253 crores in March 2000. The railways were unable to pay their creditors and payment of Rs. 1500 crores of dividend to the government had been deferred. Investments which were essential were being delayed. [*Indian Railways Report 2001: Policy Imperatives for Reinvention and Growth*; Page 295]

Broadly, the other issues mentioned in the report were already recognised by the Government and recorded in various documents, some of which have been referred to in this narrative. The issues identified were: (i) cross subsidy of passenger by charging high rates for freight (ii) high level of competition from other modes (iii) inefficient targeting of investment (iv) costs increasing faster than revenues; saturation of trunk routes constraining ability to run trains to earn revenue. (vi) controlling of costs should be primary focus, large workforce to be reduced to improve employee productivity (v) higher level of investment required; money cannot come from Government, it will come from lenders.

The Expert Committee recommended that without structural changes, Indian Railways would not be in a position to meet future traffic demands. It also recommended introduction of a robust Management Information System based on computerised data. The Centre for Railway Information System (CRIS) had been set up in 1986. The work on computerisation of freight data and monitoring of operations started rolling out through the Train Management System (TMS) from the late 1990s. The TMS became a robust and effective tool for management of freight operations. However, other important changes suggested by the report, such as in the system of accounting were not implemented.

More Liberalisation of Coal Marketing Policies

The coal sector saw a major shift in policy aimed at liberalisation of the choice of consumers from the non-core sector. In the year 2000, the Colliery Control Order of 1945 was replaced by a new Colliery Control Order Referring to this change, the Ministry of Coal observed:

> Government of India has amended the Colliery Control Order, 1945 and the new Colliery Control Order, 2000 has been notified according to which the price and distribution of all grades of coal have been deregulated with effect from 1.1.2000. Coal Companies/Coal India Limited are allocating coking coal to steel plants for their requirements. For core sector, sale of coal is guided by linkages and allocations by the competent authorities. For non-core Sector consumers, with a view to reaching the benefit of decontrol of coal as per Colliery Control Order, 2000, Coal India Limited has decided to authorize its subsidiary companies to formulate their own system and procedure for sale of coal to this sector. The new policy of Coal India Limited is aimed at providing a simplified, transparent, and customer-friendly system and procedure. In the new policy framework, the system of linkage and sponsorship for the purpose of coal supply to non-core sector is being done away with. In the emerging new policy framework for coal sale to non-core sector, stress is being given on bilateral agreement between supplying subsidiary company and consumer for well defined commitment on the part of both buyer and seller. (Colliery Control Order 2000)

Hence, the consumers of the non-core sector would now deal directly with coal companies instead of routing their demands through the Director of Industries of the states. The demand accepted by the coal companies would be submitted to the railways for allotment of wagons. Clearly, the Ministry of Coal was of the view that sufficient coal was available, and if not, the coal companies would moderate the acceptance of demand.

Comments on Policies of Railway in Plan Documents

An Approach Paper to the Tenth five Year Plan (2002–07) was published in September 2001. The paper made the following comments about the investment and tariff policies of the Railways:

> 3.97 The most important policy distortion is the skewed tariff policy which overcharges freight movement in order to subsidise ordinary passenger traffic. This is accompanied by an investment strategy which has placed excessive emphasis on opening new lines for passenger traffic and not enough emphasis on expanding capacity in areas where there is potential commercial traffic. The net result has been an alarming deterioration in the financial condition of the Railways and an inability to undertake the investment needed to improve Railway transport services.
>
> 3.98 The heavy cross subsidization of passenger fares is economically irrational and cannot be justified on social grounds since the beneficiaries of the subsidy are not the poor. This system must be phased out gradually over the Tenth Plan period. Consideration should be given to establishing an independent Rail Tariff Regulatory Authority for tariff fixation on technical and commercial considerations. [Approach Paper for X Plan, Government of India]

The Approach Paper also called for the restructuring of the railways, the setting up a Tariff Regulatory Authority and a reduction in administrative costs.

Clearly, there was awareness about the problems facing the Indian Railways and government documents flagged the relevant issues repeatedly for several years. However, as happens in a developing nation with multiple demands on scarce resources, and a multiparty democracy, the issues could not get addressed and the necessary funds were not provided.

The government commissioned another two studies in 2011 and 2012 to examine the issues facing the railways. Both the studies recommended a number of measures to improve the performance of the railways. We shall turn to these recommendations presently.

The averments in various documents, such as the Five Year Plans and the Economic Surveys, as well as the report of the expert committees leave no doubt that the problems facing the Indian Railways were known at the apex level. It was clear that enhancing the transport capacity of the railways and repairing its financial health were crucial for the functioning and growth of the industrial sector of the country. Decision to progress on a clearly defined path was awaited.

In elections held in 2004, the United Progressive Alliance led by Dr. Manmohan Singh as the Prime Minister came to office and Mr. Lalu Prasad Yadav was appointed as the Minister for Railways. During the first decade of the twenty-first century, some very bold policy changes introduced in the sphere of freight and passenger operation brought about a paradigm shift. We turn to those events now.

Paradigm Shifts (2003–2023)

New Approach

In a complete departure from the recommendations of the Rakesh Mohan Committee report (2001), the new Railway Minister announced in 2004 that there would be no increase in passenger tariff, no restructuring and no retrenchment of staff. It was the belief of the hon'ble minister that the railways had potential to revive on its own, without external help. To implement the revival strategy a number of administrative actions were initiated to enhance the capacity of the system to carry traffic.

The BOXN wagon, which carried most of the loose minerals, had a carrying capacity (CC) of 58.08 tonnes stencilled on its body. This had been increased to CC+2 tonnes in 1998 for coal and some other commodities. In 2004, a set of routine checks on freight consignments of minerals revealed that many wagons were actually carrying much more cargo than the permissible limit. The technical issue was whether it was safe to carry more cargo than the permissible limit. A series of consultations and study reports convinced the apex level management that with proper attention to track and the wagons, the weight of the cargo carried in BOXN wagons could safely be increased. From 2004, the South Eastern Railway notified that the BOXN wagon would carry CC+4 tonnes of power house coal and washed coal (plus some other commodities), and tariff would be charged on that weight. Gradually, routes were identified where carriage of CC+4, then CC+6 and finally CC+8 tonnes was allowed. An increase of 6 to 8 tonnes per wagon to the carrying capacity of the major commodities like coal, iron ore, steel on a stated capacity of 58.08 tonnes meant a quantum jump of more than 10 to 13 per cent in the loading of minerals, with the same set of wagons. This initiative was supplemented by increasing the intensity of examinations and reducing the frequency of mechanical examinations of freight wagons; by ensuring that all major loading and unloading terminals were able to accommodate full trains and that they were kept operational round the clock with proper illumination to facilitate work. The availability of more powerful locomotives, which had been inducted in the 1990s, allowed trains to run with the enhanced payloads. With these initiatives, the mobility of trains improved significantly.[50]

In 2005 another important change was introduced in the sphere of charging of freight. IR had a tradition of charging freight on the basis of two conditions known as the CC condition (carrying capacity), for commodities of higher density and the 'W' condition for commodities of lower density, whose weight would be less than the carrying capacity of the wagon even if the wagon was fully loaded with the commodity. Commodities under the 'W' condition were, therefore, charged at a 'minimum weight condition'. The government took a decision to do away with the two systems of charging freight. All commodities would henceforth be charged on the basis of the volumetric capacity of the wagon, irrespective of the actual weight of the consignment.

The Goods Tariff of the Indian Railways classifies commodities into distinct categories based on the type of commodity. For example, coal and various types of coal (such as coke) would be one category and iron and steel would be another category. For each category the 'base class' or rate of charge is specified and each base class is assigned a number. For example, salt could be class 110 and steel class 180. Higher base class implies a higher freight rate. The base class rates are low for items of mass consumption such as salt, and high for value added goods such as steel and petroleum products. The freight charge paid by the consumer depends on base class at which the commodity is charged, the weight of the consignment and the distance over which it is moved. There is a tariff table available to calculate the charge for a given distance and weight for each base class. The whole process is computerised now and the freight for a commodity between two points can be ascertained from the FOIS website.

Earlier, the freight table had class ranges from 40 to 300, the ratio between the lowest and the highest being 1:8. This system was rationalised and the ratio between the minimum and maximum class rates was reduced to 1:2. The

---

50 The frequency mechanical examination of a freight is laid down through policy circulars. A typical freight wagons takes 8 to 10 hours from its arrival at an examination point to its departure after examination. Reduction of number of examinations saves this time and improves mobility, without sacrificing safety.

All loading and unloading points cannot accommodate a full train (rake). Splitting a rake in parts for loading/unloading and reassembling it consumes time. Converting the sidings to accommodate full rakes saved time and ensured greater mobility of wagons. Opening the sidings for working round the clock added further flexibility.

break-even class rate was nominated as 100 and the maximum as 200, i.e. double the break-even price. After rationalisation of tariff, there were only 11 classes, uniformly increasing from 100 to 200 in multiples of 10. Earlier there were as many as 27 classes, and the increment was in steps of 5 between 40 and 190 and in increments of 10 from 190 to 300. The taper in the tariff for long distance traffic was also made uniform. [*Bankruptcy to Billions: Sudhir Kumar & Shagun Mehrotra, Oxford University Press, New Delhi 2009, Chapter 5*]

The new tariff structure was clearly more logical and simpler. There were some protests regarding the charging of freight at full carrying capacity for commodities which had very low density or which were discrete items with specific weights like steel coils, whose total weight was less than the carrying capacity of the wagons. These protests were not accepted. Some consumer friendly changes in the tariff pattern were introduced. For example, the tariff for transport of iron ore was increased, but that for steel was reduced.

The additional cargo per wagon due to enhancement of carrying capacity by six to eight tonnes per wagon and the charging of freight on volumetric capacity of the wagon, instead of the actual weight of the consignment, resulted in a dramatic increase in freight carried and revenue. The freight loading and the financial position of the Railways improved significantly. At the end of the Tenth Plan period (2007), the freight loading of Indian Railways had touched 727.75 mt of which coal constituted 313.33 mt (43 per cent). Continuing its upward trend, the freight loading increased further to 833.39 mt in 2008–09. Due to the enhancement in carrying capacity, coal loading increased from 223 million tonnes in 2000–01 to 369.63 million tonnes in 2008–09, i.e. by 65 per cent. Freight earnings increased from 23,305 crores in 2001 to 47,435 crores in 2008. This spectacular turn round of the Indian Railways was hailed all over the world.

Dedicated Freight Corridor

In 2006, the Minister for railways announced that two dedicated freight corridors, one from the east to north and the other from the north to the west would be constructed to provide seamless movement to freight cargo, reduce unit costs and improve customer satisfaction. A company named the Dedicated Freight Corridor Corporation of India (DFCCIL) was set up in October 2006 and mandated with constructing and running the DFC. The eastern DFC was to be from Ludhiana (Punjab) in north India to Dankuni in West Bengal (1875 kms.). The western leg would be from Dadri (near New Delhi) to Jawaharlal Nehru Port on the western coast (1506 kms.). This initiative was welcomed by the country as a radical departure from the staid planning processes of the past. Initially the eastern corridor would be constructed from Ludhiana to Sone Nagar and not up to Dankuni as the major coal traffic from the North Karanpura fields of CCL joins the Grand Chord at Sone Nagar. The stretch from Sone Nagar to Dankuni would be constructed later. It has now been decided that the Sone Nagar to Dankuni leg would also be constructed.

A map showing the planned alignment of the two DFCs is placed at Appendix 5.

It was decided that the track of the DFC was to be fit for 25 tonnes axle load of traffic, i.e. the gross weight of each wagon could be 100 tonnes, instead of the existing 91.6 tonnes. The bridges would be designed to carry 32.5 tonnes per axle. The decision was prompted by the vision of carrying heavy mineral traffic, particularly coal, on the east-north axis in the future. The estimates of traffic were perhaps too optimistic and the slow migration away from fossil fuels for energy was not foreseen. However, even if the expected mineral traffic does not move, the DFC could be used to carry parcel and container trains moving at high speeds to deliver cargo on a time tabled basis. This would help to divert a lot of traffic from road to rail and would boost the revenue earning of Indian Railways.

The eastern and western legs of the DFC were commissioned in 2023, after protracted delays due to issues of land acquisition, as the track alignment chosen for the two DFCs was not alongside the existing tracks. It is a moot point whether adding additional tracks to the existing congested routes with the same track standards and converting them into freight corridors would have been a simpler and faster exercise as in most areas the railways had land available alongside the existing routes.

As the eastern DFC was commissioned progressively, diverting coal trains on to it helped to relieve congestion the saturated trunk route and enhanced the speed of travel considerably.

New Policy for Coal

Progressing further on the path of liberalisation, the government announced a New Coal Distribution Policy (NCDP) in 2007. The major changes introduced by the NCDP were:

- The distinction between the core and non-core sector consumers was eliminated. Instead, each sector and consumer would be treated on merit, subject to regulatory provisions and other relevant issues.
- There was a new scheme for the pricing of coal for different consumers. The supply of coal to the railways and defence sectors would be at notified prices and the demands of these two sectors would be met in full.

- For the power sector, including independent power producers, captive power plants and the fertiliser industry, the full normative requirement of the industry would be considered through the agency of a 'Fuel Supply Agreement' (FSA) at prices to be decided by Coal India Ltd.
- Those power stations whose requirement had been assessed by the Standing Linkage Committee (Long Term) and who had been issued Letters of Assurance/linkage, would also be covered under the FSA.
- For other consumers, the assurance was for 75 per cent supply of the normative requirement at prices fixed by CIL. The balance 25 per cent would have to be procured through participation in e-auction of coal by CIL or through imports.
- Coal for the steel sector would be supplied on the basis of FSAs and the pricing would be on the basis of the existing system of import parity after adjusting for quality.
- Consumers requiring less than 4200 tonnes of coal per year would have to procure coal through nominated state agencies. The state governments would assess the requirements of consumers falling into this category and convey the demand to CIL. The coal would be distributed by the state governments or their authorised agencies. The nominated agencies would enter into FSA with CIL on behalf of the consumers. CIL would supply coal at the notified price and the agency would be allowed to charge a markup of 5 per cent as service charge.
- The system of coal linkage was to be replaced by what was claimed as a 'more transparent bilateral commercial arrangement of enforceable FSAs'.
- There was a clear enunciation of policy for new consumers also.
- The SLC (Long Term) would continue to be the recommending authority for issue of Letters of Assurance (LOA) to consumers in the power, captive power, steel, sponge iron and cement sectors. Other consumers would receive LOA from CIL based on recommendation of the nodal ministries.
- The e-auction of coal was introduced earlier for consumers who were unable to get coal under the existing system or did not require regular supply of coal. A new system for e-auction of coal would be introduced.

  [Source: Ministry of Coal]

The Fuel Supply Agreement was a legal document that had to be created and all the requirements of the consumers taken care of. Naturally, the new scheme threw up a fresh challenge for the coal industry, particularly for Coal India and the Singareni Coal Company. The most important departure of the new scheme from the earlier arrangement was the migration from a 'best effort' arrangement to a system of penalties in the event of noncompliance. The first task was to sign agreements with the existing power houses and this process started in 2009. For all consumers an Annual Contracted Quantity (ACQ) was calculated and the FSA stipulated a certain percentage fulfilment of the ACQ by the supplier, below which penalties would be triggered. Similarly, the consumer would be penalised for inability to accept the stipulated quantity. In case of domestic production falling short of requirements, the coal suppliers could import coal to meet the commitment of the contract.

The NCDP was introduced with laudable motives, but it seems to have overlooked certain developments in the power and coal industries and the railways. The factors were:

a) Addition to power generation capacity, which steadily increased from 16,730 mw during the Eighth Plan to 19,251 mw in the Ninth Plan and 27,283 in the Tenth Plan. It was to increase much more sharply thereafter, but that was not anticipated by the policy makers.
b) The captive coal mines which were supposed to produce additional coal, were not meeting their promises and the major companies like CIL and SCCL would have to absorb the burden of additional demand.
c) The higher price of imported coal prompted most users to opt for domestic coal.

The total production of coal in India, in 2009 was only 492.76 mt and even at this level, the import of coal was 60.88 mt, that is, about 12 per cent of the production. The power sector had not started importing coal, but would start very soon.

As addition to power generation capacity was more towards the west, north and the south of the country and the shift in the production pattern of coal was in favour of three states of Chhattisgarh, Jharkhand and Odisha, the additional coal traffic was getting concentrated on a very few railway routes which were already congested.

The quantum jumps in railway freight output achieved with the new policies was tapering off as the demand for transport was increasing very fast and the advantage accruing out of the increased carrying capacity of wagons was rapidly getting neutralised.

As mentioned earlier, the SLC (Short Term) used to consider coal allocation among major consumers in detail and produce a stable matrix of origin-destination (O-D) flows, which was helpful for the producer, the consumer and the transporter. Movement volumes on these routes were large and the distances considerable. The railways had created streams of traffic flows based on the SLC linkages and developed wagon and locomotive maintenance facilities along these routes. The sudden change in policy seemed to assume that movement from any origin to any destination would be feasible. This was true in theory, but in practice, given the state of saturation of the rail network, this was a bold and perhaps very optimistic decision.

All the factors mentioned above combined to create an imbalance between coal demand and supply. More developments were to take place very soon.

E Auction of Coal: The e auction of coal was placed on a firm footing and progressively expanded over the years to cover major sectors including power stations. The quantum of coal sold through e-auctions was small compared to the total production of the two leading coal companies CIL and SCCL. However, the price discovered through e-auction was higher than the notified price of coal and hence increased the revenue earning of the coal companies.

Developments during the Eleventh Plan (2007–12)

The growth of the railway network continued at its earlier staid pace. The demand for coal was growing rapidly and the network was getting more and more congested.

The award of the Sixth Pay Commission was announced in 2008. It entailed an additional expenditure of 73,000 crore Rupees on staff payments. The freight traffic had been projected to increase from 728 mt in 2007–08 to 1020 mt in 2011–12. The actual achievement was 970 mt with a CAGR of 5.9 per cent, less than what had been achieved in the recent past, but better than the performance of the 1990s. Coal loading was 455.8 mt (47 per cent of total freight), of which 300 mt, or about 66 per cent went to power stations. The financial position of the railways was again coming under strain.

CIL's Public Issue: In November 2010, divestment of 10 per cent of the government held shares of Coal India Ltd. was permitted. These shares would be traded in the stock market. The Initial Public Offer (IPO) was made on the 4th of November 2010. It was a great success and was soon oversubscribed many times over, bringing in a huge capital flow for the government. In that same year, Coal India was accorded the Maharatna status, which is the highest ranking for government owned companies in India.

Coal Production and Demand for Coal

The total production of coal and lignite increased from 491.1 mt (457.1 mt plus 34 mt lignite) in 2007–08 to 582.3 mt (540 mt coal plus 42.3 mt lignite) in 2011–12, yielding a CAGR of 4.4 per cent. The production from CIL increased from 379.46 mt in 2007–08 to 435.84 mt in 2011–12, a growth of 56.38 mt at a low cagr of 3.5 per cent. One of the reasons for slow growth was the stringent environmental norms which did not permit some new projects to take off.

The demand for coal increased at 6.6 per cent per year leading to higher demands for imports. The data presented in Table 5.1 illustrates the rapidity with which demand for coal from the power sector was growing:

Table 5.1: Thermal Power Generation Capacity (in Mega Watts) at the end of Five Year Plan Periods 2002 to 2012

	Coal/ Lignite	Gas	Diesel	Total	Hydro	Nuclear	RES	Total	Coal Based Generation Capacity Added during Plan (in MW)
31-3-02 end of Ninth Plan	62131	11163	1135	74429	26269	2720	1628	105046	
31-3-07 End if 10th Plan	71121	13692	1202	86015	34654	3900	7760	132329	8990
31-3-2012 end of Eleventh Plan	112022	18381	1200	131603	38990	4780	24504	199877	40,901

Source: Ministry of Power, CEA, 2022. (Last column added by author)

The mismatch between the coal production and demand led to rise in imports as seen it Table 5.2:

Table 5.2: Coal Imports by India 2006–12

	Total Import of Coal (In million tonnes)	Import for Power Sector (In million tonnes)
Year	(Data from Ministry of Coal)	(Data from PIB Release by Ministry of Power)
2006	41.21	
2007	47.77	
2008	54.04	
2009	60.88	
2010	75.62	23.2
2011	70.40	30.5
2012	105.11	44.99

Source: PIB release of 6th December 2023. Coal Ministry Annual Report 2014–15

The gap between demand and supply of coal for the power sector would worsen very soon.

Grading of Coal on basis of Gross Calorific Value

In 2012, the Government approved the pricing of coal on the basis of Gross Calorific Value (GCV), instead of Ultimate Heat Value (UHV), as done earlier. The difference was that GCV considers the calorific value that would be generated by burning the coal and other elements that may be mixed with the coal, whereas, UHV considers only the heat produced by coal and is thus more conservative in terms of grading of coal. GCV is the norm that is universally used.

Under the GCV regime, coal was divided into three categories of coking coal, semi-coking and non-coking. Coking coal was divided on the basis of ash content into eight classes starting with steel grade I, steel grade II and then moving on to Washery grade I to washery grade VI. Semi-coking coal was divided into semi-coking grade I and II. Non-coking coal was put into 17 classes based on energy levels of kilocalories per kilogram, with Grade I starting at the value exceeding 7,000 kcal/kg and Grade II with calorific value 6,700 to 7,000 kcal/kg. and so on in bands of 300 kcal/kg each up to 2,200–2,500 for the lowest grade G-17. The price of coal was increased after the change from UHV to GCV. The justification was that this was international practice and the price of coal in India was one of the lowest in the world. The increase in prices did not go down well with the consumers, grappling with the environment of coal shortage.

Shortage of Coal

The stage was getting set for a major coal supply related issue to develop. The major coal producer in the country CIL, had been signing FSAs with existing power sector entities and other consumers. The stipulation in the NCDP was that demand of all consumers had to be met. It is the opinion of some experts that this stipulation of the NCDP was based on a perception that the total planned increase in power generation capacity would not fructify, as had been the experience in the Ninth and Tenth Five Year Plan periods. P.S. Bhattacharya, who was Chairman of CIL between 2006 and 2011 observes:

> The provision was inserted on the basis of a perception that the coal demand, particularly from the power sector, was unduly inflated and unlikely to materialise. It was based on the experience during the Eighth, Ninth and Tenth Five Year Plans when capacity addition in the power sector fell short of the planned target by margins of 50 per cent or higher. However, the preparation on the ground to mitigate the constraints against accelerated growth in power capacity addition was markedly different during the Eleventh Five Year Plan, a fact that policy makers did not visualise. This failure to

> read the writing on the wall made the situation untenable as the aggregate demand in all consuming sectors increased fast and far exceeded CIL's planned production. (Bhattacharya, P. S., When Coal Turned to Gold, Penguin Random House, Gurugram 2018, pages 84–85)

There were two categories of power plants. Those that were functioning at the time of signing the first FSAs and those that were under construction and would be commissioned by 2015. CIL was willing to sign FSA with plants that were functioning but baulked at signing FSAs with new power stations as the amount of coal to be delivered was difficult to produce within the given time frame. The new power consumers, whose power plants were under commissioning, met the Prime Minister and requested him to intervene.

A Presidential Directive was issued to CIL in 2012 stating that all plants which were functioning as of 2009 were to be provided coal for 90 per cent of their requirement and those that were under commissioning, and were likely to be onstream by 2015, should be provided coal to 80 per cent of their requirement. This was a very difficult task and the contracts provided for stiff penalties for noncompliance. After considering the issue, some amendments were made by the CIL Board with respect to the penalties that were to be paid by CIL in the event of failure to supply at the rate of 80 per cent. The Ministry of Coal confirmed that if the power plants did not receive adequate coal, it would be imported by CIL. The power plants had the option of importing the coal directly or through CIL.

The Indian Railways was the main transporter of coal to the power stations. Despite the introduction of new wagons and powerful locomotives and daily coordination with coal companies regarding coal loading and movement, the capacity to carry traffic was getting stretched as the traffic was growing on a few specific corridors. Between 2010 and 2015, a total of about 93,000 mw of coal based power capacity had been added either by expansion of existing facilities or by installing new power stations. The western and the northern sectors added the largest capacities.

Table 5.3: Coal based Power Capacity added between 2010 and 2015

Sector	States	Capacity Added in MW	Per Cent of Total
Eastern	Bihar, Jharkhand, Odisha, West Bengal	13555	14.5
Northern	Punjab, Haryana, Rajasthan, Uttar Pradesh	18320	19.6
Western	Chhattisgarh, Madhya Pradesh, Gujarat, Maharashtra	46224	49.4
Southern	Andhra Pradesh, Karnataka, Tamil Nadu, Telangana	15,400	16.5

Source: Derived from List of Thermal Power Stations in India, Ministry of Power, CEA, 2021.

Due to the location of the demand centres, the greatest pressure of movement came on the following sections:

a. Jharsuguda-Bilaspur-Raipur-Nagpur
b. Bilaspur-New Katni-Bina
c. Talcher-Cuttack Paradip and Talcher-Khurda Road Waltair
d. Tori-Garwa Road-Sone Nagar-Deen Dayal Upadhyay-Kanpur ('A'-route of old Northern Railway, now North Central Railway)
e. Tori-Garwa Road-Sone Nagar-Deen Dayal Upadhyay-Lucknow ('B'-Route of Northern Railway).

Line capacity enhancement works were in progress in all these areas, but the works were not completed in time to meet the surge in traffic. For example, two critical line capacity works, the Jharsuguda-Bilaspur third line was completed only in 2020, the Bilaspur-Anuppur doubling was completed only in 2019.

A map showing the coalfields and important coal routes under considerable pressure is placed at Appendix 6.

Expert Committees

To find a solution to the issues facing the railways, the government set up two committees, in 2010 and 2011. The first Committee was known as the High Level National Transport Development Policy Committee (NTDPC). The committee submitted its report in 2014. The NTDPC committee had formed a special group on movement of bulk materials, particularly coal.

The NTDPC report was very large in its ambit as it considered the transport sector as a whole and also addressed issues of energy use. It stated that the demand for freight transport was expected to rise sharply in the next two decades and the rate of growth of passenger traffic demand would be even higher than freight. In the freight segment, Indian Railways had been steadily losing market share which had reduced from about 90 per cent in 1950–51 to about 30 per cent in 2012. The present trend of growth in the transport sector would not be sustainable in the long run as the energy implications of this pattern would imply greater dependence on imported crude oil and the higher levels of pollution caused by road transport. The report emphasised that steps should be taken to increase the modal share of the railways.

While reiterating the problems faced by Indian Railways in terms of inadequate growth of network, congestion of arterial routes, insufficient investment, cross subsidisation of passenger traffic by freight, the report called for major increase in investment in the railways. Other issues of an independent tariff regulatory authority, better investment planning and execution of projects were also flagged.

The second report was from an expert group on the modernisation of the Indian railways. It was named "The Report of the Expert Group on Modernisation of Indian Railways (2012)," and was headed by Sam Pitroda. In the final report the committee stressed the need for an immediate expansion of the network and the need to dedicate money for this purpose. It called for a rebate in the dividend payment and a reduction in sourcing of funds from extra budgetary resources. Among the priority projects, the report mentioned the need to expedite completion of and increase expenditure for doubling of single tracks, new lines and electrification projects.

Basically, both the expert committees had reiterated issues which had already been flagged since the Ninth Five Year Plan. The availability of resources and the political will to fund the expansion proposed by the committees was the crux of the issue.

Beneficiation of Coal and Pit Head Power Plants

In the absence of rapid expansion of the railway network, the washing of non-coking coal could have provided relief for transportation, as carrying 45 per cent ash over long distances was a patently wasteful exercise. However, the performance on this front was dismal. According to the report of Coal Controller for 2016–17, there were 20 washeries in the country, 3 in the public sector and the rest in the private sector. The total installed capacity for washing of non-coking coal was 105.24 mt and the output of these washeries was a paltry 45.12 mt

Another way of reducing the load on the transportation system, and reducing the cost of generation of power would be to set up more power stations near the coal sources. This process had been started but did not really take off due to concerns of environmental degradation at the locations where major power stations were set up. According to the CEA, at the end of the second decade of the twenty-first century, there were 180 coal based power stations in the country, of which 18 were based at the pit heads and 15 were based on use of imported coal. The coal requirement was:

Table 5.4: Coal Requirement of Thermal Power Stations in Million tonnes

Total Coal Required	690.2
Requirement of Domestic Coal Based Plants	645.2
Requirement of Plants Based on Imported Coal	45

Source: Ministry of Power, CEA, 2021, pp. 58–9.

Clearly, the number of plants based on imported coal was a rather small fraction of the total. Two types of plants used imported coal. First those which depend exclusively on imported coal for generation and second, those which use imported coal for blending along with domestic coal. Imported coal has high calorific value and thus exerts lesser demands on the transport system. However, the total volume is very small.

In the year 2020–21, the Indian Railways transported a total of 1230.94 million tonnes of freight traffic, which included 541.82 million tonnes of coal (44 per cent). As 75–80 per cent of the coal transported is for the power sector, the transportation requirement is well over 400 million tonnes. Considering the fact that the preponderant quantity was emanating from the three major coalfields of Korba, Talcher and North Karanpura, the pressure on the already congested corridors was steadily increasing

Captive Coal Mines

The allocation of captive coal mines had continued unabated from 1993 to 2011. In all 218 mines had been allocated via two routes. First, through the Screening Committee route, in which a committee headed by the Additional Secretary, Ministry of Coal and other officers of various departments scrutinised applications and allocated mines. The second route was through the Government Dispensation route, which allocated mines for Public Sector Enterprises for captive use. 'The Comptroller and Auditor General (C&AG) of India in its Performance Audit (PA) Report No. 7 of 2012–13 for the year ended March 2012 highlighted the issues of lack of transparency and objectivity in the allocation process of coal blocks and financial gains of (Rupees) 1.86 lakh crore to the private parties, a part of which could have been tapped by the Government by taking timely decision on competitive bidding for allocation of coal blocks.' (Comptroller and Auditor General, 2012)

Following a public interest litigation [Manohar Lal Sharma V/s the Principal Secretary & Others (Writ Petition (CRL.) No. 120 of 2012], the Supreme Court of India held, (in August 2014), that the allocation of coal mines since 1993 were arbitrary and illegal. Allocation of 204 coal blocks was cancelled. This was a major milestone for the production of coal in the country as the demand for coal, particularly from the power sector was growing very rapidly.

The period was one of great stress on the coal supply front. On October 10, 2014, a report by Reuters stated:

> A power plant in India's capital New Delhi is among 37 across the country that have either exhausted their coal or have less than four days' supply, a shortage that has forced some states to ration power for industries and homes.

> Many states have been hit by a severe power deficit which has dealt a blow to small-scale factories that produce everything from steel to textiles and cannot afford alternatives such as diesel generators. (Reuters, 2014)

The projection of coal production for the terminal year of the Twelfth Plan (2016–17) was 795 mt, which included a growth of 179 mt from CIL at a cagr of 7.12 per cent, up from 3.5 per cent for the Eleventh Plan, a very ambitious target. Another ambitious target was to increase coal production of captive blocks from 36 mt to 100 mt. Assuming an overall demand of 980 mt for the terminal year of the Twelfth Plan, the import component would have to be 185 mt. The actual import in the fiscal year 2017 was 191mt. The inability of domestic production to meet demand continued. The steady increase in import of coal can be seen from Table 5.5:

Table 5.5: Coal Imports 2013–17

Year	Total Import of Coal in million tonnes	Import for Power Stations in million tonnes
2012–13	137.56	62.7
2013–14	166.85	79.5
2014–15	212.10	90.10
2015–16	203.95	81.1
2016–17	191.01	66.1

Source: PIB Communique, 6 December 2023, Ministry of Coal, 2021.

The Twelfth Five Year Plan could not run its full course. In the general elections of 2014, a new government of the National Democratic Alliance (NDA), led by Mr. Narendra Modi came to power. The Planning Commission was disbanded and replaced with the NITI Ayog. The Press Information Bureau, stated in a press communique:

> The NITI Aayog, established in 2015, is one of Indian democracy's youngest institutions. It has been entrusted with the mandate of re-imagining the development agenda by dismantling old-style central planning. As the Indian economy rapidly integrated with the global economy contradictions arose between central planning and increasing private capital flows. The NITI Aayog was mandated to foster cooperative federalism, evolve a national consensus on developmental goals, redefine the reforms agenda, act as a platform for resolution of cross-sectoral issues between Centre and State Governments, capacity building and to act as a Knowledge and Innovation hub. It represented a huge mandate for a nascent organization. (PIB Communique, 2017)

New Initiatives

The new government took some important decisions regarding the Indian Railways and the coal industry, which would help the progress of these two industries.

In the case of the railways, the Minister for Railways Mr. Suresh Prabhu presented a White Paper on Indian Railways before the Parliament in February 2015. The paper stated very candidly the problems the railways had faced in the past and the planned course of action. At the outset the White Paper stated:

> The expenditure on Railways as a percentage of total transport expenditure has declined considerably. Railway expenditure as percentage of transport sector expenditure used to be about 56% in 7th Plan (1985–90). It has reduced to 30% in 11th Plan (2007–12). IR in last two decades has remained under-invested whereas the road sector has witnessed a surge in investments. The share of IR in overall GDP has been static at 1% and has, in fact, gone down to 0.9% in 2012–13 ...."In the last 64 years while the freight loading has grown by 1344% and passenger kilometers by 1642%, the Route kilometers have grown by only 23% and Doubling & Multiple route length by only 289%. (Ministry of Railways, White Paper on Indian railways February 2015)

The paper provided data to show that the traffic density on IR was comparable to the leading railway systems of the world, but the growth of its network had been extremely slow and this had resulted in severe congestion on most of the important routes right across the nation. The only way out of the impasse was to create track capacity on a massive scale. In the Railway Budget presented in February 2015, the railway minister proposed an investment plan of Rupees 856,020 crores of which 45 per cent would be spent for network decongestion and network expansion. The Plan outlay was increased significantly and it was decided that money for financing the expansion would be raised from the market if required.

This, indeed, was a bold departure from the past. The experiment of raising the cargo carried per wagon had been a spectacular but short term solution. The limitation on the ability of the existing track network to carry additional load had been exploited and now additional tracks or massive expansion of the existing network was required. Fortunately, the new Government decided that additional tracks was the correct answer.

Another committee on the railways with broad terms of reference submitted a report in 2015. This was the report of the Committee for Mobilisation of Resources for Major Railway Projects and Restructuring of Railway Ministry and Railway Board, headed by noted economist Dr. Bibek Debroy. It made a large number of recommendations in the areas of organisational restructuring, accounting methods, revenue generation etc. to revive the position of

Indian Railways. Without going into all the suggestions, the most important ones are mentioned here. (a) Transition to a commercial accounting system (b) setting up an independent Railway Regulatory Authority, which would be independent of the Ministry of Railways and would have a separate budget. It would have far reaching powers regarding tariff and safety regulation, setting of technical standards and also have jurisdiction in several other areas. (c) The government should review its dividend policy and provide the railways with gross budgetary support net of dividend. (d) The number of services of Group A officers should be combined into one or two cadres. The Committee preferred the two-cadre option with the technical services belonging to one group and the non-technical services falling in the other group. (e) The Committee also made a number of recommendations for offloading non-essential services like running schools. It was recognised that the wide-ranging changes suggested would have to take place gradually and a graded approach was recommended.

In a historic move in 2016, the central Government decided to amalgamate the Railway Budget with the Union Budget with effect from the financial year 2017–18, putting an end to the separation which had started in 1924 following the Acworth Committee Report. The merger of the budget had very important implications for the railways. First, the 'Capital at charge', which was the legacy capital received from the government and on which the railways paid dividend to the government, would be wiped out. There would be no dividend payable henceforth on the capital provided by the government. This would save the railways about Rupees 5,000 crores every year. The capital for investment in the railways would be provided in the general budget. Borrowing from the market could be resorted to by the railways, if required. [PIB Communique on merger of Railway Budget with General Budget]

Funding Capital Investment

Due to the enhancement of carrying capacity of wagons introduced in 2004, the revenue position of the railways had improved and up to 2008–09, a large portion of capital funding came from internal resources. However, from 2009–10, the government had to undertake the major share of the funding. From 2015–16, with the change in the policy of the government, a large portion of funds was raised from the market. This continued till 2020–21, after which the funding from the government increased as it was decided to provide a thrust to infrastructure growth. Total capital investment in the railways more than doubled between 2015–16 and 2022–23. Consequently, a lot of projects for laying of new tracks and augmentation of existing routes received funds.

To revive the production of coal from the captive mines, the new government 'within a short span of time, laid down the framework and successfully auctioned 29 coal mines in two tranches by March 2015' [CAG report referred above]. The production of coal from captive mines was a welcome addition to the total basket. Starting from a level of level of 51 mt in 2012–13, the production increased steadily and reached a level of 90 mt by 2021–22.

Total production of coal increased from 609.2 mt in 2014–15 to 730.8 in 2019–20, at a CAGR of 3.71 per cent. Import of coal continued to rise and touched a figure of 248.5 mt in 2020. The freight loading of Indian Railways increased from 1101.5 in 2015–16 to 1221.5 in 2018–19, but dropped to 1208.4 in 2019–20, yielding a CAGR of only 2.3 per cent between 2015–16 and 2019–20.

New Environmental Norms for Power Stations

In 2014, the earlier norm (of 1997) of a distance of 1000 kilometres for using beneficiated coal was modified. Now it was mandated that plants located at distances less than 1000 kms would also have to use beneficiated coal with ash not exceeding 34 per cent. Captive power plants and stand-alone power plants within distances of 500–749 kilometres and 750–1,000 kilometres would also have to use coal of similar ash content on a quarterly basis.

In December 2015, the environmental guidelines were tightened further and stringent limits for emission norms with respect to oxides of sulphur (SOx), oxides of nitrogen (NOx) and mercury were specified. The norms were graded for plants commissioned before 31 December 2003, between 2003 and 31 December 2016 and after 2016. The new guidelines necessitated the retrofitting of or replacement of electrostatic precipitators (ESPs) at the functional power stations. New Flue Gas Desulphurisation (FGD) units would also have to be added to new plants.

In 2020, 'The Energy and Resources Institute' (TERI) prepared a report on 'Economic and Environmental Impact of Coal Washing in India' for the NITI Ayog. This report cited the benefits of using washed coal, but added a caveat that the judicious use of the rejects of the washing process was equally important to control pollution. The study noted that it was difficult to conclude that beneficiation was an unmixed blessing. This was because developing a direct correlation between ash percentage and GCV was a challenge. Coal with lower ash percentage could have a lower GCV than coal with higher percentage of ash. One pilot study conducted on behalf of TERI had shown that overall cycle efficiency of the power plant deteriorated after using beneficiated coal. Thus, a number of pilot studies were required and decisions would have to be taken on a case by case basis regarding use of beneficiated coal for a power station.

In 2018–19, there were 22 non-coking coal washeries in India of which four were under CIL and eighteen under private operators. The total installed capacity was 16.22 mt for the CIL washeries and 100.47 mt for the others. The installed capacity of 116.69 mt does appear to be rather small compared to the requirement of coal by the power sector. The issue of beneficiation received less attention after the report of TERI was circulated, and the washing of non-coking coal hardly progressed. In fact, the report from the Ministry of Statistics and Programme Implementation for the year 2022 mentioned that the total installed capacity for washing non-coking coal in 2022 was 115.13 mtpa. There were a total of 41 non-coking coal washeries in the country. Of this five were under CIL and thirty six in the private sector. Of the five under CIL, only three with a total capacity of 11.0 mt were functioning. Out of the thirty six in the private sector, only eighteen were functional, with a total capacity of 104.13 mtpa. Two washeries under CIL and as many as eighteen under the private sector had closed down. In April 2022, PIB reported that CIL was going to set up a 10 mt washery at Ib Valley as capacity of washing non-coking coal continued to be inadequate. It is heartening to note that the total installed capacity of coking coal washeries in 2022 was 37.18 mt and CIL planned to set up ten more coking coal washeries.

Expansion of Railway Network

Three major joint venture companies had been formed between 2013 and 2015 for specific railway projects designed to evacuate coal from new coalfield expansion programmes. These were collaborations between the coal companies under CIL, the railways (represented by Indian Railway Construction Company, IRCON) and the state governments for evacuation of additional coal production from the Korba/ Mand Raigarh coalfields under SECL in Chhattisgarh, the Talcher coalfields in Odisha under MCL and the North Karanpura coalfields in Jharkhand under CCL. The names of the three companies were:

- Chhattisgarh East Railway Company Limited (participants: SECL, IRCON, Government of Chhattisgarh) – Line from Kharsia-Dharamjaigarh-Korba (192 kms), projected traffic 62 mt for phase 1 and 25 mt for phase 2. Transportation of coal from Mand-Raigarh field of SECL. Line up to Dharamjaigarh has been completed and coal loading has commenced.
- Chhattisgarh East West Railway Company Limited: Line from Gevra to Pendra Road on Bilaspur-Katni route (135 kms). Projected traffic 63 mt. This would probably include some traffic emanating from the CERL project.

  When fully functional, the projects would provide new routes for coal transportation by rail.

- Jharkhand Central Railway Company Limited: (participants: CCL, IRCON, Government of Jharkhand): Tori-Shivpur (50 kms). Projected traffic 32 mt The line has been completed and is functional. An extension is proposed from Shivpur via Khatautia to Koderma to meet the Dhanbad-Gaya line at Koderma. This is uncertain at present.
- Mahanadi Coal Railway Company Limited: (Participants: MCL, IRCON, Government of Odisha) laying additional lines on the existing double line routes for additional movement of about 40 mt of coal.

Some other projects which are being executed for catering to large increase in production are:

Jharsuguda-Barpalli line for movement of about 60 mt of coal. This is being executed by the Indian Railways and funded by MCL. Additional infrastructure is also being created on ECL for clearance of coal traffic from the Sonepur Bazari and Rajmahal projects.

Schematic maps showing the lines planned for the Korba and Mand Raigarh fields and the North Karanpura coalfields is placed at Appendix 7.

After these projects are completed, the ability of the railways to evacuate coal from the four coalfields of Korba/Mand Raigarh, North Karanpura and Talcher and Ib Valley coalfields will increase substantially. The work on the main railway routes which would carry away the additional coal would also have to be expedited. Some additional works are already in progress in areas such as: third line on the Bilaspur-Katni route, a fourth line on the Jharsuguda-Bilaspur route, a third line on the Jharsuguda-Chakradharpur-Tata route, a third line on the Khurda-Waltair route and a third line between Tori and Son Nagar. Line capacity augmentation beyond these railway zones will also be required and this has also been planned.

The railways had also introduced some schemes such as the 'Own Your Wagon Scheme', the 'Special Freight Operator Scheme' and the 'Private Freight Terminal Scheme' to augment the rolling stock and terminal handling capacity of the railways. Coal was kept out of most of the schemes. However, procurement of wagons by private players for transportation of other commodities would release rolling stock for coal loading.

Commercial Mining of Coal

In view of the growing demand for coal and the steady increase in imports, the government decided to open up the coal sector for commercial mining. The Mineral Laws (Amendment) Act was passed in 2020. The coal sector was thrown open for private players and earlier conditions of captive use were withdrawn.

Participation of foreign investors was allowed. A revenue sharing model was developed through which the state governments would benefit substantially. Twenty mines were auctioned in 2020 and by March 2023, eighty-seven mines had been successfully auctioned. The new mines would create large employment opportunities and add an estimated revenue of more than 33,000 crore Rupees for the states. The scheme also offered incentives for adoption of cleaner technologies like coal liquification and coal gasification. Extraction of coal bed methane was also allowed to the successful bidders. Production of coal from the new mines would take some time. It is hoped that with the new ventures contributing to the production, the country will become self-sufficient in non-coking coal (PIB Communique, 2023).

The Covid pandemic which hit the world in 2019, travelled to India in early 2020. Economic activities were hit badly. However, amidst these challenging circumstances, the coal industry and the railways continued to deliver services to the nation. The performance of these two industries is presented in table 5.6. The data is drawn from the information available from website of Ministry of Coal and Year Books of Ministry of Railways.

Table 5.6: Coal Availability and Coal Transported by Indian Railways (Data in Million Tonnes)

Year	Total Coal Production from (CIL+ SCCL+ Captive and Others)	Share in Total from Captive and Private Sources	Coal Imported	Total Coal	Coal trans-ported by Railways	Total Freight Loading of Railways
2019–20	730.87	64.70	248.53	979.4	586.87	1,208.41
2020–21	716.08	69.29	215.25	931.33	541.82	1,230.94
2021–22	778.21	90.56	208.93	987.13	652.80	1,415.87
2022–23	893.19	122.85	237.67	1,130.86	727.24	1,509.10

Source: Ministry of Coal, Indian Railway Year Books.

By the second half of 2021, the economy was slowly emerging from the throes of the pandemic and demand from industry, particularly power, was increasing. Despite the commendable performance of the two industries during the pandemic, another crisis of coal availability for power plants developed. As in the past, the strong cooperation between the railways and the coal industry led to concentration of resources to fulfil the coal demands of the core sector of the economy and the problem did not last for very long. The Indian Railways transported 652.80 mt of coal in 2021–22 and 727.24 mt in 2022–23. Of this 74 per cent in 2021–22 and 78 per cent in 2022–23 was for the power sector. The high percentage of power sector movement was a positive indicator of industrial revival after the Pandemic. The progressive commissioning of the eastern DFC enabled freight trains to be run at high speeds on the DFC and this helped to increase the mobility of coal movement to the north. A crisis of low coal stocks was averted.

First Mile Connectivity Project

A laudable initiative of CIL is the 'First Mile Connectivity Project'. This scheme aims to install rapid wagon loading systems at all mines producing more than 4 mt per annum. The mined coal would move via conveyors to the loading system where it would be crushed to small size and then loaded into the wagons. The advantage would be the elimination of road interface from mine to colliery siding and use of payloaders for loading wagons. Complaints of oversized coal from consumers are likely to reduce and quality parameters are expected to improve. The mobility of the railway wagons will also improve as loading time of a train would be about two hours. It may be recalled that a similar suggestion had been made by the Kumaramangalam Committee way back in 1983. Those suggestions were, unfortunately, implemented at only a few locations.

The rapid increase in the production of captive coal mines, many of whom were located near the power plants reduced the pressure on the transport system. The production from captive and other sources was about 10 per cent of the total production.

Another initiative of the government, the Gati Shakti scheme, was launched in 2021. It aimed at fast tracking the sanctioning and execution of engineering projects for enhancing the capacity of railway to carry freight traffic. There has been a perceptible improvement in the execution of projects.

Power from Renewable Sources

India made commendable progress in the generation of electricity from renewable sources of energy (RES). According to data of the CEA, the percentage breakup of installed capacity for power generation at the end of March 2020 was:

Coal: 56.36 per cent, Hydro: 12.75 per cent, RES: 21.8 per cent, Nuclear: 1.9 per cent, Diesel:0.18 per cent and Gas 7 per cent.

The growth of generation capacity based on renewable energy sources was a commendable achievement. However, in terms of gross electricity generation, the coal-based power stations contributed 71.87 per cent due to their higher PLF, while the renewable energy based power stations contributed only 10 per cent. India has a long way to go before transitioning from coal to cleaner sources of energy.

The world is slowly moving towards cleaner energy and India will doubtless follow suit. The growth of the Indian economy and the consequent growth in energy needs, particularly that for power, makes the choice of technology extremely delicate. Policy makers have to consider the ways of achieving the goal of providing reliable energy supply to all citizens by 2030, and the fuel mix that will enable this goal optimally while moving towards the sustainable development goals. We turn to examining the various options available and the likely road ahead in the next chapter.

CHAPTER 6

Looking Ahead

From a humble beginning in the middle of the nineteenth century, the coal industry and the railways have traversed a long journey spanning one hundred and sixty-eight years. During this long period, policies, administrative structures and management practices have changed to suit contemporary conditions. Technology has been upgraded as science has progressed. Administrative exigencies have, sometimes, resulted in sudden changes in management practices. The two industries have taken all these revisions in their stride and continued their mutual cooperation to provide a crucial energy resource for the nation.

Coal production increased spectacularly since 1855 to satisfy the increasing demand for the steadily expanding railway services. Other industries slowly developed and claimed their own share. As late as the 1950s, the railways used almost a third of the coal produced in the country. The requirement of the railways dwindled slowly with the introduction of diesel and electric traction. However, the rapid increase in demand from industries, particularly coal-based power generation, stretched the resources of both industries. In the present century, coal is being imported to supplement indigenous availability. Close coordination between the coal producers and railways along with technological innovations, changes in administrative policies and management practices helped to deliver sufficient coal to the consumers.

Use of coal and oil have undoubtedly promoted industrial development, but this has come at a great cost to the environment. The world has realised that the unfettered use of fossil fuels cannot continue. During the COP 28 conference in December 2023, Indian climate justice activist Licypriya Kangujam, held aloft a placard inscribed 'End fossil fuel. Save our planet and our future'. She was all of 12 years of age, and her action may be put down to the exuberance of youth, but she drew instant applause from the audience before she was escorted off the stage.

The action of this young girl underlined the importance that the generation of today, and indeed the entire world, attaches to climate change and the role of polluting fossil fuels. Though the final declaration of the conference mentioned 'transitioning away' from coal, oil and natural gas, instead of the more direct 'phase out', the writing on the wall was clear. Fossil fuels like coal would have to go, sooner rather than later.

To move towards a carbon free world, research on non-fossil fuels is progressing at a frenetic pace. A number of new frontiers such as green hydrogen, are emerging. This new form of energy is extremely important as it can be stored. The cost of solar panels is also reducing rapidly. Any disruptive change in technology, such as the possibility of achieving nuclear fusion at room temperature, may change the scenario suddenly. For the present, we can try to assess what the future has in store for us, given the present state of technology.

In the COP 26 meet at Glasgow in 2021, India had made five commitments (Panchamrit):

- Increase its non-fossil electricity generation capacity to 500 GW by 2030, from 172 GW today.
- Meet 50 per cent of its energy requirements from renewable energy by 2030.
- Reduce the total projected carbon emissions by one billion tonnes from 2021 till 2030. The IEA's WEO (International Energy Agency, World Energy Outlook) estimated India's net emissions from energy use at 2.3 billion tonnes in 2020.
- Reduce its economy's carbon intensity by 45 per cent by 2030, compared to 2005 levels.
- Achieve the target of net-zero carbon emissions by 2070. (PIB Communique 3 February 2022)

What trajectory would the transition curve follow, and how would the demand for coal be affected? This is a complicated exercise as a number of issues such as the energy security of the nation, environmental protection and the geopolitical scenario have to be considered.

The primary energy demand in the country has been growing steadily due to industrial development and urbanisation. The rate of growth of demand for energy would be determined by the progress of industrial development and increase in urban population. India is today the third largest electricity market in the world and the per capita consumption of electricity in the country doubled from 631 Units to 1,255 Units between 2005 and 2022. The economy has come out of the impact of the Covid pandemic, and it is expected that the demand for electricity will continue to grow rapidly.

At present, the main providers of energy remain the fossil fuels, coal and oil, with renewables gradually increasing in importance. According to the Energy Statistics for 2023 published by the Department of Statistics and Programme Implementation, in 2021–22 (P), the two major contributors to the total energy supply in the country were coal, which accounted for 56.13 per cent of the total and Crude Oil which accounted for 33.40 per cent. The power sector consumes about 70 per cent of the coal used in the country and the demand for coal in the future will depend greatly on the requirement of the power sector. For this reason, the present narrative will focus primarily on the future role of coal with respect to power generation. If the demand for power rises at a very fast pace in the future, renewable sources may continue to be supplemented by additional coal based generation. The energy generation mix for the future would have to be assessed keeping in view the anticipated sharp growth in demand and the resource constraints.

The total production of coal in the country in 2022–23 was 893.19 mt and the total coal availability (including imports) was 1130.86 mt, a positive growth of 14.56 per cent over the previous year. The total imports were 237.67 mt including 181.61 mt of non-coking and 56.05 mt of coking coal. In the energy mix for power generated, electricity generation from coal based plants contributed about 74 per cent of the total. The relative share of coal remained the highest amongst all fuels. However, it has begun to exhibit a slight downward trend due to increased contribution from renewables.

The National Electricity Plan (NEP) for the period 2022–32 assesses the energy demand for the medium term. A statement published by the PIB on 31 May 2023 mentioned the following salient points:

- According to the NEP, the projected All India peak electricity demand and electrical energy requirement is 277.2 GW and 1907.8 BU for the year 2026–27 and 366.4 GW and 2473.8 BU for the year 2031–32 as per 20th Electric Power Survey (EPS) Demand projections. The Energy Requirement & Peak Demand are inclusive of the impact due to increased adoption of Electric Vehicles, Installation of Solar roof tops, Production of Green hydrogen, Saubhagya scheme etc.
- The likely Installed Capacity for the year 2026–27 is 609,591 MW comprising of 273,038 MW of Conventional capacity (Coal-235,133 MW, Gas–24,824 MW, Nuclear-13,080 MW) and 336,553 MW of Renewable based capacity.
- The likely Installed Capacity for the year 2031–32 is estimated to be 900,422 MW comprising of 304,147 MW of Conventional capacity (Coal-259,643 MW, Gas–24,824 MW, Nuclear-19,680 MW) and 596,275 MW of Renewable based Capacity

- The projection of total capacity addition is in line with the target of the country to achieve a non-fossil based installed capacity of around 500 GW by the year 2029–30.
- Share of non-fossil fuels is likely to be 57.4 per cent by 2026–27 and 68.4 per cent by 2031–32.
- The average PLF of the total Installed coal capacity of 235.1 GW is likely to be about 58.4% in 2026–27 and that of 259.6 GW of coal based capacity is likely to be about 58.7 % in 2031–32. (PIB Communique of 31 May 2023).

The plan is to add 24,510 mw of coal-based capacity between 2026–27 and 2031–32 and the total coal based power generation capacity installed would be 259,643 mw, up from the level of 211,055 as on 31 January 2023 (CEA data). However, due to rapid growth in the installed capacity of renewable sources, the share of coal in installed capacity would drop to about 38 per cent of the total in 2026–27 and further to 28 per cent in 2031–32. Clearly, the rate of growth of demand for coal would decelerate to some extent.

The Ministries of Coal and Railways have attempted projections of coal demand and movement by rail. According to the Ministry of Coal, the domestic coal production would be about 1500 mt by 2031–32. The demand for coal from the power sector would be about 1055 mt by that time, which would include 29 mt of imported coal for shore-based plants. The projection of the Ministry of Coal roughly matches with the requirement of coal for power stations as projected by the NEP, using the current coal use norms. The use of the residual coal by other industries is difficult to quantify. If some coal is surplus to domestic requirements, perhaps India could once again export some non-coking coal as in the past.

At present the Indian Railway transports about two thirds of the coal consumed in the country. The National Rail Plan (NRP,2021) of the Ministry of Railways presents the rail traffic projection for 2031 as 3167 mt, with the share of coal being 1050 mt. The Ministry of Coal has projected the demand from the power sector alone as 1055 mt. Thus, the forecast of the NRP for coal movement is less than that of the Coal Ministry. It is possible that some more power stations at pit heads would come up, reducing the dependence on railways. The NRP also forecasts that the share of coal in the freight basket of IR would reduce to 33 per cent from the present 49 per cent. This seems to be a plausible scenario and would be in line with the policy of the government of India.

There are some avenues for putting the abundant coal reserves of India to good use in a non-polluting manner. Some options being explored are:

Gasification of coal is considered as a less polluting option than burning of coal. The gas is used for generation of electricity and the bye-products for other industries. The new coal exploration policy announced in 2020 has provided for incentives for methods like gasification and liquefaction of coal. The National Coal Gasification Mission under the Ministry of Coal aims to achieve a level of one hundred million tonnes of coal gasification by 2030.

We have seen that the coal used in India for power stations is of poor quality. If the coal is beneficiated, the pollution caused would be less. Modern coal washeries produce reasonably high yields and the rejects are not usable for power generation. Somehow, this route has not been followed assiduously in India, although it is the norm in most countries using coal for power generation. It is hoped that modern beneficiation technology will be put to use to reduce pollution and also reduce the load of expending energy to carry ash over large distances. This measure would help to reduce the load on the railway system.

To move towards net zero emission, reduction of use of fossil fuels would also have to be accompanied by steps to absorb the greenhouse gases emitted. To this end, the only method followed in India is afforestation. Other methods such as carbon sequestering are expensive. The declarations during the COP meetings on climate change have mentioned that the developed countries would contribute towards implementation of cutting edge technologies for carbon absorption. It is only through sustained international cooperation that these technologies could be implemented.

Executive decision making regarding future of coal based technologies is extremely complex as the energy security of the nation has to be balanced against the costs of pollution. The most important factor considered by the decision makers would be the rate of growth of demand for electricity. India is likely to have 500 gw of renewable capacity by 2030 as promised at the COP 26 meeting in Paris. However, the rate of growth of demand for electricity may dictate that reliance on coal may have to continue for a slightly longer period than anticipated earlier.

The demand for energy in any country also depends on a host of other circumstances, such as strategic geopolitical configurations. With the beginning of the war between Russia and Ukraine, the flow of gas into Europe from Russia was stopped and this led to an immediate increase in the demand for coal for power generation in countries like Germany. Similarly, the uncertainty of future green energy supply has prompted Britain to reassess its earlier decision to slow down exploration for oil in the North Sea. In November 2023, just before the COP 28 meet, Reuters reported that India was planning to add 17 Gigawatts of coal based power generation capacity in the next 16 months to keep abreast of the burgeoning demand for power. [Report of Reuters of 29 November 2023].

Similarly, the growth in generation of green energy, particularly solar powered electricity, depends on the import of components of solar cells from other countries. Any disturbance in these areas could jeopardise the imports. On the other hand, coal deposits are abundant in India and there may be a case for keeping thermal power stations operating at a lower level of generation, which could be increased if the need arose. In any case, a base load[51] requirement would need to be maintained and that can only be coal based, which could reduce only if battery energy storage systems (BESS) are sufficiently augmented. These systems are quite expensive and it is uncertain how much progress will be made.

Demand for coal in India is at its zenith at present and the stellar journey of rail and coal is likely to continue in the next decade. The future, however, will surely see the demand for coal moving from its present zenith towards the sunset of the coal industry. Though that would be some years away, Indian Railway would do well to start planning for the future where coal is a lesser component of railway freight traffic.

Other than the power sector, the steel, cement and fertiliser industries generate demand for railway movement of bulk commodities. Though all these sectors are expected to grow rapidly in the future, none of them would be able to substitute the reduction in volume of traffic from the power sector. Hence the Indian Railways will have to return to the smaller, break-bulk traffic for future growth. The challenge would be to locate traffic streams which could slowly replace coal when its demand starts slowing down. Infrastructure planning for the railways is a time consuming and expensive exercise. In the National Rail Plan, the share of the basket of other commodities, euphemistically named 'balance other goods' (BOG), has been projected to increase from the level of 6.6 per cent in 2019 to 17.9 per cent by the year 2031. The plan has identified corridors and provided other suggestions for helping the growth of 'other traffic'. With the Dedicated Freight Corridors in place, the railways should be able to run time tabled freight trains and that would divert a huge amount of traffic from road to rail. The ancillary infrastructure such as logistics parks and goods sheds have to be set up in time to absorb the traffic. We now turn to some suggestions for dealing with a scenario where the demand for transportation of coal is declining.

---

[51] Base load is the minimum level of demand on an electrical supply system over 24 hours. Base load power sources are those plants that can generate dependable power to consistently meet demand.

Future Planning for Indian Railways

At the present juncture, the railway probably has about ten years in which to organise an action plan to sustain freight traffic in the future. The concept of 'bigger and heavier' trains would have to coexist with trains carrying low weight high value products, moving to a time table to deliver consignments on time.

In a sense, this is the second tectonic shift which would occur in the life of the railways in India. Since its inception, the railways operated to a system of loading small and large consignments and catering to the demand of all consumers on a best effort basis. The first tectonic shift occurred when, from the late 1970s, IR decided to shift to the block rake system of operation and gradually refused to deal with cargo of less than a full train load. The segregation of BOX (and later BOXN) and other large wagons into rake formations led to the small customers migrating mainly to road. The primacy of mineral traffic over the years led to the composition of IR's wagon fleet shifting in favour of top-open wagons with high sides. The smaller wagons were completely phased out. Containers handled some break bulk cargo. With the volume of the predominant mineral traffic, coal, likely to reduce gradually, the time has come for the wheel to turn a full circle and for IR to return to the system of accepting small traffic and catering to multiple customers from all industries.

At one time, the Indian Railways had a tariff schedule with more than 4000 entries. These were the legacy of the era when the railways carried small and large consignments. As the era of block rake operation came in, many of the commodities were no longer carried and after the rationalisation of tariffs in 2005, many of the items were deleted. Some of the commodities from the deleted list may well have to be brought back.

To propose an action plan for facilitating the growth of BOG on IR, it is worthwhile to breakup the future planning into segments and examine what could be planned for each.

(a) Market Survey: The unique selling proposition (USP) of IR as a carrier of bulk traffic is that in the case of minerals like coal and iron ore, it provides a direct service from production area to the consumption point. A good example of this would be a coal consignment moving from a coal mine to a power plant or steel plant. In the case of products of manufacturing industries, the cargo has to be loaded or unloaded at the railway handling facilities. Thus, an interface with other transport modes is involved. The multiple handling adds to costs, which the customers naturally try to avoid. With the introduction of multi axle road carriers capable of handling heavy cargo and the great improvement in the kilometrage and quality of roads, the railways have been facing stiff competition even for commodities like steel and cement, which are loaded in bulk from large industrial establishments. The task of winning over small traffic moving in truck loads to railways would be very challenging.

The first task, therefore, would be to conduct a detailed market survey to assess the volume of traffic available and amenable for diversion from road to rail. This has to be done at an all India level covering as many industries as possible.

(b) Line Capacity: The USP of IR for the BOG segment would have to be the running of time tabled trains and delivery of consignments with a degree of assurance. At present, some container trains are being run to time tables, details of which are available at the FOIS website. However, doing this on a large scale would necessitate the development of adequate line capacity on all the important freight routes and connectivity from the first mile to the last mile. Frequently, capacity gets developed on trunk routes, but when the consignments transit from trunk routes to the branch lines, there are serious hold ups due to lack of line capacity. The NRP has suggested augmentation of capacity on certain routes. There are two dedicated freight corridors at present. It would be necessary to plan multiple tracks on all major routes as soon as possible. The new tracks need not have designs for carrying very heavy wagons as the proportion of heavy wagons would slowly reduce. The new tracks could be alongside the existing railway routes. This would save time required for land acquisition, reduce construction costs and provide ease of interface with the existing network.

(c) Speed: In the case of high value low weight cargo, the total time between despatch from factory door to arrival at the storage point for sale in the wholesale or retail market would determine the competitiveness vis-a-vis road. As we have observed earlier, the main impediment to running freight trains at high speeds is the presence of passenger and freight trains on the same track and the precedence that has to be accorded to passenger traffic. Hence, the issues of line capacity, speed of freight trains and adherence to a time table acquire great importance. The availability of dedicated freight lines would enable the freight trains to run at high speeds.

The Indian Railways should aim at designing new wagons for carrying small volume high value cargo in units of 15 to 20 tonnes and capable of speeds up to 120 kmph. The stipulation of minimum number of wagons to be loaded could be decided after a market survey and interactions with prospective customers. There would have to be multiple points of aggregation and dis-aggregation of the cargo. This would need careful planning of terminals.

(d) Wagons and Goods Sheds: A slowing down in the demand for coal would require a change in the procurement policy of wagons. The percentage of top-open high sided wagons in the total wagon fleet increased from 29.6 per cent in 1990–91 to 55.4 per cent in 2021–22. Similarly, the average carrying capacity of a broad gauge wagon increased from 36.95 tonnes in 1990–91 to 61.75 tonnes in 2021–22. The requirement of such wagons would decline over the years and wagons with new designs for new traffic would have to replace them. The Indian Railway has designed a top-open high sided wagon named BOXNS, which has a carrying capacity of 80 tonnes of cargo, fully 14 tonnes more than the existing BOXN, with the carrying capacity of 66 tonnes on CC+8 routes (after enhancement of CC post 2004). Very few routes on IR are capable of carrying such a heavy wagon. Yet, this wagon is already being manufactured, and once in service will remain available for thirty years. It is time that such decisions are reviewed.

Some specialised wagons for carrying high value cargo such as the BLCA wagons for container traffic, special wagons for carrying cars and tank wagons for carrying liquid petroleum products, milk etc. are available at present. However, even in the case of cars, there is no wagon suitable for transporting SUVs, small freight carriers, large trucks and two wheelers. Less than 10 per cent of the cars manufactured in India move by IR. The origin-destination flows of this traffic are well known and plans to attract this traffic will produce rich dividends as this is an expanding industry.

There is no wagon which is designed to carry high value consumer durables such as refrigerators, television sets or washing machines. The assumption is that the container operators would take care of this traffic. However, this would require some innovation. A normal 20 foot container, when loaded with consumer durables like refrigerators, weighs about 2 to 3 tonnes, whereas the minimum charge of IR for a loaded container is for 7.5 tonnes. It is understood that CONCOR has ordered 12 feet high containers, which would permit loading of about 8 tonnes of white goods in a container. In a similar manner, the market survey may throw up the need for special wagons required for a variety of other products amenable for transportation by rail.

The parcel vans available with the railways could be redesigned to carry consumer durables. The parcel vans are capable of high speed travel and could be a game changer for providing timetabled delivery of consignments. The manufacturing capacity of these vans would perhaps require augmentation.

Consumer durables are manufactured at several locations in the country and the manufacturers would need to have easy access to all the rail loading points, which they do not have at present. The biggest container operator in the country, the Container Corporation of India has only 66 Inland Container Depots and about 185 container rail terminals (CRTs). The reach of Indian Railways is much larger. A sample of six railway zones, the Central, Eastern, East Central, Northern, Southern and South Eastern shows that they have a total of 428 goods sheds capable of handling full and half rakes, and this list excludes the industrial sidings. Depending on emerging demand patterns, the challenge would be to make many of the railway sidings suitable for loading high value commodities of small bulk. These terminals should be easily accessible by the consumer or the freight aggregator and the small consignments should be aggregated at some point for movement to destination.

(e) Unloading: The facilities at the unloading points would have to match those at the loading points and easy egress from the unloading point to the final destination should be planned.

(f) First and Last Mile Connectivity: Ensuring first and last mile connectivity for a door-to-door type of logistics configuration is essential for attracting high value customers to rail. This would require excellent coordination with road transport operators for picking up and delivery of cargo based on a mutually agreed time schedule with the customer. The running of trains would have to be synchronised with the delivery schedules.

(g) Pricing Policy: The pricing policy of IR would have to be reviewed and recast to deal with the cargo of the future. At present, the policy is to charge for the full rake from origin to destination. In the case of two-point rakes, which are also permitted now between notified pairs of terminals, the pricing is for each terminal. A multi consumer, multi-product train could have the consignments loaded and offloaded at various points of its run between two major terminals. The freight charges for each would have to be calculated separately and fairly. Whether the road movement portions would be included in the railway freight or dealt with separately with the road transport provider is a matter of policy, which would also have to be decided.

(h) Hub and Spoke: For developing a web of small loading and unloading points and aggregating the cargo at a central point, a hub and spoke type of arrangement would be ideal. The Indian Railway has a policy for movement of containers under its 'hub and spoke' policy. The stations covered this policy are notified from time to time.

(i) Shift of Focus from Tonnes and NTKMs to Revenue Earning: As the tariff charged by the Indian Railways is technically controlled by the government, the focus of officers dealing with traffic has always remained on the tonnage of freight loaded and the NTKMs earned. The revenue is an outcome of the tonnage and the distance moved. With the change in traffic configuration away from bulk commodities, the growth in tonnes of freight carried and hence the NTKMs logged would not increase very rapidly. However, the growth in revenue earnings would be great if the planning is appropriate to the requirements. The focus of the management would have to shift from what has been the norm for many years now. The most important change would be that the power of fixing tariff would have to be delegated from the level of the government to lower levels of the hierarchy to enable quick response of tariff to market stimuli. True flexibility to respond to market forces would come if the decision making is delegated to the head of the railway zones. This would indeed be a paradigm shift and it would be an interesting exercise for the government to consider.

The Indian Railway is about to face a great challenge for management of a major change in the structure of its freight market. As we have noted earlier, the IR and the coal industry dealt with one challenge in an exemplary manner in the 1980s. The challenge which would confront IR about a decade from now would be far more formidable. The challenge of the 1980s was to convince some industries to adhere to the requirements of a monopolistic transport service provider. The fact that many of these industries were government controlled, made the task comparatively easier. The management of change of the 2030s would be to adjust technology, investment and commercial policies to the dictates of the market. This calls for an organisational structure that is flexible and responds to market requirements quickly. The organisational structure of IR would perhaps have to be looked at afresh to imbue it with the characteristics of a huge but very flexible and responsive organisation. It is a tall order, and it is hoped that with the expertise and dedication of railwaymen in India, this battle too shall be won.

***

Appendices 1 to 7

Appendix 1

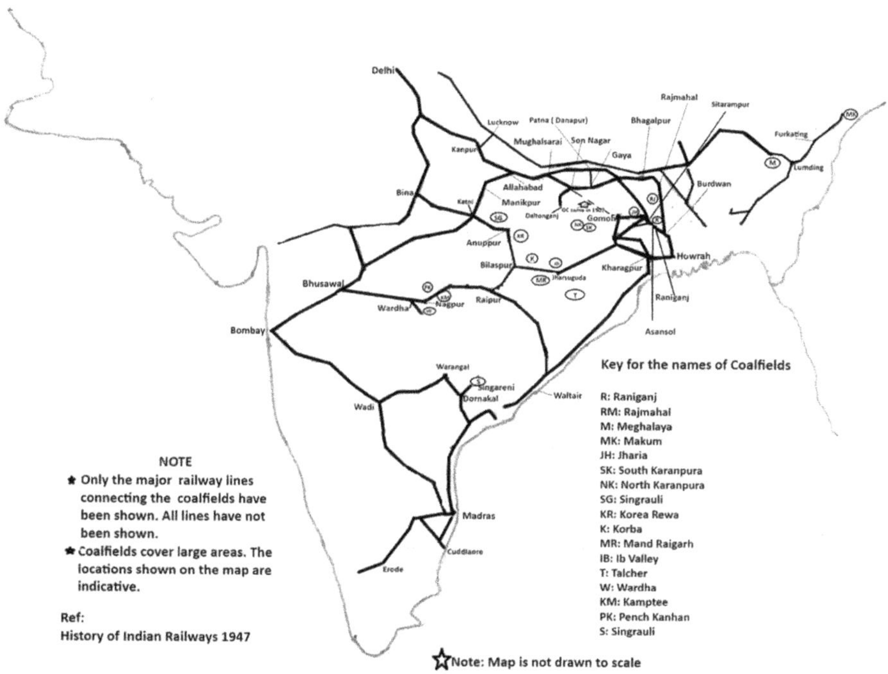

Map 1: Year 1903: Major Coalfields of India and adjoining railway lines for coal movement

Appendix 2

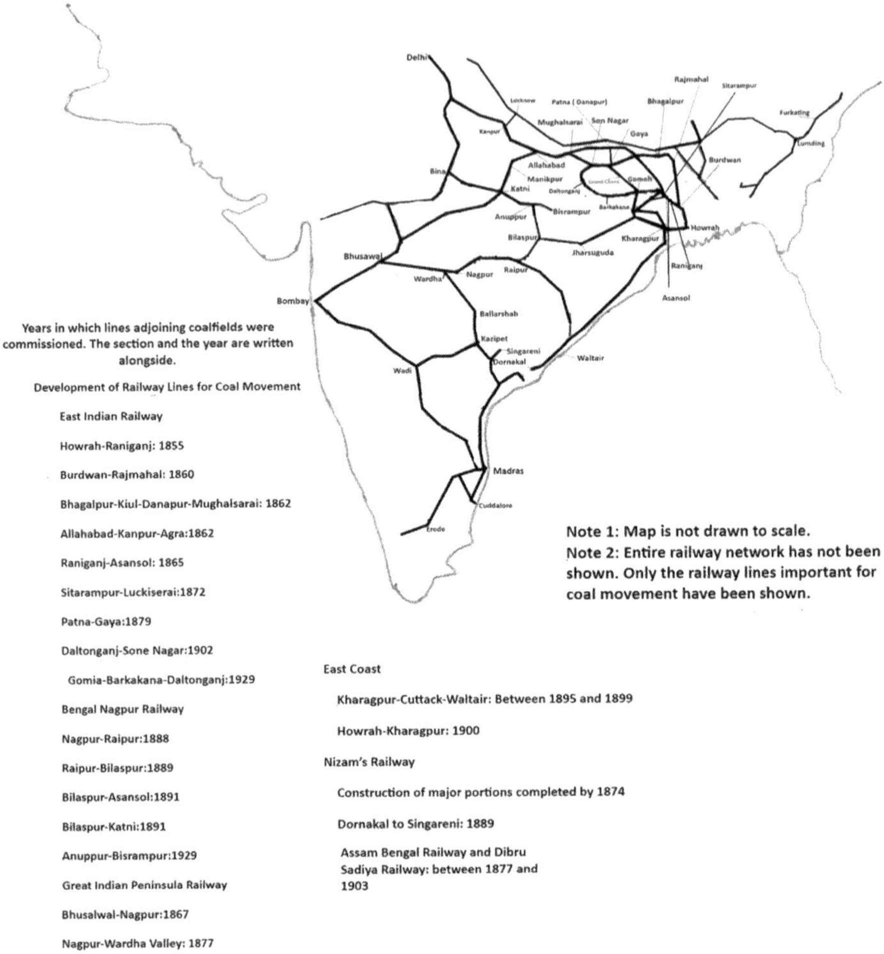

Map 2: Map of railways in India in 1939 showing important lines adjoining the coalfields and the year in which the lines were commissioned.

Appendix 3

Map 3: Map showing the six routes of the Golden Quadrilateral and two diagonals. These routes comprise 15 per cent of the route kilometrage but carry 58 per cent of the freight and 52 per cent of the passenger traffic

Appendix 4

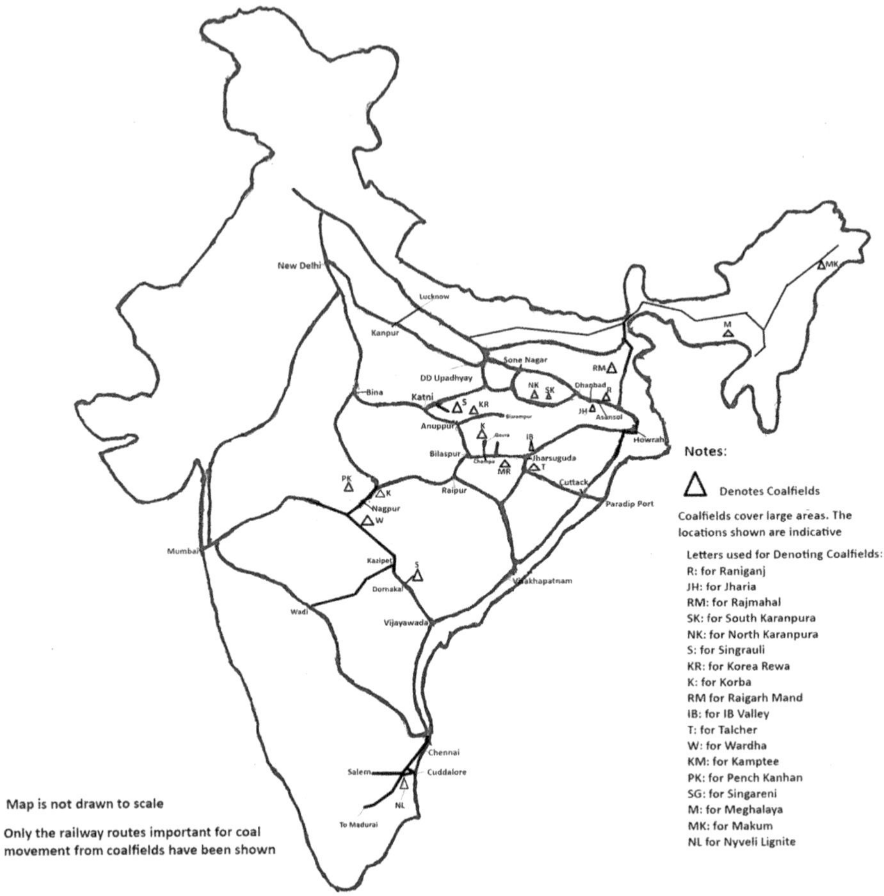

Map 4: Coalfields and adjoining Railway Routes in 1990s

Appendix 5

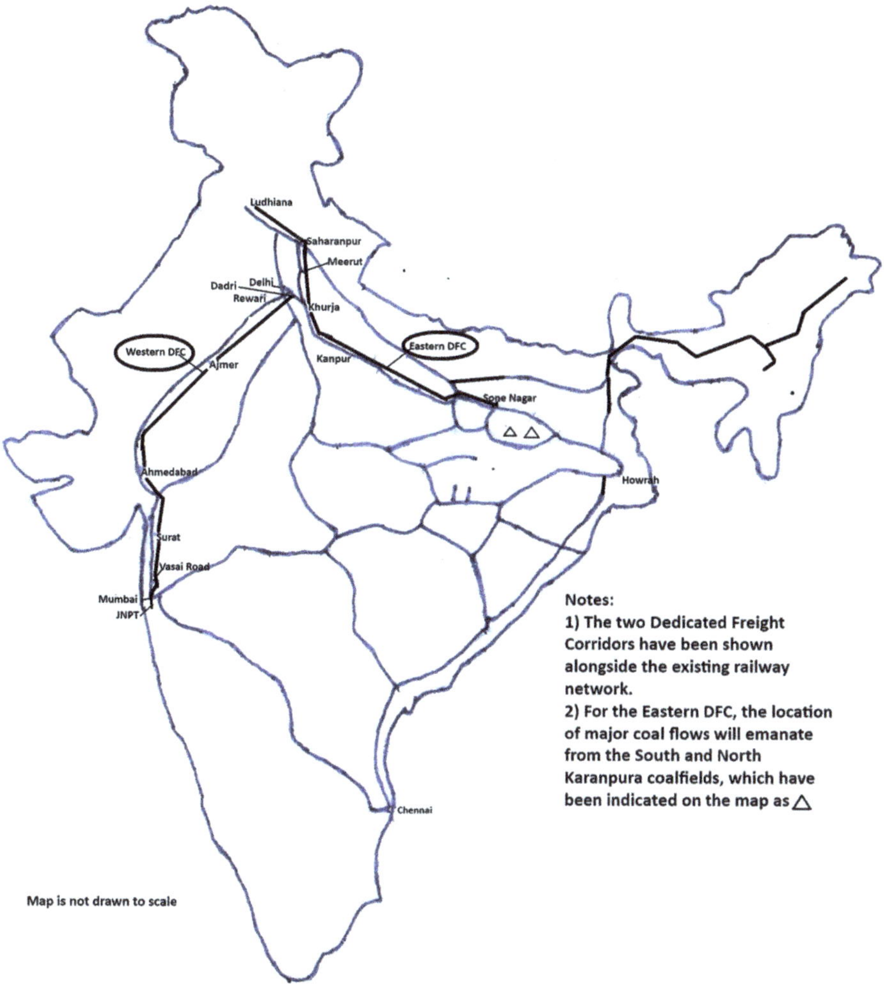

Map 5: The two Dedicated Freight Corridors of IR

Appendix 6

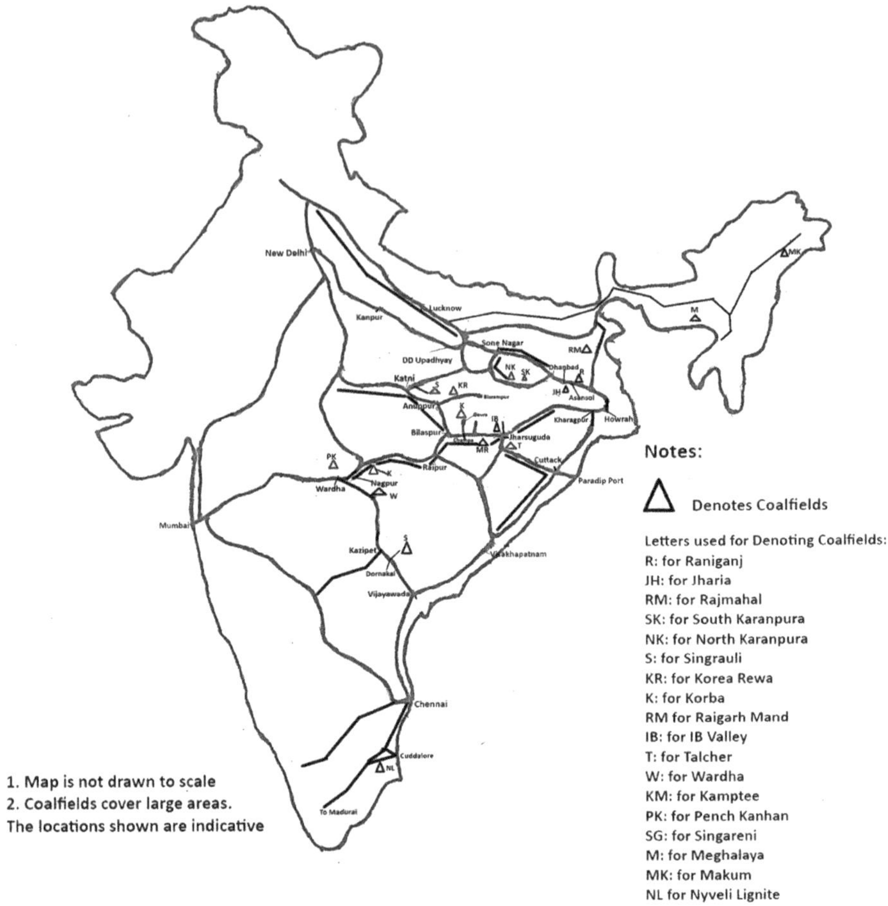

Map 6: Coal Routes Facing Acute Congestion

The coal routes under intense pressure are shown with bold lines alongside the railway route.

Appendix 7

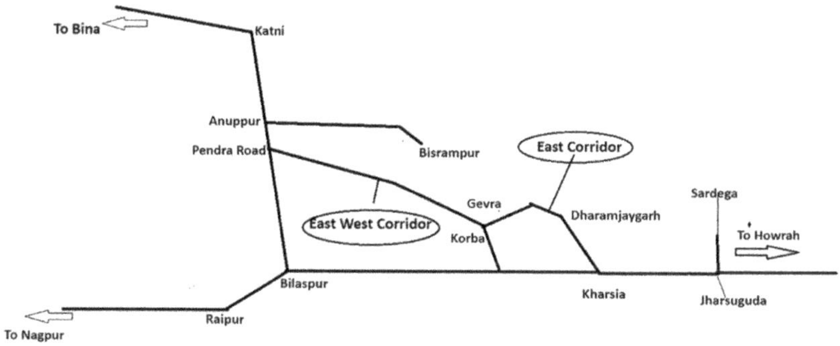

Schematic map of New Projects for coal evacuation from coal projects in Korba and Mand Raigarh fields

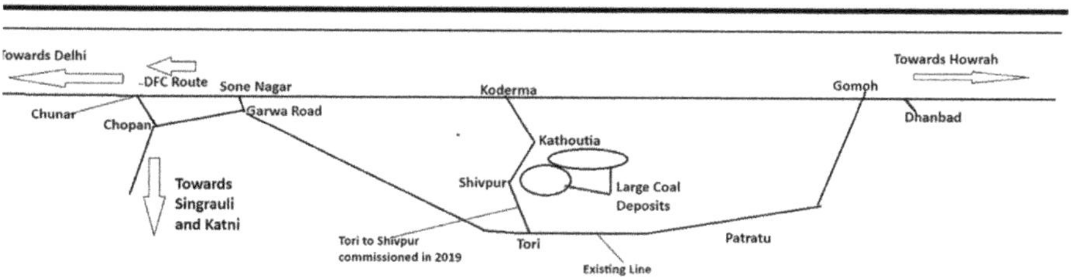

Schematic map of new projects for evacuation of coal from the Central Coalfields, North Karanpura area.

Map 7

Bibliography

Bagchi, A., *Private Investment in India 1900–1939* (Cambridge: Cambridge University Press, 1972).

Benjamin, N., *Fuels for Railway Locomotives in Colonial India: Proceedings of the Indian History Congress, 2014*, Vol. 75, Platinum Jubilee (Indian History Congress, 2014), 653–658, accessed 20 February 2021.

Bhattacharya, P. S., *When Coal Turned to Gold* (Gurugram: Penguin Random House, 2018).

Bhattacharya, S., and Maitra, A. K., 'Impact of Coal beneficiation on Rail Transport in India', *International Journal of Coal Preparation and Utilisation*, Taylor and Francis, Vol. 27 (2007).

Brereton, A., *Administration Report on Railway for 1901* (Simla: Government Central Printing Office, 1902).

Central Electricity Authority, 'Norms of Coal consumption for Thermal Power Stations' (2019), <https://cea.nic.in/old/reports/others/thermal/tppd/acq_norms.pdf>, accessed 15 November 2024.

Central Electricity Authority, 'List of Thermal Power Stations in India as on 31.03.2021' (2024), <https://cea.nic.in/wp-content/uploads/pdm/2021/06/list_power_stations_2021.pdf>, accessed 17 November 2024.

Colliery Control Order 1945 (Government of India, New Delhi, 1945).

Comptroller and Auditor General of India, 'Report for 2014' (2023), <https://cag.gov.in/uploads/download_audit_report/2014/Union_Compliance_Railway_Comptroller_and_Auditor_General_26_2014_chapter_2.pdf>, accessed 9 February 2023.

Comptroller and Auditor General, 'Report on Captive Mines' (2012), <https://cag.gov.in/uploads/download_audit_report/2012/Union_Performance_Commercial_Allocation_Coal_Blocks_and_Production_Ministry_Coal_7_2012_chapter_6.pdf>; <https://cag.gov.in/uploads/download_audit_report/2012/Union_Performance_Commercial_Allocation_Coal_Blocks_and_Production_Ministry_Coal_7_2012_exe_sum.pdf>, accessed 22 November 2024.

Review of Trade in India (Simla: Government Central Branch Press, 1889).

Danvers, J., 'Report to the Secretary of State for India in Council on the Railways in India for 1859' (London: Secretary Railway Department, 1860).

Danvers, J., 'Report to the Secretary of State for India in Council on the Railways in India for 1876–77' (London: Government Director of Indian Railway Companies, 1877).

Danvers, J., 'Report to the Secretary of State for India in Council on the Railways in India for 1877–78' (London: Government Director of Railway Companies, 1878).

E Parliament Library, 'Answer of Minister of Planning and Programme Implementation on Freight Equalisation Scheme', <10_III_25031992_p383_p383_t450.pdf>, accessed 22 November 2023.

Economic Survey for 1984–85 (Government of India, 1985).

Economic Survey for 1990–91 (Government of India, 1991).

Economic Survey for 2001–02 (Government of India, 2002).

Economic Survey (Government of India, 1998).

Economic Times, 'Report on Presidential Directive on Coal', in 3 April 2012 <https://economictimes.indiatimes.com/industry/indl-goods/svs/metals-mining/coal-india-gets-presidential-directive-to-commit-fuel-to-power-companies/articleshow/12521115.cms?from=mdr>, accessed 3 October 2023.

Expert Group on Indian Railways, 'Indian Railways Report 2001: Policy Imperatives for Reinvention and Growth' (New Delhi: National Council of Applied Economic Research, 2001).

Ghose, S. C., 'A Monograph on Indian Railway Rates' (Calcutta: Government of India, 1918).

Ghosh A. B., 'Coal Industry in India Vols. 1 and 2' (Calcutta: Coal India Ltd., 1977).

Gupta, A. K., 'Events in the Coal Industry in India' (Calcutta: Business Economics, 2004).

IIT Roorkee <https://www.iitr.ac.in/>, accessed 2 October 2023.

Indian Coal Statistics for 1928, Department of Commercial Intelligence (Calcutta: Government of India, 1929).

Indian Coalfields Committee 1946, Report of, New Delhi (Government of India Press, 1947). (Popularly known as the Mahindra Committee Report, after its Chairman K. C. Mahindra).

Indian Institute of Engineering Science and Technology, <https://www.iiests.ac.in/>, accessed 2 October 2023.

Indian Railway: Key Statistics 1970–71 to 2012–13 (New Delhi: Ministry of Railways).

Industrial Policy Resolution 1948 (Government of India), <https://dpiit.gov.in/sites/default/files/chap001%20%2013.pdf>, accessed 16 January 2021.

Kelway-Bamber, 'The carriage of coal in India by rail', *Journal of the Royal Society of Arts* 67/3454 (1919) <https://www.jstor.org/stable/41347888?seq=1>, accessed 10 August 2022.

Khosla, G. S., *History of Indian Railways* (New Delhi: Ministry of Railways, 1988).

Kumar, S., and Mehrotra, S., *Bankruptcy to Billions* (New Delhi: Oxford University Press, 2009).

Kumaramangalam, S. Mohan, *Coal Industry in India: Nationalisation and Tasks Ahead* (New Delhi: Oxford & IBH Publishing Company, 1973).

Ministry of Statistics and Programme Implementation, Coal Washeries in India, 2022.

Minister for Railways, Speech of Nitish Kumar, Railway Budget, 1998.

Ministry of Coal, History, <https://coal.gov.in/en/about-us/history-background#:~:text=On%20account%20of%20these%20reasons,coking%20coal%20mines%20in%201973>, accessed 21 October 2023.

Ministry of Coal, Data on import of coal from 2013–14 to 2022–23, <https://coal.gov.in/sites/default/files/2021-01/Import-of-Coal-and-Coke-last-ten-years.pdf>, accessed 20 October 2024.

Ministry of Coal, Grading of Coal on Basis of Gross Calorific value, <https://coal.gov.in/en/major-statistics/coal-grades>, accessed 10 October 2023.

Ministry of Coal, National Coal Gasification Mission Target 100 mt coal gasification by 2030, <https://coal.gov.in/sites/default/files/ncgm/ncgm21-09-21.pdf>, accessed 15 September 2024.

Ministry of Coal, New Colliery Control Order of 2000, <C:\FrontPage Webs\Content\distr (coal.gov.in)>, accessed 16 February 2023.

Ministry of Coal, New Policy for Coal Distribution, Office Memorandum No. 23011/4/2007-CPD dated 18 October 2007 <https://coal.nic.in/sites/default/files/2020-01/28-06-2018-b.pdf>, accessed 11 October 2022.

Ministry of Coal, Production of Coal, 2023, <https://coal.gov.in/en/major-statistics/production-and-supplies>, accessed 10 October 2024.

Ministry of Coal, Report on Coal India, 2009–10, 2010, <https://coal.gov.in/sites/default/files/2019-11/bchap10_0.pdf>, accessed 31 January 2023.

Ministry of Power, Government of India, Growth of Electricity in India from 1947 to 2020, New Delhi, October 2020, <https://now.solar/2021/04/07/growth-of-electricity-sector-in-india-from-1947-2020/>, accessed 5 September 2022.

Ministry of Power, CEA, List of Thermal Power Houses in India, New Delhi, 2021, <https://cea.nic.in/wp-content/uploads/pdm/2021/06/list_power_stations_2021.pdf>, accessed 25 January 2023.

Ministry of Power, CEA, Government of India, CEA, Growth of Electricity Sector in India from 1947–2022, June 2022, <https://cea.nic.in/wp-content/uploads/pdm/2023/02/Growth_Book_2022_PDF.pdf>, accessed 23 September 2023.

Ministry of Power, CEA, Government of India, Annual Report of CEA for 2020–21, <https://cea.nic.in/wp-content/uploads/annual_reports/2021/CEAAnnualReport_final.pdf>, accessed 15 September 2024.

Ministry of Railways, Government of India, Key Statistics 1970–71 to 2012–13, New Delhi, 2014.

Ministry of Railways, Report of the Committee for Mobilisation of Resources for Major Railway Projects and Restructuring of Railway Ministry and Railway Board, New Delhi, June 2015, <https://indianrailways.gov.in/railwayboard/uploads/directorate/HLSRC/FINAL_FILE_Final.pdf>, accessed 17 February 2023.

Ministry of Railways, White Paper on Indian Railways, 2015, accessed 6 January 2023, <https://indianrailways.gov.in/railwayboard/uploads/directorate/finance_budget/Budget_2015-16/White_Paper-_English.pdf>, accessed 15 September 2022.

Niti Ayog, Climate Energy Dashboard, <https://iced.niti.gov.in/energy/fuel-sources/coal/production>, accessed 20 October 2024.

O'Conor, J. E., Assistant Secretary to Government of India, Department of Finance and Commerce, Review of Trade in India for 1878–79 (Simla: Government Central Branch Press, 1879).

O'Conor, J. E., Assistant Secretary to Government of India, Department of Finance and Commerce; Review of Trade in India 1888–89 (Simla: Government Central Branch Press, 1889).

O'Conor, J. E., Assistant Secretary to Government of India, Department of Finance and Commerce; Review of Trade in India for 1890–91 (Simla: Government Central Branch Press, 1891).

O'Conor, J. E., Review of the Trade of India 1900–1901 (Calcutta: Office of the Superintendent of Government Printing, 1901).

Planning Commission, Approach Paper for X Plan, Government of India.

Planning Commission, First Five Year Plan (New Delhi: Government of India, 1951).

Planning Commission, Mid Term review of Sixth Five Year Plan (New Delhi: Government of India, 1983).

Planning Commission, Ninth Five Year Plan (New Delhi: Government of India, 1997).

Planning Commission, Preface to Eighth Five Year Plan (New Delhi: Government of India, 1992).

Planning Commission, Second Five Year Plan document (New Delhi: Government of India, 1956).

Planning Commission, Seventh Five Year Plan (New Delhi: Government of India, 1985).

Planning Commission, Third Five Year (New Delhi: Government of India, 1961).

Press Information Bureau, Coal imported by Power Sector in India PIB release of 6 December 2023, <https://pib.gov.in/PressReleseDetailm.aspx?PRID=1983084#:~:text=There%20are%20a%20number%20of,23.8%20MT%20in%202019%2D20>, accessed on 31 March 2024.

Press Information Bureau, Communique of 31 May 2023 regarding future course of power generation, <https://pib.gov.in/PressReleaseIframePage.aspx?PRID=1928750>, accessed 15 June 2023.

Press Information Bureau, Communique on Coal washeries to be set up by CIL, <https://pib.gov.in/PressReleasePage.aspx?PRID=1813244>, accessed 5 January 2023.

Press Information Bureau, Communique on Formation of Niti Ayog, <https://pib.gov.in/newsite/printrelease.aspx?relid=170000>, accessed 4 April 2022.

Press Information Bureau, PIB Communique on merger of Railway Budget with General Budget, <https://pib.gov.in/newsite/PrintRelease.aspx?relid=153672>, accessed 10 April 2022.

Press Information Bureau, PIB Release on India's Stand at COP 26 Summit, <https://pib.gov.in/PressReleasePage.aspx?PRID=1795071>, accessed 18 June 2022.

Press Information Bureau, Release on Commercial Mining in Coal Sector, <https://static.pib.gov.in/WriteReadData/specificdocs/documents/2023/apr/doc2023424184801.pdf>, accessed 20 February 2024.

Press Information Bureau, Status of Coal Consumption by Power Plants in the Country, <https://pib.gov.in/PressReleaseIframePage.aspx?PRID=1947383>, accessed 20 October 2023.

Rail Tariff Enquiry Committee Report (New Delhi: Ministry of Railways, 1980).

Railway Board, Administration Report for Railways in India for the Year 1929–30 (New Delhi: Government of India, 1930).

Railway Board, Administration Report for Railways in India for the Calendar Year 1906 (Simla: Government Central Printing Office, 1907).

Railway Convention Committee, Report on the Infrastructural Requirements for Indian Railways in the Ninth Plan period (1996, submitted in March 1997).

Railway Convention Committee, Report for 1971 on Wagon Supply, April, 1973.

Railway Convention Committee, Sixth Report, 1973, Rates of Dividend and Other Matters <https://eparlib.nic.in/bitstream/123456789/58306/1/rcc_05_06_1971.pdf>, accessed 27 December 2022.

Ray Indrajit, Paul Krishna; Beginnings of the Coal Industry in Bengal; Proceedings of Indian History Congress, Vol 61, Part One, Millenium 2000–2001, accessed 9 August 2022.

Review of the Trade of British India with Other Countries for the Official Year 1878–79, Department of Finance and Commerce; Government of India, Superintendent of Government Printing; Calcutta, 1879.

Reuters, Article of Reuters on addition to power capacity in India, 2023, <https://www.reuters.com/world/india/india-scrambles-add-coal-fired-power-capacity-avoid-outages-sources-2023-11-29/>, accessed 6 June 2024.

Reuters, Report on coal shortage in India, <https://www.reuters.com/article/idUSL3N0S51UO/>, accessed 18 July 2023.

Sanyal, N., Development of Indian Railways (Calcutta: Calcutta University, 1930).

Sriram, S., Indian Railway Finances: Critical Issues and Emerging Options, Vol 35, Number 12, March 18–24, *Economic and Political Weekly* (2000).

Statistics of Mines in India, Vol 1 (Coal), for 2011, Directorate General of Mines Safety (DGMS), Ministry of Labour & Employment, Government of India, 2014.

Statistics of Mines in India, Vol 1 (Coal) for 2015, Directorate General of Mines Safety (DGMS), Ministry of Labour & Employment, Government of India, 2017.

TERI, Report for NITI Ayog on Economic and Environmental Impact of Coal Washing in India, <https://www.niti.gov.in/sites/default/files/2021-08/CoalWasheryReport.pdf>, accessed 20 July 2023.

Thorner, D., Patterns of Railway Development in India; Far Eastern Quarterly, 1955.

Trevor, W. S., Col; Administrative Report on Railways in India 1880–81; Director General of Railways; Simla, 1882.

Vikalpa, Tiwari, Bhattacharya, Raghav, A Discussion on Non-Coking Coal Pricing Methods Adopted in Different Countries, IIM Ahmedabad, March 2015, <https://journals.sagepub.com/doi/10.1177/0256090915573615>, accessed 31 January 2023.

Index

D

E

F

G

H

I

J

K

www.ingramcontent.com/pod-product-compliance
Ingram Content Group UK Ltd.
Pitfield, Milton Keynes, MK11 3LW, UK
UKHW020720041026
15590UKWH00002B/773

9 781803 745671